PRAISE FOR *I WILL FOLLOW YOU ANYWHERE*

"In this powerful and inspirational book, John Feal expertly demonstrates what it means to be a leader, organizer, and activist. Through fierce determination and relentless perseverance, the FealGood Foundation, Jon Stewart, and a devoted array of sick and dying first responders show us the true meaning of Never Forget."

—STEVE BUSCEMI

"John Feal made me famous . . . I'd follow him anywhere."

—JON STEWART

"John created a system never seen before that others can learn and use for their own causes."

—MICHAEL MCAULIFF, REPORTER FOR *NEW YORK DAILY NEWS* AND *DAILY BEAST*

"Blunt and relentless, *I Will Follow You Anywhere* is a story of loyalty, accountability, and courage that didn't end when the dust settled."

—JAKE WOOD, COFOUNDER OF TEAM RUBICON AND AUTHOR OF *ONCE A WARRIOR*

"I have never read a more accurate, responsible, and heartbreaking rendering of the events of that day and all those long days afterward. Feal brings the reader on a 'mission after the mission' journey, from the perspective of a humble citizen who stood up when it counted."

—ROBERT JOHN BURKE, FILM AND TELEVISION ACTOR, VOLUNTEER FIREFIGHTER, AND 9/11 RESPONDER

PRAISE FOR JOHN FEAL

"A true get-in-your-face New Yorker who doesn't back down from a fight."

—SPIKE LEE

"The toughest son of a bitch I ever witnessed in my forty years in DC."

—NANCY PELOSI (D-CA 11TH DISTRICT)

"I have never met anyone whose empathy matches their anger (like John)."

—KIRSTEN GILLIBRAND (D-NY)

I WILL FOLLOW YOU ANYWHERE

The True Story of the 9/11 Responders Who Took On Congress

JOHN FEAL

with Charles Daly

BenBella Books, Inc.
Dallas, TX

BENBELLA

BenBella Books, Inc.
8080 N. Central Expressway
Suite 1700
Dallas, TX 75206
benbellabooks.com
Send feedback to feedback@benbellabooks.com

BenBella is a federally registered trademark.

Printed in the United States of America
10 9 8 7 6 5 4 3 2 1

Library of Congress Control Number: 2026022782
ISBN 9781637748749 (hardcover)
ISBN 9781637748756 (electronic)

Editing by Rick Chillot
Copyediting by Scott Calamar
Proofreading by Ashley Casteel and Rebecca Maines
Text design and composition by Aaron Edmiston
Cover design by Sarah Avinger
Front cover photo by FEMA / Andrea Booher
Back cover photo by Faye Murman-Dorsey
Printed by Lake Book Manufacturing

For my mother, my hero,
You did good.

Must you have battle in your heart forever? The bloody toil of combat?
Old contender, will you not yield to the immortal gods?
—Homer, the *Odyssey*

CONTENTS

FOREWORD

On June 11, 2019, I had the privilege of sitting next to Luis Alvarez as he delivered his testimony to a half-empty dais of a House Judiciary Subcommittee. The purpose was to convince a reluctant Congress to once and for all fully fund the Zadroga Act, a 9/11 victim compensation fund, and end the tortuous cycle where sick and dying first responders had to come hat in hand to DC to plead for help. Luis was a marine, an undercover cop in the NYPD narcotics division, and when all that didn't put him in enough danger, he asked to be moved to the legendary NYPD bomb squad. None of that killed him, however. That was a job colon cancer took on. A cancer that was born of Luis's service working at Ground Zero after 9/11.

Luis was tired. He had postponed his sixty-ninth round of chemotherapy to plead with these mildly interested lawmakers not to forget all the still-sick and dying victims of that terrible terrorist attack. Luis was worried that others who were suffering wouldn't be as fortunate as he was . . . to have healthcare . . . while he was dying. Luis told these lawmakers, "You all said you would never forget. Well, I am here to make sure that you don't. I am here because others cannot get here."

Luis never made his sixty-ninth chemo appointment. After he dragged himself down to DC to once again advocate on behalf of others,

Luis's liver failed. Hospice followed, and by the end of the month he was gone.

It was a painful replay of the previous fight to renew the Zadroga Act in 2015. At that time I had the privilege of roaming the halls of Congress with another legend, FDNY veteran Ray Pfeifer. I was Ray's DC wingman in 2014 and 2015. It was, ironically for a firefighter, a good cop/bad cop arrangement. Ray, cancer ravaged from his time serving on the Pile, was the endlessly patient good guy. We would chase down senators and representatives, my anger slowly building as we experienced their disinterest and disrespect. I would sprint to catch them, challenging their lack of humanity . . . Ray right behind on his scooter to apologize for his friend's intemperance. Ray would be the voice of reason and conciliation, a role that is hilarious if you knew his stubborn wild-man rebel streak.

His calm came from a sense of perspective. I would fume at being handed another business card from another legislative aide trying to shield their boss from having to answer personally to these heroes. Ray would tap his jacket pocket, pull out a wad of prayer cards he kept from all those he had already lost in the FDNY from 9/11 and the ensuing illnesses: "I got all the cards I need right here." Ray considered himself lucky. He had lost so many friends on that day, and so many more since.

Like Luis, Ray was advocating not for himself but for all those whose illnesses hadn't yet been covered, whose families were having to choose between medicine and rent. Ray's cancer had advanced by then . . . it had already claimed a kidney and parts of his femur, but he was relentless. His passion and advocacy got Zadroga over the finish line in 2015. By 2017 he was gone. One of the most difficult phone calls I have ever received was the one where Ray asked me to speak at his funeral from hospice care. When I asked him how he was holding up, he said "can't complain." That was Ray. I loved him, even though he was an Islanders fan.

Ray and Luis were just two of hundreds of advocates who had given selflessly of their time and energies to make sure that Congress never forgot their obligation to the people. Whether those folks had volunteered at Ground Zero, or had the misfortune of just living near it, or had taken the oath to protect and defend the Constitution and had been exposed to burn pits and other toxins while serving overseas . . . These men and women inspired me over all those years, and the man who inspired all of them was John Feal.

Feal had become active in the 9/11 community after losing part of his foot during the rescue and recovery operations at Ground Zero. He saw a community that was sick and struggling, and he made it his mission to not allow our elected officials to escape accountability. I first became aware of him in 2010 when he and his merry band of Feal-Good Foundation warriors furiously lobbied Capitol Hill to get the original Zadroga Act over the finish line. I was immediately struck by this unlikely lobbyist for his plainspoken, forthright passion, and by the fact that he was clearly even shorter than I was. We tried to book him to come on our show as the deadline for the legislation approached, but he said no. He had to stay in DC. He had to keep the pressure on. Instead he recommended four of his guys: Chris Baumann, ex NYPD; Ken George, NYC Highway Department; John Devlin, operating engineer; and Kenny Specht, ex-FDNY. All four had either responded to the call on 9/11 or had served on the Pile during rescue and recovery, or both. All were suffering terrible health effects of those efforts. They made for an incredible panel. People who had done the right thing by our city and country and were made to suffer by government's indifference. Their outcry, and John Feal's efforts, helped push reluctant officials (*McConnell, cough cough*) to finally do the right thing and pass the Zadroga Act.

And that was the last I ever heard from John Feal.

Kidding, of course. John was exhausted from the effort but knew that getting a bill passed was the least of it. Now came the hard work of implementing the bill, getting the word out to those affected by the bill, and making sure Washington didn't sabotage the bill. I told John if he ever needed anything to please let me know . . . and that was a huge mistake. John did, often. We became fast friends and partners in crime. I learned John was a much more sophisticated general than he let on and that all of his actions . . . as wild as some of them got . . . were rooted in strategy to achieve wins for people in need. I also learned he orders egg-white scrambles with an unholy amount of egg whites . . . and eats them with grape jelly. So . . . there are real issues there.

I hope this book gives the reader some insight and nuance into the man who has taken me on an invaluable fifteen-year odyssey of frustration, tenacity, resilience, camaraderie, and into the lessons in selflessness and compassion he has graciously bestowed. I would follow him anywhere . . . although as I mentioned earlier, it is sometimes not easy given how short he is.

Jon Stewart
2025

Prologue

THE VIEW FROM THE THROGS NECK BRIDGE, SEPTEMBER 11, 2001

On Saturday, September 8, 2001, I played golf with both feet for the last time.

When I finally get back on the course, in late spring 2002, I will beat the doctor who told me I might never play again.

If you worked construction in the early 2000s, you'll remember Nextel, the cell phone carrier known for indestructible phones and a nationwide walkie-talkie network. In the days of limited minutes and pricey overage fees, this feature let you talk to any Nextel user anywhere for free with a push-to-talk function. On September 11, 2001, this will be the only way for civilians in New York to communicate as phone calls overwhelm the cell towers.

On that day I'm at work as a foreman on a large-scale demolition job in Nanuet, New York, about an hour outside the city. I wear my work

Nextel and a personal cell phone clipped to the neck of my shirt, so I can hear them ring on a loud job site.

My Nextel chirps a little before 9 AM.

It's one of my guys saying that a one-engine Cessna has gone off course and hit one of the Twin Towers.

But on such a sunny day?

We keep working.

A series of chirps and radio chatter follows with conflicting reports, saying it might have been a passenger jet. When we get the call confirming that a second plane had hit the South Tower, we know this isn't just an accident. So I send everyone home and start locking up the site, which takes about an hour. There's probably a TV somewhere—maybe in the trailer we use as a break room—but I don't need to see what's happening in Manhattan.

I need to be there.

I peel onto the highway and head back to the office in Brentwood, Long Island, where I'll pick up some gear and drive into the city to see if I can help in some way. There are bound to be casualties.

Maybe I'll hand out water.

Maybe I'll give blood.

If there's broken glass and wreckage from the planes in the streets, I'll help with the cleanup. I'll do whatever's needed.

As I cross the Throgs Neck Bridge and the Manhattan skyline comes into view, I screech to a stop. I get out of my car and stare, mouth hanging open, hands on my head, awestruck by a scene I can't comprehend. A dark cloud, like the aftermath of an A-bomb in the place where the towers once stood, is carried thousands of feet into the air by the heat of burning rubble and blown out to sea by a gentle breeze.

At 9:59 AM, 9-1-1 logs report a female caller concerned about the respiratory effects of the dust and ash settling outside her apartment window on Duane Street. This is the first person we know of to have raised such a concern, a wildly inappropriate reason to call 9-1-1 at the time.

Standing on the bridge, beside my parked SUV with my hazards on, I have no way of knowing that for the next two decades, the evil cloud will occupy my waking hours and rob me of sleep. The dust will introduce me to the greatest friends I'll ever know. And the dust will take my friends away, slowly and painfully. Working on the Pile, we will eat in the dust, sleep in the dust (or try to), and cry in the dust. We will absorb the toxic cocktail of mutagens and carcinogens through our noses, mouths, and skin. We will later learn that the dust is made up of everything you can think of and a lot of things you wouldn't imagine, from pulverized concrete, glass, and metal to the mercury from thousands of broken lightbulbs. The pH of the dust is roughly the same as Drano. The fires at Ground Zero create what *Scientific American* will later dub a "chemical factory," superheating elements to form new, lethal compounds.

We'll be told that the air is safe. The coughs we develop immediately, our burning eyes, and the illnesses and deaths that follow testify that it's not. We will carry the proof in our lungs and in our tissues and bones. That dark cloud will hang over us for the rest of our lives. The dust will never settle.

Somewhere in that plume of destruction that I'm staring at are the men and women who will stand shoulder to shoulder with me over the next two decades in the fight for post-9/11 healthcare. Among those who answer the call that morning is Michael O'Connell, a twenty-five-year-old probational firefighter, not yet even a graduate of the Fire Academy. He joins Kenny Specht and hundreds of his brothers rushing to the scene, with an official FDNY response time of five seconds following the first plane hitting the towers.

There are guys like firefighter Billy Gormley, who aren't on duty that day, racing to their firehouses to find that all the trucks have left. They get to the World Trade Center any way they can: on foot, carpooling, or in Gormley's case, requisitioning a city bus with a reluctant driver.

Ray Pfeifer is off duty that day and golfing with a group of firefighters. They all hurry to their firehouses, suit up, and head for Ground Zero.

Lou Alvarez, an NYPD bomb squad detective, is there as a first responder and investigator, gathering evidence in a crime scene that's on fire. Phil Rizzo, a captain in the Department of Corrections ESU (SWAT team), locks down Rikers Island and heads to Ground Zero along with many of his fellow corrections officers, unsung heroes of the cleanup.

Uptown, FDNY paramedic Ivonne Sanchez is working to free a large, older gentleman who fell between a wall and the toilet in his penthouse bathroom. Sanchez and the firefighters on the scene are cutting away the toilet and a section of drywall when the chatter over the radio becomes impossible to ignore. They drop the big man off at the hospital and head downtown.

Tom Wilson is at the scene of a burglary in Brooklyn, taking statements from an elderly couple, when he's summoned by repeated "1013" Mayday calls over the radio. The burglary case will go unresolved, as far as Tom knows.

Rafael Orozco, NYPD community affairs, is stuck in a car wash when he gets the news. It's primary day in the city, and he wants the police van to look presentable.

Meanwhile, in Washington DC, FBI Special Agent Thomas J. Mohnal is stuck in traffic on his way to respond to the attack on the World Trade Center. He watches American Airlines Flight 77 hit the Pentagon.

In the language of post-9/11 healthcare and compensation, these are the "responders." As cleanup becomes the main objective at Ground Zero, this group will include people in the construction trades, sanitation workers, and many random volunteers who are as brave as they are unqualified.

The "survivors" are made up of everyone below Houston Street on September 11 and during the cleanup that follows. People like Lila Nordstrom, who watches the towers burn from her classroom at Stuyvesant, one of New York's elite public high schools, where she is starting her senior year. Michael Barasch, a personal injury lawyer for cops and firefighters hurt on the job, is at his law firm, just two blocks from the World Trade Center. Paralyzed by the view of people jumping from the towers, his staff delays evacuation. Barasch will be the first to put it in the public record that all the firemen working on the Pile have developed a signature "World Trade Center cough."

The Daily Show host and professional night owl Jon Stewart is still in bed in his Lower Manhattan apartment when he hears and feels the roar of the first plane flying overhead, lower and faster than commercial jets ever fly. His show that night, scheduled to feature rock star Dave Navarro, will be canceled. Jon will become a 9/11 responder in his own right, responding to the tragedy and the political absurdities that follow with his gift for rhetoric and satire. And when the responders and survivors start getting sick and dying, he will become an advocate and friend like no other.

With no idea of all that's to come, I take a deep breath of fresh late-summer air and compose myself. I get back in my Ford Expedition, gear up, and drive into the dust.

Testimony

LILA NORDSTROM

September 10th–12th were school picture days at Stuyvesant High School, where I had just started my senior year. I'd had my picture taken on the 10th and hated it.

On September 11th, I picked out a special outfit—not dressed up, just a shirt I liked better than the one I had on the day before. I wore makeup. The plan was to get my photo retaken with my classmates who were having theirs taken on the 11th. Obviously, nobody got their picture taken that day.

They ended up retaking everyone's pictures sometime later that fall. It was like we all had new faces. I ended up liking the first picture better.

Lila Nordstrom was a senior at Stuyvesant High School, in Lower Manhattan, on 9/11. She is the author of *Some Kids Left Behind* and the founder of StuyHealth, an advocacy group representing former students who were in Lower Manhattan during 9/11 and the resulting cleanup.

You can look up, and have probably already seen countless times in news reruns, what we saw from our classrooms three blocks from the towers. I don't want to talk about that, and to do so wouldn't add anything to your understanding of what New Yorkers experienced that day. The ground shook when the first tower collapsed. The lights flickered. We were all frightened. The Applebee's across the street disappeared in the dust. We were evacuated just before the second tower fell. I walked away with a classmate for miles, uptown and all the way into Queens in brand new, silver flats that were a terrible choice for covering miles of pavement.

My experience as a survivor should have ended that morning when I found clearer air and blue skies north of Houston Street. But, due to decisions made for me and my classmates by adults in a position to know better, our ordeal was just beginning. On September 18th, Christine Todd Whitman, head of the EPA, released a written statement that said: "I am glad to reassure the people of New York and Washington, DC, that their air is safe to breathe and their water is safe to drink." Based on that assessment and the attitude that getting back to "normal" as soon as possible was the patriotic thing to do, we were sent back to school in a building that would not be decontaminated until January 2002. In addition to all the dust deposited in and around the building when the towers collapsed, the barges that would haul the toxic rubble away from Manhattan were loaded just across the street from the intake vents for the school's heating and air-conditioning, introducing and recirculating more dust.

I live with GERD, the most common post 9/11 illness after PTSD, an esophageal condition that can lead to throat cancer, among other complications. I had asthma and allergies before 9/11, but now I have super asthma and super allergies that require stronger, more specialized, and expensive medication. During the gap in care between moving out of my parents' place and becoming eligible to stay on their health insurance thanks to Obamacare, I used to rely on my doctor sneaking me enough free samples of my asthma meds to get me through the semester when I would come home from college. And I'm one of the lucky ones healthwise. As I told the congressional subcommittee in 2019: I haven't had my twentieth high school reunion, and I know five people with lymphoma. My friend Michelle has thyroid cancer. And classmates are starting to die.

Since I made that statement over five years ago, those cancer numbers have ballooned significantly, to the point where I don't have an exact number, but I know of at least twenty-five. I have been to more funerals, of classmates and of other survivors I've come to know through my work. Michelle is still with us.

As minors, the choice to spend a school year in an environmental disaster area wasn't legally ours to make, and the adults who made it for us had been lied to and misinformed.

We were not "heroes."

We didn't respond or search or rescue or recover.

We're not who you remember when you say "never forget."

One

WHY WAIT?

Growing up on Long Island in the late '70s/early '80s, my childhood was a little different from Lila's. What we have in common is that we both went through things no child should be exposed to, and those experiences made us into the relentless activists we grew up to be.

Dad stops beating us when I'm big enough to stop him. I'm sixteen years old; it's 1983. I come home from school and interrupt him as he's winding up, standing over my mother in the kitchen of our little house in Commack, Long Island. Mom is sobbing, not from pain or fear, but embarrassment. My being there to witness this makes it worse. I've seen what will happen next so many times, I'm sick of it, but I'm also helpless. This time it's Mom. Next time it will be me, her baby, or my brother or my sisters. On a good day, he'll pay us ten bucks to leave him alone. He'll go out, get drunk, hold one or all of us accountable for whatever resentment he's seething with, whatever personal disappointment or shortcoming is standing between him and the life he thought he deserved. When it's all over, he will be so, so sorry. "It will never happen again." But it will, of course. Over and over until it's normal for four children and a woman who deserve better.

We are his hostages.

He is our terrorist.

I step into the kitchen. This ends today.

Taking on my father is the fight I've been training for all my life, with an undefeated record on the playground. I was eleven years old when my brother and his friends showed up while I was in the middle of getting my ass kicked. I thought the cavalry had arrived, but they told me:

"If you don't get up and kick their asses, we're going to beat your ass when they're done."

It was like the eighth rule of *Fight Club: YOU HAVE TO FIGHT.* My brother's words stung worse than the fists or the pavement. I regained my composure, got to my feet, and proceeded to whale on the bully who had been clobbering me. Between that brawl and high school graduation, I must have been in eighty fights. Undefeated. But here's the thing; in every one of those bouts I was defending someone who was being bullied, protecting my sisters or my friends, or putting a creep in their place. Living with constant abuse meant living in constant fear. Bullying scared me, even when I wasn't the one on the receiving end. The violence at home and in the schoolyard didn't desensitize me, it made me overly sensitive. Some jerk would want to amuse himself at the expense of a special-needs kid, and I would get so upset that I had to stop it the only way I knew how. We all knew that one kid in school who got picked on something awful. Maybe we didn't stand up for them, or maybe we joined in. That feeling made me so distressed that I had to act, even if it meant I was about to get hurt or suspended again.

At that age, there's all this posturing and arrogance that goes along with physical intimidation. I hated that and had no patience for it. One of my many suspensions happened when this kid challenged me to meet him on the corner after school.

"Let's do it right here," I said and laid him out with one punch, right there in the hallway.

If we're going to fight, let's do it, right here, right now. Why "take it outside"? Why wait for the dismissal bell? The number of times I punched someone in the mouth as they were getting the words out, "I'm gonna kick . . ."

Why wait?

When the bullying was personal, I did some of my best work. One time my sister, April, the nerd, "the Quaker" as we call her because she wouldn't fight, is getting picked on for doing well in science class. This kid is saying she sucked the teacher's dick. He's a varsity bench warmer. I'm captain of the wrestling team at this point. Friday is game day for him. It is also spaghetti day at lunch. Brett is sitting at a table for eight with some jocks and their friends. I open a can of whoop ass right then and there, and not one of his jock pals lifts a finger to help him. They're all wearing spaghetti when I'm done with Brett.

I would imagine it's a typical response for a young man who's getting abused to become an abuser, as an outlet, or a way of imitating what he learns at home, or a means to feel powerful and in control instead of being controlled. In my case, I wasn't above choosing violence, but unlike your typical repeater of the cycle of abuse, I put violence to use as a protector. And that, I owe to my mother's example. Without her, I would have been a thug. God knows where I would be today without her love and example. Not helping people. Nowhere near the halls of Congress.

Whimpering, shaking on the floor of her kitchen, hands up in a pathetic defense, Mom needs me. She's screaming, "Please, don't."

Her sobbing is only encouraging my father to get rougher.

It's time to pay her back for everything she's given me and put that moral backbone to good use. Four kids by the age of twenty-five, countless beatings, all the excuse making.

I'm not a boy anymore. I refuse to be "the good man who does nothing." I want her to have options besides being a punching bag or a shield for her kids. I want her to live.

Dad is a Green Beret, he has killed in the hills of Korea; he's a machinist who shapes steel. But I'm not afraid of him. The one thing holding me back is the dread of my mother seeing my violent side; that reservation is at odds with a love that would have me kill for her.

"Mom," I say, "I got this."

The room goes silent. Dad stops looming over her and focuses on me.

He squares up. "You want a piece of this?"

"Yeah, actually, I do."

"You little shit, I'll kick your ass!"

There's that posturing again.

"Let's take this outside," he says.

He readies his old weapon of choice with me—the belt. As he pulls it off, in an intimidating whipping motion, his pants drop around his ankles. Pathetic. In an instant I go from getting ready to kill him to just feeling so sorry for the guy. While he's tangled up in his pants, I grab him in a half nelson and drag his ass out the front door. I come back into the house and lock the door behind him. I throw his car keys out the window.

"Let me in, I'll kick your ass."

"Go fuck yourself."

His shouts and pounding fade into the background, like a screen door rattling in a storm.

Back in the kitchen, I say the obvious thing: "Mom, why don't you just divorce this guy. He's no good, and you deserve better."

What she does next remains the bravest thing I've seen anyone do. She divorces that loser and starts over, moving into a small apartment, where I live with her while I finish high school. She gets a job at a stationery store in a strip mall. She will live in that apartment and work in that store for the rest of her life. She will never have money or nice things, and that fact will never bother her or keep her from being generous. During those last Thanksgivings and Christmases at home, and every year after when I come home for the holidays, there are people I've never met joining us at our table, people with nowhere else to go or no family of their own. There is always enough room. There is always enough of everything. I will carry on this tradition, picking up the tab for the next table over, paying for the person behind me in line, buying donuts for the homeless dude outside my building and sitting with him while he eats because he must be hungry for companionship too. This is my self-care pick-me-up when I'm down. And I think of her whenever I do it.

Anyone can throw a punch. Most people can take a punch. Strategy is what separates a thug from a warrior. I was lucky to have training from a young age because Coach Schuster saw something in my physical aggression besides grounds for suspension. He found a place for me on the wrestling team where I made captain and went on to be ranked sixth in Suffolk County, where there are over fifty schools, and around twenty-eighth in New York state.

Everything I went on to do in Washington I did without having ever studied civics or law. But none of it would have been possible without the lessons I learned as a wrestler. On the mat is where I learned to savor the feeling of proving people wrong, a feeling I will chase all the way to DC. Tell me I can't do it. Tell me "No!"—I love that word. Just don't call it a fluke when I prove you wrong. At the first big tournament of my senior year, I beat Chris Lauria, who was ranked number one in the state (a great guy by the way, who's now with the NYPD). They call it a fluke. That lights a fire under me. When I beat him again, at which point I'm ranked fourth in the county, they say it's an "early season loss."

Those matches with Chris teach me a lesson about earned respect that will stick with me. The first time I beat him, he won't shake my hand. The second time I beat him, he hugs me like a brother.

I wrestle in over four hundred matches in my career, in junior high,

high school, and every summer. My mother makes sacrifices to get me to wrestling camps. She's on the edge of the mat, shouting:

"That's my son, don't hurt my boy!"

I have to tell her, "Mom, just let me wrestle."

It gets to where we have to kick her out of the gym; she was too enthusiastic. Watching me cut weight between football and wrestling, she worries, "You look like you're killing yourself, I hope you know what you're doing."

The only match my father ever attends, I lose.

Going into a match is the one time I don't give a firm handshake. No disrespect, I just don't want to know how strong my opponent is. Don't give me the odds. I always help a guy up after. When I play football, I hand the ball to the ref; I don't spike it.

In 1984, my senior year at Commack South, my last match, I wrestle Chuck Sciabba, who was the JV wrestler under me. I make him wrestle for six minutes and I intentionally hurt him, putting all my weight on him with my takedown, throwing a cross face that was more like a punch. He's furious. But I end up taking first in the tournament, and he takes second, making us the only school to have the varsity and JV first and second from the same school.

I sit with Chuck after the match and say, "I'm sure you're mad, and you have every right to be. But lemme tell you something . . . You're gonna have somebody who trains underneath you next year when I'm gone, and they're gonna look up to you and want to be as good as you. They're gonna want to beat you. Two things happened today: One, I made sure you couldn't beat me. And two I made sure you were ready to take the mantle from me."

After that match, I cry for the first time since my grandfather died and the last time before 9/11. I cry because it's over and soon, I won't be a champion or a wrestler, a teammate or a rival.

The summer before my junior year, at a tournament at George Washington University, in front of a bunch of college scouts, my hand touches my shoulder backward, breaking my elbow in three places. It happens in a bout I could have won in thirty seconds, but I force the guy to go six minutes to give me a workout. I paid for my ticket to be there, I wanted to enjoy the ride. It ends up being an expensive ticket.

I lose my shot at a scholarship with the injury. And in any case, I'm looking at schools that keep me on the island or elsewhere in state when all I want to do is get away.

I find an army recruiter who laughs in my face. "How old are you, kid?"

I tell him I'm going to be the best damn soldier the army's ever seen. I'm ready to kick ass for Uncle Sam. I'm Bo fucking Jackson.

He sends me home with a permission slip. At seventeen, I need my parents' signatures.

My father makes a point of letting me know he doesn't think I'm army material. My mom doesn't want her baby going to war; I sit with her a long time before she signs. Looking back, I think nobody in their right mind would have signed me over to the army if they knew what was in my head and my heart: I'm cocky, young, arrogant, and naive. I want to be badder than Dad, out-hero him. I want to die on the battlefield. I want to die a hero. At seventeen, I can't yet understand that wanting that means wanting to break my mother's heart.

I'm ready physically, but I have a lot of growing up to do. And that happens fast at basic training. Indoc at Fort Hamilton, in Brooklyn, is intimidating. Like a jail environment, waiting for orders, the soldiers not yet separated from the guys who don't belong there. We get on a plane to Georgia. In basic, our staff sergeant is a small but terrifying man built to scare some sense into cocky kids like me who swagger into the army, thinking they'll never let someone yell at them. As a Yankee in the South, I can't win with the drill sergeants. If I say I'm from New York, I'm a mugger and a rapist and a murderer. If I say I'm from Long Island, I'm a spoiled rich kid. Either way, I'm getting singled out for some remedial attention.

Staff sergeant wants to use me as an example during pugil stick training, those giant padded Q-tip–looking things soldiers use to practice clobbering each other as if with rifle butts. I'm putting on my football helmet for the drill, but staff sergeant doesn't wait, he clocks me under the chin with a cheap shot before I'm ready, and I bite my tongue so hard I end up needing stitches. There's a limit to how many days of basic training you can miss before you wash out or have to start over. My case is borderline. It works in my favor that he really wasn't supposed to do that. This is around the time drill sergeants are no longer allowed to hit soldiers. This guy didn't get the memo, I guess.

Just because I'm in the army doesn't mean I have to take that kind of abuse sitting down. Tradition allowed me to challenge him in "the pit," a place reserved for setting aside rank and settling differences man-to-man. We get in there and I wrestle him; I don't punch or kick, I sweep him, I want him to know that if we're not throwing cheap shots, he poses no threat to me. I can end it in twenty seconds, but I drag it out. He needs to feel the embarrassment.

My tongue heals. I learn quick. I run quick. All the way to the top four in my basic training class. On the last day of basic, I smoke everyone in the two-mile run, like nine minutes.

As graduation draws near, we start looking at places where we might want to go. A lot of us don't have much choice. And that is why I made sure to graduate in the top four of my class. For next duty assignment, I get my first choice—101st Airborne, air assault. That's an easy one for me, a screaming eagle. Not that there's anything wrong with 10th Mountain Division, but they're stationed in New York state, and the whole point of joining the army was to get out of there. The 101st sends me to Air Assault School where I learn to rappel out of helicopters and how to get the chain-link count right, hooking a helicopter up to a Humvee to pick it up. We "Australian rappel" down the side of buildings, face-first, after mastering it upright. We learn to jump and fall and land without hurting ourselves, but mostly, we march and run. A lot.

Every so often, we are told, "You guys are up."

Nobody says anything; we all know what to do. We get our stuff, get in the back of a deuce-and-a-half truck, and get driven to the airport where we sit in a C-41 transport plane and wait. It could be an hour. I wait as long as a day one time, telling myself: *This is the one. This is the one.* Then they tell us to stand down, with no explanation, and the army's largest deployable unit goes back to training and killing time.

I miss Grenada by a year. I miss Panama by a year.

Meanwhile, back on Long Island, my sister, April, is in trouble again. I had a long-standing beef with a kid I'll call "Sonny," who claimed his dad was in the Mafia and tried to intimidate everyone he crossed paths with, using violence with anyone who wasn't stupid enough to believe his tough talk. He and his pals, a bunch of wannabe thugs, would go into Grand Union to steal and to harass customers. One day, toward the end of high school, they started bothering my sister in the store where she was working. She said:

"You know who my brother is; he'll kick your ass."

They stole some money from her pocketbook. I started looking for Sonny as soon as she told me. I caught up with his crew at a local deli, but there was no sign of him. Rather than "take this outside," I beat one of them senseless with the cash register and told the others to tell your buddy I'm looking for him. Later, a bunch of his friends jumped me at a local shopping center. They gave me an out, saying, "What are you going to do, there's four of us and one of you." I took them all down with the shopping cart. But I never found Sonny, and before long, it was time to ship out for basic training.

While I'm at Fort Campbell, April and her nerdy friends go to a sad amusement park on Long Island called Adventureland. She runs into Sonny, who's there with his friends, his sister, and her friends. They get hold of April, break a bottle in front of her, and use the glass to cut her face up.

I come home on leave and resume the manhunt, this time as a

soldier. I find one of Sonny's friends at a pizza parlor. I tap on the glass. I go inside. I throw him through the glass and out into the street. I go back outside, stepping through the broken window, and throw him back into the pizza place again. I walk back through the broken window and throw him back out again. I go nuts. I play with this creep. But I never find Sonny. Years go by and he remains a ghost. One Saturday afternoon, I'm home, lying on the couch while April is out working one of her many jobs, selling jewelry at a flea market at the Long Island Arena. She calls to tell me Sonny's there.

I get up, get in my car, and drive to the flea market. The place is huge, and April has no idea where he is, so I wander around looking. I shout his name as soon as I see him. He knows what's coming. I take him to the ground and punch his face until it's soft and lumpy like mashed potatoes. He has a wife and two kids with him, and I kick his ass in front of them.

I feel a hand on the back of my shirt. Security pulls me off him and drags me away. He shouts through the blood:

"Are we good now?"

"Yeah, we're good."

There's an interview with an FDNY lieutenant, Mickey Cross, who was in the towers and got out before they collapsed. He remembers climbing the stairs with all his gear, struggling under the weight. He fell back on a cadence from boot camp he sang as an eighteen-year-old marine:

"ONE TWO THREE FOUR I LOVE THE MARINE CORPS."

And that helped him keep moving up. The greatest lesson from the army, the one I will lean on when I get hurt and on our trips to DC, has nothing to do with war or fighting or fitness. It's that mental toughness you can draw from as a reserve when you think you've got nothing left. Once a month, we do a thirty-mile road march as a unit. I carry a sixty-pound ruck with all the standard-issue gear plus an additional twenty-four-pound AN/PRC-77 radio plus batteries. That's on a Saturday. If you don't complete the march in the allotted eight hours, you have to do it again on Sunday.

I will never use my road marching skills in combat, but I will use the toughness I acquired on those marches to teach myself to walk again from one end of a hospital room to the other. And to walk the marble halls of Congress, in pain but undaunted.

I'm stationed at Fort Campbell, Kentucky. I visit Nashville, Memphis, Chicago, and towns you've never heard of. In Paducah, Kentucky, I attend a wedding between one of our guys and his cousin. One of my roommates is from Livingston, Tennessee. His high school didn't have a yearbook, it had a pamphlet. It's a town full of pickup trucks and bluegrass music. And drinking. The first time I visit, I'm talking to this girl at a party in a field. She's wearing overalls, and she's beautiful. She hands me her beer in a red Solo cup and says she has to go pee. She walks over about four feet away from me, drops her overalls, squats, and pees. You don't see that on Long Island.

The life expectancy of a radioman in the last war, Vietnam, was like two seconds of combat. The radio puts a big target on your back, because taking you out means silencing an entire platoon, often while simultaneously decapitating its leadership by greasing the lieutenant or captain holding the phone. In my experience, in war games, the job has its pros and cons like any other, the main drawback being the weight of the radio and batteries. The upside is not having to dig a foxhole and enjoying some of the fringe benefits of rank, quartered with the officers while working as the company commander's bitch. This means sleeping in a Jeep sometimes instead of in the dirt. Another downside is this annoying habit officers have of pulling you by the radio phone while they're talking and trying to do other things at the same time.

A highlight of my time in the army is an exercise at Fort Drum, New

York, in 1985. They pit our squad of seven against a battalion of reservists, about 1,100 men. The idea is to give these citizen soldiers a chance to go up against an elite unit and see how they do. Their job is to find us in the woods and take us out. They put graders and spotters everywhere. Early in the battle, I get lucky and score a couple of "kills," like, "BANG, you're dead." The slain enemy put stickers on to indicate their KIA status.

I get the bright idea to commit a soft war crime. I swap uniforms with one of the dead guys. He protests—but he's supposed to be dead—and I proceed to walk right into their base, where I find their headquarters' radio tent. I take all their information, their codebooks, and everything we need to compromise their comms. I walk it back and bring it to my sergeant and Captain Laufenberg, our company commander. We listen to their comms all night and make a plan. At dawn, we take out their company commander and his HQ. We tie him to a pole, like something the Vietcong would do, and ransack the mostly sleeping camp, stickering whole squads.

"You're dead . . . you guys are dead . . . you over there, you're dead too . . . this whole tent is dead."

We get an achievement medal for the op and a reprimand for going overboard with the mistreatment of prisoners.

It goes without saying that I had a little insubordination problem that would eventually come between me and a career in soldiering. The rules and regimental way of living became tedious. There are opportunities for advancement and selection for specialized training, but many of these come with commitments to lengthy enlistment contracts that increasingly start to feel like signing up for more years of getting yelled at and chewed out over minor infractions while doing nothing but practicing and playacting at war. The physical toll starts to add up. Ruck marches, drills, time in the field, it all hurts. The human body is just not made for that kind of punishment over years and decades, the constant wear and tear. It stops being fun.

I'm out jogging one afternoon. We do a five-mile run every morning, but I supplement it with additional running after work. When we're not in the field, garrison life is like a nine-to-five job, with an earlier start. You do formation in the morning, you get told what to do, you get it done, you have formation and a head count again in the afternoon, you go home, and you show up again. So simple it makes you crazy. So one day, I'm out on my after-work run on base. Cars, jeeps, and other military vehicles pass me, and I don't think anything of it. One car passes, stops, turns around, and pulls up next to me. The driver rolls down his window and says:

"Do you know who this man is?"

I salute and say, "No, sir, I don't, should I?"

He introduces the base commander, Lt. Col. Thompson.

I straighten up and say, "Thank you, sir, for everything, I'm proud to serve in the 101st Airborne, SIR!"

"Son, next time I drive by, you salute. Is that understood?"

"Sir, you're driving past me at thirty-five miles per hour, and I'm focused on running so I can kill babies and be the best soldier I can be, sir."

He proceeds to rip me a new one. He has me doing push-ups on the side of the road and drives past me again to have me practice saluting him. Later, he calls my company commander, and I get chewed out in front of 110 guys. I ask my CO what am I supposed to do, not run? Not stay in shape? Salute every car just in case there's an officer riding in it?

He tells me to watch my mouth.

I think about becoming a cop but rule that out for the same reason I get tired of the army. I look at my friends who are cops; the Suffolk County guys are all married, 3.2 kids, white picket fence, boat in the marina, etc. The city cops I know are divorced, alcoholics, drug addicts. Neither life sounds appealing, and chasing delinquent kids around and issuing summons doesn't sound like the life I want.

My father had taught me how to fabricate and weld. I get into construction and use the endurance I honed in the army, and my lack of family commitments, to work crazy hours in foreman and manager positions.

In 1998, I start with Diversified Construction as one of five foremen in a company of two hundred. As the only one who isn't married, I work later, start earlier, and take on the more thankless tasks. I reward my guys for their hard work by letting them keep and sell copper and scrap out of the demo jobs. We do large-scale demolition, transforming the suburbs from what they are to what they're becoming. Leveling tenement blocks to make way for shopping malls, scraping old malls for multifamily housing developments. The broom in a culture of more more more.

I buy a house with a big sofa and TV and recliner; I buy a Corvette, a Ford Expedition, a Jeep, and a Harley. I'm saving to retire young to someplace sunny. I take up golf.

Life is good.

ACTION FOR ACTIVISTS: FIND YOUR MINIMUM VIABLE ACTIVISM AND START NOW

When someone tells you they want to "take it outside," or whatever their professional or bureaucratic version of that may be, they're usually bluffing and hoping to scare you off because the last thing they want is to take it outside. So, call their bluff. Better yet, force them to "do it right here."

Get them into the pit.

When the 9/11 responders went to DC, that meant meetings in the hall, with cameras rolling with reps who wouldn't give us meetings. Our timeline was defined by the urgent need of sick and dying responders and survivors, not the schedules of congressional representatives who wanted us to engage on their terms at times that suited their agendas.

The time to start your activism is NOW. Don't let someone else dictate your timeline. Don't wait for things to get worse or for the need to become more urgent. Delays are inevitable; there's no point in further dragging things out through procrastination. Procrastination kills. A mother had to lose a child before Mothers Against Drunk Driving (MADD) was founded. A great organization that does great work, but a kid shouldn't have to die before we get together and confront something as obviously harmful as drunk driving.

To do this well, you have to be ready to go and seize the initiative. Simplify your message. Not everyone has to agree with you, but they must at least understand you. Cut through context and concepts and get at the heart of what needs to change and how you plan to act. Don't wait!

To quote General Patton: "A good plan violently executed now is better than a perfect plan executed next week."

Testimony

MIKE O'CONNELL

As a rookie firefighter, you're told to keep your eyes and ears open and your mouth shut. It's how you learn the job. I was still on probation in September 2001, after starting with the fire department in May. I hadn't yet graduated from the academy.

There were one hundred of us in my academy class. Two quit when they saw their first paychecks. Six died in the towers.

Mike O'Connell, aka "Lush," is an FDNY lieutenant who was medically retired in 2010 due to 9/11 illness. He testified before Congress in 2019 and continues to work with families navigating the VCF (Victim Compensation Fund) and WTC (World Trade Center) health programs.

The summer had been all classroom work and physical fitness. After that phase, they put us through a fourteen-week program with seven weeks in an engine and seven weeks in a truck. After that, we were scheduled to graduate and get our next assignments sometime in late October, early November.

We were sent throughout all five boroughs, assigned alphabetically by last name. I wound up doing my training with my buddy Robbie O'Korn in Flushing, Queens.

I was at home on Long Island the morning of September 11th. My phone rang. It was my buddy who was working in Brooklyn at the time and could see the towers in flames. I wasn't sure if I was going to get called into this, but I hung up and called the firehouse to see if I was due. I turned on the news and saw the second plane hit, at which point I raced to the firehouse. It was like *Total Recall*, you had the guys who were there working, and the guys like me who showed up. Shea Stadium was a staging area, and they started busing in guys from there to Lower Manhattan. All we knew is that the country was under attack, and we were on our way to a massive fire. On our way, we hear the Pentagon's been hit, and there's another plane down.

I thought about it in terms of all the skills I was learning and fire department operations. I was thinking: *The elevators are out of the question, so guys are walking up. In a regular house fire, we pull up with a fire engine, hook up to a fire hydrant, and get water through the truck, and you can go all day long like that. The Twin Towers, like all skyscrapers, worked off standpipes, so these guys had to carry two-and-a-half-inch roll-ups, weighing about thirty or forty pounds, up seventy-plus flights of stairs, and who even knew if the standpipe system was functioning after a plane severed so many if not all of the pipes, so maybe they would get all the way up there and have no water.* All of this is racing through my head. I'm getting ready to have to do it myself. My eyes and ears are open, ready to take cues from the senior guys. But they've never seen anything like this either.

Then the towers collapse.

Every thought of training, and firefighting, and my own safety, got replaced in that instant by the one we were all thinking; one of the senior guys, Louis Minutoli, turned to me and said it out loud:

"Do you have any idea how many guys we just lost?"

We became firemen because of the value we place on human life and the lengths we will go to save a life. None of us have a frame of reference for loss on this scale. My racing thoughts returned to Father's Day, 2001. We worked Monday through Friday in the academy. Father's Day was on a weekend. There was a fire in a hardware store. A bad place for a fire. One guy went through the floor and got trapped in the basement, where he died. Two other guys were killed in the front of the building when it collapsed. On Monday, I came back to the academy, and everything felt somber and heavy. We were already at a stage where we understood and felt that this isn't just a job, it's a brotherhood. We lost three brothers. That's tragic enough, but each one of these guys is married with kids. Wives and children crying because Daddy's not coming home. Our instructors told us something like, "Let's hope in your careers, this is the worst you ever see or hear of."

We lost 343 on the morning of September 11th. Among them was my closest buddy at the academy, Anthony Rodriguez. He was one of the oldest in the class, at thirty-six, because he had served in the navy, and the department allows veterans to take the test and pause while they're in the service and not age out of the job. He was already married with three kids, and his wife was pregnant with their fourth. Anthony worked in Red Hook, Brooklyn, Engine 279. All of 279—he and five other guys—were lost that day. We lost the youngest guy in our class too, Mike Cammarata, twenty-two. Calixto Anaya, Engine 4, and Richard Allen, Ladder 15, had been at those firehouses because of their last names. I lost my dear friend Mikey Kiefer, a high school buddy of mine; his whole truck, Ladder 132, was killed.

It was tragic then, all that loss and sacrifice, but I understand on a whole other level now that I'm a father and a husband. At twenty-five, speeding toward those burning towers, I didn't have anything to lose or to sacrifice besides my own life. Now, I think of my kids and my wife, and the void my loss would leave in their lives. At the time, I was thinking about the job and the tactics of firefighting and rescue. When I remember that morning, I think about what it must have been like to go in there and climb those steps, knowing you're not getting out of this. I think about the people diving ninety stories to their deaths because nobody wants to burn.

You don't need me to tell you what it looked like when we got to the scene. There are so many pictures. We all know what it looked like. The sound is what sticks with me. For one thing, it was quieter than you might imagine. That is because the dust in the air and on every surface absorbed a lot of the sound, the way snow does. As we approached the Pile all we could hear was the shrieking of PASS alarms that each firefighter wears that activate when he has been motionless for thirty seconds or more. We realize that these alarms are not coming from the guys working on top of the Pile. They're coming from guys trapped under the Pile who we can't get to. The alarms sound continuously as long as their battery packs supply power and they are not consumed by the heat and flames under the rubble. They chirp for hours, days, maybe weeks. I'm the wrong person to give you an exact time, because I can hear them to this day.

That sound changed my life in an instant. Walking into the Pile, I made a pact with myself, I swore with that sound as my witness that I would try to live a life that means something and is worthy of their sacrifice. I will never amount to who those guys were on that day, but I will try my best to live a life that's about giving more than I take and loving more than I'm loved.

I told Congress about the alarms and my pact when I testified in 2019. I tell students when I speak at schools, and I pass those lessons on to my kids. You don't have to be a first responder or a graduate of the fire academy or a survivor of a historic event to live up to that example, it's enough to be human.

Two

IF NOT ME, THEN WHO?

Now that those of us who responded to the September 11 attacks are all sick and dying, or waiting to get sick, everyone's favorite question is whether we would still go knowing what will happen to us. Many first responders agree with Michael O'Connell and would say "absolutely." But they would also appreciate not being lied to about the dust and the long-term risks. I don't want to say anything to diminish the courage of someone who feels that way, and I have no doubt that jobs like firefighters, police, and the military inspire and require that kind of courage. So for men like Michael, maybe that attitude is just part of the job. On the other hand, we all know we're supposed to say that. It's the sound-bite-friendly answer that affirms everyone's belief in heroes and our fond memories of how we all came together on that awful day and in the days after. It's one of those Hallmarkisms you find in war movies, like "you would have done the same for me . . ."

I would have to know a few important details before I could answer that question honestly.

If you could stop me on the bridge as I watch the plume drift out over the Atlantic and tell me *exactly* what's going to happen: "John, this morning you woke up after the last good night's sleep you'll ever have. You are going to hurt, mentally and physically, nonstop from this day forward. You will be lied to and disrespected by the very people for whom you put your health and safety and sanity on the line without having to be asked. A week from today, you will be disabled, disfigured, and disqualified from the only work you know how to do. You will see things you'll never get out of your head. When you get under the covers every night, they will visit you, the ones you couldn't help. You will hate yourself for surviving. You will be hard to be married to, hard to know. But the people who were there with you and in the long fight after will become closer than family to you—together you will do amazing things. You'll be on TV and honored in the halls of government, and the president will shake your hand. You will give each one of 'your guys' a nickname because it's easier that way when they're gone. Death from the dust will be slow and agonizing. One by one, they'll suffer, waste away, and die. And every time, you'll wish it was you instead, not just because you would die for these people but out of envy that, for them, it's all over. You'll have to keep living."

If I knew all this, would I still go?

Fuck no. That's my answer.

Everyone remembers the blue sky. They start every 9/11 story with a nod to the weather, as if horror doesn't happen in the sunshine. The cause of the pristine weather is a high-pressure system spinning down from Canada on a jet stream, creating a phenomenon meteorologists call "severe clear."

As far I'm concerned, September 11 and the days that follow are dark. As soon as I drive into the dust cloud, the ash and dust block out the sun. My brain searches for something familiar to make sense of these strange surroundings, and what I come up with is foggy London

Joanne Capestro (left), who worked on the 87th floor of the North Tower, and colleague fleeing the World Trade Center covered in dust. (Photo/Phil Penman, Collection 9/11 Memorial Museum)

in Jack the Ripper's day as seen in old movies. As for the odor, there's nothing before or since that I can compare to how it smells and what that smell means—the loss of life, the evil content of that dust. The best I can come up with . . . it's like the devil threw up on a pile of his own shit. Approaching the Pile, all my senses are telling me this is a bad spot. I silence that voice and go toward the smell and the heat and into the thickening dust.

I drive in with the head of our company, with a Nassau County police escort. We tow in a heavy machine, cut it loose from the trailer, and get to work. Our job is to clear and recover. Our sector is the area near World Trade Center 7, a forty-seven-story building on fire that will collapse at 5:20 PM on September 11.

WTC 7 had been home to the city's emergency command center, which had to be relocated. It's one of the most secure buildings in the world, because it is where several federal agencies have their New York offices. As we get to work clearing, a swarm of guys in windbreakers and ball caps with various three-letter acronyms on their backs are nosing around—ATF, DEA, FBI—getting in our way and putting themselves in danger. There's no security or perimeter yet, and they're anxious to make sure nothing sensitive gets lost or falls into the wrong hands. There's talk of drugs, weapons, gold bars, cash. These guys are seriously full of themselves if they think anyone down here is thinking about anything other than the horror all around and how we can help. I make a managerial decision and tell the feds to stay on the other side of a barrier and supervise us from a safe distance. If we find anything, we'll tell them. They're also looking for evidence and items of forensic value. They post pictures of the bright orange cockpit voice recorders and flight data recorders (CRV and FDR), aka the "black box." And they tell us over and over to say something if we find one. They will find parts of Flight 11's landing gear in an alley blocks away.

By late in the day on the 11th, the trades, ironworkers, and construction crews at the Pile outnumber first responders something like four to one. We will be dubbed "the Unbuilders" by William Langewiesche in *The Atlantic.* They need us to access the site and to carve out pockets of relative safety where they can do the hero's work of search and rescue in a place that makes a mockery of the first rule of first aid: "make sure the scene is safe." When their dogs catch a whiff of something, a whistle blows, and we all stop working and get quiet. Before long, we all realize that there are no living casualties to rescue. Soon, we lower expectations even further and give up hope of finding whole bodies.

Legs and arms are easy. I know what a foot in a boot looks like, and when I find one, I call over someone who's working the recovery to take the parts to the makeshift morgue nearby. Most of the parts we find are much smaller and not immediately recognizable. Some people will tell stories about slipping on a kidney or a liver. I don't buy that. Nobody knows what a kidney or liver looks like the first time they see one. It's more like a slow realization—you're looking at something that just doesn't look right and doesn't belong with the twisted rebar and pulverized concrete, and then it hits you like "oh, that must have come out of a human body that was torn apart." You call for a paramedic, or a firefighter, and you keep clearing. The folks working the morgue are meticulous and have a method to keep from identifying the same part repeatedly. They will be assisted in their efforts by an NYPD highway cop with a background in computers who I will get to know well. James Ryder puts together the database and spreadsheets they will use to cross-reference DNA from body parts, tissue, and hair recovered from the Pile with samples provided by next of kin, who will be asked for anything that might contain genetic material from the missing: hairbrushes, toothbrushes, even dirty underwear.

Firemen are more likely to be found intact due to their protective gear. Women working office jobs in skirts and stockings are shredded by the steel and burned up by the fire. Years later, firefighter Billy Gormley will have a flashback and a panic attack while grocery shopping with his family. He will turn down an aisle and see a woman with toes painted the same color as a pedicured foot he found in the Pile.

Clearing away a heap of steel is simple in theory: You start at the top and work your way down until it's all gone. But that simple whole is made up of complex and deadly details. It's like a giant game of Jenga, where you can't move a single piece without considering how doing so might affect everything else. The challenge is to remove stuff without destroying the structural integrity of the Pile. It's like a glacier of metal, with entire floors of office buildings balanced precariously on unstable stacks of rubble. Steel trestles teeter overhead, "widow-makers" in the language of loggers. A physicist would look at the Pile and see an unstable system for storing potential energy. We are all being given the final exam before anyone has taught the lesson. Steel of any size wants to spring back to its original shape. At the scale of the structural beams of a skyscraper, this means a beam under tension, weighing many tons, has the potential to sweep wildly with enough force to swat a person away like a fly or knock a pile of rubble loose in a cascade when the tension is released. Working to clear those beams, we watch that tension and keep an eye on what each piece might be holding in place. The machinery is heavy, but the work is delicate.

The instability of the Pile would be hazardous enough on its own. Now remember that everything is on fire. The fire will burn for ninety-nine days. It flares up as we clear away debris, delivering fresh air to smoldering material deep under the Pile. Steel conducts heat, so beams far from any obvious source can glow white-hot and burn anyone who isn't careful. Standing on heated debris melts the soles of my work boots. I go through six pairs. As the firefighters turn their hoses on the Pile, the water boils on contact, and we are scalded by superheated droplets landing on exposed flesh, leaving us covered in red sores, which are further irritated by the caustic dust. The plexiglass shields on our excavators melt.

The work continues. The fire is not our problem. The Pile is five to seven stories high. We carefully dismantle it and break everything down to fit in the trucks that just keep coming. The trucks carry the wreckage to barges, which take it to the Fresh Kills Landfill where NYPD and FBI Evidence Response Teams from every field office in the country sift through it all and "de-homogenize" the rubble, which is a fancy way of saying separate the tangle of steel from human remains, evidence, and personal effects. The tugboat crews are assisted in this work by seabirds. They notice gulls flocking to barges that carry human remains in their load of rubble.

At Fresh Kills, these loads are spread out in debris fields. There is a vehicle graveyard for fire trucks and ambulances.

One FBI agent remembers, "I had already seen the worst of humanity, working homicide investigations. Then (at Fresh Kills), I found a charm bracelet with a little silver baby carriage . . . I really have a hard time talking about this. I'm sorry."

The Pile and the people on it are covered in dust. The air is thick with it. My eyes burn from the moment I arrive. Everyone is coughing. People compare it to breathing sand or flour. It drifts knee-deep in places like snow. We have masks, but we don't wear them because they clog with dust and make breathing impossible. It burns to breathe, with or without a mask. My skin burns—a chemical burn like bleach, I will learn later. Apparently, the dust has the same alkalinity as Drano due to the lye content of all the concrete. My nose runs constantly. My eyes are red. The inside of my mouth is caked with dust. My tears congeal into mud.

In another sector, Corrections Captain Phil Rizzo has the good sense to order his men not to eat near the Pile.

Firefighter Ray Pfeifer remembers watching the wind direction and doing his best to stay upwind of the cloud, saying to his guys "we don't want to get cancer today." Ray is not a doctor, a scientist, or a public health official, but his common sense and training tell him the dust is extremely toxic. But what's he going to do? His brothers are under the Pile. An eleven-year-old boy asks him, "Are you going to find my dad today?"

The evidence teams will face the same exposure. Dust blows all over the landfill. The surfaces in their makeshift plywood break rooms are coated with dust. They get masks fitted by OSHA, and the masks do nothing. They will get sick and die.

When I look back on this, I will block out the gore, the carnage, the devastation, and all the things I wish I hadn't seen. I will look past the anti-Muslim graffiti, scrawled in anger on concrete and steel and drawn with fingers in the dust coating windows and vehicles. What I choose to "never forget" is the humanity and heart of the responders. Big guys breaking down. Firefighters with mustaches like poodles consoling each other, a cop weeping in his buddy's arms. We're all desperate for comfort, so we comfort each other. You look around, it looks like the end of the world, and the response from everybody is love and compassion for one another. Everyone says "thank you." These are New Yorkers; we have a reputation for being rude and abrasive. This tragedy has revealed a kindness most of us keep close to the chest in our ordinary lives. Now we're all hugging and saying "thank you" for that water bottle, "thank you" for everything. Television doesn't capture the horror, but it doesn't fully capture the humanity either.

We eat at the Pile, we sleep there or at makeshift barracks at local schools that are just as dusty. There is always food and coffee. High-end restaurants and bakeries donate food. Massage therapists rub the shoulders and aching backs of workers on the Pile. There are Porta Potties like on any construction site and volunteers who clean them. They take their job as seriously as anybody else down there. The Red Cross and civilian volunteers hand out water bottles, which are as much for eye washing as drinking. There are pop-up "flea markets" full of donated goods you can help yourself to when you need something. Every time I melt through another pair of work boots, I find another size 8.5, donated by some thoughtful stranger from who knows where. They have gloves, hats, anything we need. The USS *Mercy*, a hospital ship, is moored at Chelsea Piers, initially as a place for triage and medical care, but she soon becomes just a barracks and a canteen as there is nobody to treat. Coughs echo down her iron corridors.

Also at Chelsea Piers, Eric Kant sets up an on-site data center and IT hub. These are the days before cloud computing, when servers have to be on premises. He is an expert in disaster modeling, and his computer models will help the improvised command center keep tabs on the various zones of the cleanup. They will overlay thermal imaging and all the data they can get about the safety and stability of the site. Which is to say they find a way to quantify what we all know—the whole thing is unsafe and unstable. Eric was working in Florida on September 11, simulating a plane crash carrying radioactive materials as part of a training exercise for first responders down there. Eric grew up on Coney Island, where his family ran the amusement park. He says growing up in a circus gave him an education in chaos that now helps him use computers to make sense of disaster areas. None of us on the Pile know anything about the IT and comms work happening behind the scenes; we just know our cell phones start getting signal again.

Meanwhile in Washington, DC, FBI agents Dawnele Holbrook and Thomas Mohnal respond to the attack at the Pentagon. Like the World Trade Center, the building was hit with a plane carrying enough jet fuel for a transcontinental flight. The fire is intense, but the scene is not as complex as the Pile in New York. Dawnele works counterterrorism. Tom is an explosives expert. They have no illusions about the potential for an event like this. Dawnele was already hunting Bin Laden before the attack. They would know better than anyone what the 9/11 Commission Report means when they say, "The system was blinking red," and yet nothing can prepare them for what they're walking into. As FBI agents, after helping first responders any way they can, their main task is evidence collection. It's heartbreaking work. Dawnele recovers to-do lists that won't get done and photos in wallets and lap seat belts from the plane. As in New York, there's no logic to which pieces remain intact and which are consumed. Parts of the plane are warped beyond recognition, while papers and clothing are preserved. She finds a child's shirt that says "Princess" across the front and a boy's pajamas with airplanes up the sleeve. She thinks of her own babies at home.

Shanksville, Pennsylvania, is the most straightforward attack site, being just a plane crash in a field, uncontaminated by building materials or urban rubble. For this reason, it is the most forensically sterile and the easiest place to collect evidence, there being no benign explanation for the presence of box cutters or Saudi passports as there would be at the Pile or the Pentagon.

I work for about thirty-eight hours straight after I first get to the Pile, with the occasional ten-minute break to eat something. I don't stop or talk to anyone about anything other than the job we're there to do—clearing and making the scene safe enough for the first responders to do their jobs. When my boots melt, I go to Church Street to find new ones. I pour talcum powder down my pants to prevent crotch rot. I feel like a zombie. Eventually, I hit a breaking point, and I go home to get some rest. I feel like a stranger in my own house. The cars in the driveway and the Harley in the garage no longer excite me, like toys I used to play with as a kid. I'm not just exhausted, I'm a different person from the cool guy with fast cars who left for work on Tuesday morning, already thinking about next weekend and the golf course. I take a bath. The dark ring of dust and grime will never rinse off. I sleep for about six hours. I get back in the Expedition and return to the Pile. I don't want to. I have to.

On my way back into the city, traffic slows to a walking pace along the West Side Highway. The road is lined with I don't know how many people. Someone reaches through the open window and hands me a bunch of surgical masks.

"Take these, you'll need them where you're going."

Most of them are holding up pictures of their loved ones and printed *MISSING* posters. They're handing out flyers with photos and personal information. A lot of the pictures are wedding photos or family portraits with the missing person circled. They talk through my open windows, hundreds of them all the way to the parking area near the Pile, where more posters litter the chain-link fences and police barriers.

Have you seen my brother?
Please call 917-638 . . .
Have you seen my husband?
Missing from the 97th floor of the North Tower.
My sister was down there, we can't get ahold of her . . .
Have you seen my daddy?
Take my number, call me if you find him.

ACTION FOR ACTIVISTS: BE A RESPONDER

"Responder" isn't a job title, it's something you become when you decide to take action and face your circumstances head-on. A responder is someone who answers the question: "If not me, then who?" It's easy to find the courage to act when you realize nobody else is coming.

Practice "responding" by taking opportunities to stand up and take action in small ways every day. The need doesn't have to be immense for you to rise to the occasion. This could be as simple as picking up litter or reaching out to your elderly neighbor. Volunteer, and step up at every opportunity. Guaranteed, there's someone in your community who could use some help. Help them.

When it comes to physical safety, you don't have to wait for an emergency to prepare for one. Have a plan and an emergency kit, learn first aid. The 9/11 Report points out that "preparedness of individual civilians" was a major factor in who lived and who died that day. The commission report states, "One clear lesson of September 11th is that individual civilians need to take responsibility for maximizing the probability that they will survive should a disaster strike."

9/11 was unprecedented not just in the scale of the attack on American soil but as a day that will be forever remembered for the heroism of first responders and citizen responders, each one of whom answered the question, "If not me, then who?" in their own way.

History has recorded the exact words with which some of them answered that call.

Fire Captain Paddy Brown was in the North Tower when the South Tower collapsed, and his chief gave the order to evacuate. He replied over the radio:

"I refuse the order. I am on the forty-fourth floor, and we have too many burned people with me. I am not leaving them."

Aboard Flight 93, Todd Beamer said, "Let's roll" before he and a group of passengers fought their way into the cockpit, forcing the hijackers to crash the plane into a field in Shanksville, Pennsylvania, instead of the Capitol Building or the White House.

Rick Rescorla, Vietnam veteran and head of security for Morgan Stanley, saved 2,700 lives when he evacuated their offices after the first plane hit, disregarding the PA announcement telling everyone to stay put. When a colleague told him he should get out, too, he replied, "As soon as I make sure everyone else is out." He was last seen heading back up the South Tower.

In a last phone call to his wife, he said, "Stop crying. I have to get these people out safely. If something should happen to me, I want you to know I've never been happier. You made my life."

Citizen responder and former volunteer firefighter Welles Crowther, aka "the Man in the Red Bandana," helped coworkers to safety, administered first aid, and rallied survivors in the South Tower. His body was found with a group of fallen firefighters under the Pile. When his family cleaned out his apartment, they found an application to the FDNY. He had been planning to leave finance for what Mike O'Connell will tell you is "the best job in the world."

Survivors remember Crowther shouting through the smoke words that could be a rallying cry for anyone interested in doing the right thing:

"Everyone who can stand, stand now. If you can help others, do so."

Testimony

IVONNE SANCHEZ

I remember thinking: I can't go home. I can't face my kids. We're going to have to move, I'll have to take them out of school, that is, if their father doesn't get sole custody over this, because everyone is going to blame the fire department for those buildings coming down. We were supposed to stop this, and now the whole city will blame us for it.

Ivonne Sanchez, aka "Miss America," is a retired FDNY paramedic and 9/11 cancer survivor who was injured on the Pile while working on a body recovery detail.

They sent me home the first night, before I got reassigned to the Pile. I had gone in on foot that morning, because we were afraid of losing more vehicles, and I walked out again that evening, totally exhausted—my uniform covered in dust—up Broadway. On my way to Ground Zero that morning, I had kept my head down; I couldn't look at the survivors walking the opposite direction. Walking home that evening, when I got farther uptown, I saw crowds gathering. I froze, thinking "They're going to blame the fire department." I was picturing an angry mob with pitchforks or something. As I got closer, I could see they were holding candles—these were vigils. They weren't blaming us. We were heroes. When they saw my uniform, they thanked me. They hugged me even though I was covered in dust. I remember thinking, "I will never leave New York."

I wish I could tell you that everyone at the Pile behaved like heroes. But the fact is, there was some stealing. There was a lot of amateur bullshit from people who couldn't handle the intensity of the situation. I'll never forget having to shut everything down because we found pieces of bone that turned out to be chicken bones from someone's lunch they had thrown into the pit, like that's something to do at a crime scene. From then on, there was no eating on the Pile where I was. You also had pissing contests between police and fire and Port Authority. There was fisticuffs at one point, like ten on eighteen, it was a brawl. They settled it by having the cops do security outside the morgue and FDNY handling the bodies and the inside.

In the morgue and among the body recovery crews where I was working, there was a lot of drinking. When we found a body or part of someone in uniform, everybody stopped what they were doing for a moment of silence. Then one of the guys would get out a bottle and say:

"Come on, have a drink."

I refused.

The last thing I needed was to get written up for drinking on the job. On top of that, I was aware that being a woman and Puerto Rican, I had something to prove to these guys, so I did everything by the book. I thought about my family—they're all marines going back generations, from Japan to Desert Storm. My brother Eddie was in Beirut. I wanted to live up to their legacy and prove to myself that I was made of the same stuff.

We followed the dog teams. Whenever a dog would sit, we would come in and start clearing rubble really gently until we found whatever the dog was smelling. Usually, it was hair because hair doesn't decompose. We would go through the remains and check for ID; if not, it's a "J. Doe"—it wasn't always clear whether it was a "John" or "Jane." We pronounced, signed the papers, and took the remains to the morgue, where there were religious people performing last rites. In the beginning, we were finding intact remains; they were burned but still recognizable. Toward the end, it was just pieces and clumps. Bones. Hair. So much hair.

I used to talk to the parts we found. People probably thought I was crazy; I got some looks from the construction guys. I would say:

"Please don't haunt me. I did everything I could. I'm sorry I didn't find you sooner, but I'm here now, and I'll be here 'til the end, until we find everybody. I hope your family finds peace."

One day in October, OSHA was there, and they fitted us for biohazard masks. We were told if we didn't wear them, the department was going to write us up. I remember thinking, "Oh . . . So, now they think the air might be unsafe, but all through September, beginning of October, we were just freewheelin' out there." At that point, they had us decontaminate when we left the pit. They hosed down the tires of our vehicles. I knew something was wrong. We all did. And none of that biohazard gear worked. The dust and the smell still got all over you. It got in your hair and in your mouth. I wanted to jump in the river to get the smell off me.

I got hurt badly on the Pile. We found the remains of a bunch of people together. I was moving up the Pile to get to one set of remains when I looked down to see some other parts I had almost stepped on. I jumped back, slipped, and got impaled through the shoulder by a piece of rebar. I put a bandage on it and kept working. I popped Motrin, then muscle relaxers, but before long, I was done. I felt so guilty because I had to leave. I was still looking for my buddy Hector. He had five kids. I didn't want to leave him. I could have gone back to the streets before I got hurt, and maybe I wouldn't have gotten sick. But Hector was under there, and I had to find him. We didn't find him in the end. His family buried a picture in his coffin.

Fast forward to 2006. The fire department says we now have World Trade Center health monitoring. They told us about long-term exposure and its health risks based on what their studies had found. At that point, I started getting asthma attacks and sinus issues. I had bleeding ulcers which, at first, they thought was stomach cancer. On top of that, I had multiple surgeries for my shoulder rods in my back. When I meet with pain management doctors, they're expecting to see someone in a wheelchair, based on my chart.

Then they found a lump, and I became the first person in the program to get breast cancer. I say "person" because there are men with breast cancer from 9/11 dust exposure too. They told me they caught it early and I would only need radiation. I told them:

"NOPE. If I have radiation, I'm going to die."

Don't ask me how, I just knew. My friends tried to talk me out of it. The docs say that's too extreme.

I told the doctors, "Just cut them off."

I got it done at Sloan Kettering. Lying in the recovery room, the pain was so bad, I regretted my decision. One of the doctors walked in and said to me:

"Are you psychic? You had cancer all over both breasts. It was like a Jackson Pollock painting."

She went on to tell me that the cancer had moved so quickly I would have been in big trouble if they had gone with a more conservative treatment. Later I took the BRCA gene test. I don't have cancer in my family, and I wanted to prove this was environmental because we were being told that our illnesses weren't from the Pile, and there wasn't much data to support links from the dust to cancer in women, because there weren't many women working on the Pile. The test came back with all the markers of exposure cancer, not genetic.

I got sick from the Pile. Nobody can deny that now.

Today, I live with my brother as his full-time caregiver. He's a marine who survived the Beirut bombing only to get cancer from the water at Camp Lejeune. Like me, his only regret is that his service was cut short.

Semper Fidelis, Always Faithful.

When I walked through that vigil on the evening of September 11th, I knew at least nobody was blaming the FDNY. But I didn't realize just how much love the whole country had for the first responders until game three of the World Series. They turned it into this big celebration. Michael Bolton sang, and President Bush threw out the first pitch, which I guess they clocked as the fastest ceremonial first pitch of all time. I was there as part of an honor guard, dressed in my Class A's. There was a long delay, and they had us just standing there at the pitcher's mound. Eventually, we got tired of standing around, so we walked off the field. I walked right into Tino Martinez, who's like my baby daddy in my mind. I bumped into him, he turned around, and I froze and said:

"I'm your biggest fan. I love you!"

He went, "Mami, I love you too," and picked me up and kissed me.

I was in a daze from kissing my all-time sports crush, and it took me a minute to notice the crowd was going wild. The game was delayed, nothing's happening on the field. They're cheering for us, all of Yankee Stadium on their feet for the first responders.

At the Pile, there was a guy walking around taking pictures. I asked him what he's doing and he said he was working on a book of portraits of the responders: *Aftermath*. When he asked me, "Who are you?" I told him "I'm Miss September," and he put that in his book. I told him about the last time I had my picture taken, for the NYC Emergency Medical Services calendar, which had just been released and went on to be the bestselling calendar they've ever done. I didn't know who he was, the famous photographer Joel Meyerowitz. A few years later, when they launched the World Trade Center Health Program, NYCOSH [New York Occupational Safety and Health] used Joel's portrait of me in a bilingual ad encouraging responders to sign up for the program. I saw myself on the side of buses; my kids saw the ad. It was like that episode of *Sex and the City* where Carrie sees herself on the side of a bus.

A marine brought me down to earth one day. He hadn't seen the photograph by the two-time Guggenheim Fellow, but he had seen "Miss September."

He said, "We had your picture hanging up in the bathroom on a firebase in Afghanistan."

"In the bathroom," I said, "really?"

I got a more dignified tribute to that period of my life during Hispanic Heritage Month when the Smithsonian displayed the FDNY sweater I was wearing in Joel's photo in an exhibit on Latinas who made an impact in American history. My uniform stands shoulder to shoulder with Justice Sotomayor's robes and a space suit worn by Ellen Ochoa, the first Latina astronaut.

Three

TAKE ONE STEP . . . THEN ANOTHER

Speaking on September 18, Christine Todd Whitman, head of the Environmental Protection Agency, is "glad to reassure the people of New York and Washington, DC, that their air is safe to breathe and their water is safe to drink." And in case anyone has concerns about the dust that has been burning our eyes and making us cough all week, she adds, "The concentrations are such that they don't pose a health hazard. Conditions in both New York City and near the Pentagon show that the public in these areas is not being exposed to excessive levels of asbestos or other harmful substances."

And for anyone who still has a bad feeling about all this, she promises, "we're going to make sure everybody is safe."

At this point, the cough has a name: "World Trade Center cough."

On September 17, Wall Street reopens, just five days after the attack, to show the terrorists that we are undaunted and unafraid. Kids go back to schools in what will become the WTC disaster zone. About 300,000 office workers get back to work. To suggest that we do anything differently, or proceed with caution, or wait until there's any hard science from the samples they've been testing all week would be considered unpatriotic, un-American even. There's money to be made on Wall Street, make no mistake, that's the moral of the story right there. Human life, health, and safety, these things will take a back seat to economics.

At the Pentagon, they have a war to plan.

Work on the Pile becomes like any other job in a lot of ways, except the job site is still unstable and still on fire. They issue badges and designate parking areas. After September 15, we start working in twelve-hour shifts, cutting steel and rubble into pieces that fit in a truck. We average about 250 truckloads per shift. The trucks are all different sizes, and we cut the steel to fit. Up until the 15th, the site was a clusterfuck, with a lot of well-meaning, unqualified people in the way. This is not a five-dollar-an-hour job and we didn't need five-dollar-an-hour people, even if their hearts were in the right place. By the 15th, the amateurs have all been sent on their way or are volunteering elsewhere in supporting roles. You need a badge to work the Pile, either as a tradesman, police, fire, EMS, or one of the agencies with three letters. The Red Cross is there, too, handing out water bottles and flushing dust from our eyes. They remind me of the girls you see in old movies, walking around the bar with trays of cigarettes. They're young. They're kind.

I keep going to the Church Street "flea market" for new boots. The steel is still glowing hot in places. The three dimensions of danger extend below ground as well as overhead. The foundation of each tower is seventy feet deep, with subway lines, cables, and water mains running nearby, all severed by the collapse. A retaining wall holds back the Hudson River. I'm so preoccupied with the steel piled up in front of and above us that I don't think much about the void below until I am almost swallowed by it.

Early on the 17th, I'm in a Bobcat excavator, sitting behind a plexiglass shield, pulling steel from the Pile and placing it on the ground to be cut up and loaded onto a truck. There's a technique where I use the leverage of the lift to get my front wheels off the ground and hopefully avoid getting flat tires from the heat that keeps melting our boots. As I'm pushing some steel around, wedging the Bobcat against the Pile to lift the wheels, I snag on something. I keep pushing against it until something goes *BOOM*. The piece of steel gives, and I keep driving. Then I drop.

The steel I knocked loose was a plate covering a gaping chasm into the subway. I'm teetering over the hole in my Bobcat, looking through the plexiglass and down into a thirty- to forty-foot drop. I'm thinking, *This is how I die.* Guys are shouting at me to move back in my seat for balance, but what's my weight going to do against the weight of this machine? Then Kenny, working a payloader, swings his bucket over and scoops up the Bobcat, sets me down on solid ground, and swings back to nudge the Bobcat back from the edge. *Thank you, Kenny, I owe you.*

I get back to work, not knowing my time on the Pile is almost over. About four hours later, early evening, we're taking an immense piece of steel off the Pile. Even lying on its side, the top of the beam is five feet off the ground. Someone will tell me later that it weighs eight thousand pounds, and that's the number I go with when I tell my story. Beyond a certain tonnage, I'm not sure it matters. A short guy, shorter than me, is on the other side of the beam, torching the steel. With smaller pieces, the torch goes right through and out the other side, but with a piece this big, the steel ends up snapping, almost like a tree that comes down without a clear cut all the way through. A very dangerous thing to be anywhere near. I'm guiding trucks as they back in, and I don't realize the torch man is behind me. I don't see anybody on the other side of the beam, and there's no spark line or visual cue that someone's torching. I'm preoccupied because I'm making the international sign for STOP and a truck driver keeps backing up. The steel starts to come down.

I'm between the truck and the steel. If I don't jump out of the way,

I'll be the main ingredient of a deadly sandwich. When I jump, the steel lands on my foot. (It's so heavy that it bounces back up, so some people say I lifted it up. Are you kidding? I was just fast enough to move out of the way when it landed, but nobody could lift that weight.) I look down at my boot. I look up. I see blood spraying in every direction. "Like a human sprinkler" is how I will describe it to one historian of the Pile. The guy next to me turns white and gets all woozy.

I say to him, "Quick, give me your belt." I'm not wearing one.

I fashion a tourniquet below my knee by wrenching his belt down hard, and then I hobble to the curb.

I take my boot off. Bones are sticking through my sock.

"Nothing to see here, everybody back to work," I tell everyone.

The firefighters are there in two seconds. They stop me as I'm trying to cut away my sock with a razor blade. The first thing they do is drape a big white towel in front of me so I can't see my foot. But I can see their faces. I can tell it's maybe even worse than it seems. They take my blood pressure: 120/80, like nothing happened. They call that coherent shock. The fitness I had maintained since my army days probably kept me from passing out or going into deeper, more life-threatening hemorrhagic shock. A fit heart doesn't need to work as hard to supply blood and can support consciousness in a situation where blood pressure would otherwise drop critically.

There is no pain whatsoever.

They put me in an ambulance.

I tell everyone I'll be back in a couple of hours.

On the radio, the paramedics make a point of mentioning that the patient is a 9/11 responder along with the details of my injury: blunt force trauma, etc. I get a police escort to Bellevue Hospital.

When I get there, you'd think I was the pope. The doctors and nurses are waiting for me in receiving lines on either side of the ER. They're more shook up than I am; their expressions are a strange combination of eager and shell-shocked. They had been prepared for mass casualties when the towers fell. Emergency rooms as far away as Boston prepared to deal with the overflow. EMS workers from out of state were dispatched first to the Meadowlands stadium, a staging area in the event of nuclear war or something, then to field hospitals closer to the World Trade Center, and by the end of the day on Tuesday, they were all sent home because the emergency rooms in Manhattan could handle the few injuries there were. People had burns, broken bones, and flesh wounds; the firefighters working the recovery were collapsing with severe dehydration, but that was about it. The last survivor was pulled from the rubble twenty-seven hours after the attack, and it was all recovery from then on. Over 36,000 units of blood had been donated by citizens eager to do *something*. Of those, 258 units were actually used. (Which is not to say the surplus went to waste. Untold car accident and trauma victims and people with chronic illness will be saved by the generosity of 9/11 blood donations, but very little was needed by survivors and responders.)

Doctors remember the waiting. Now they have me. About an hour after I arrive, the pain hits. It's the worst pain I've ever felt . . . so far. They drug me up pretty good, so I can't say for sure when my mother and sister arrive. I had called my mom on my way to Ground Zero to tell her where I was going. She told me to be careful.

They prep her baby for emergency surgery. Tonight.

They start by doing debridement, flaying off layers of skin. Six surgeries in a couple of days. On day nine, the doctor comes in and tells me:

"Mr. Feal, you have gangrene, you're septic."

"I'm sorry, what? That's something out of the 1800s, isn't it? How did this happen?"

"Well," he answers, "we put pins through your toes when we were doing the debridement. And I'm not going to say if that's wrong or right, but you don't put metal in a crush injury where there's no blood flow."

All I can say is, the doctor is lucky my mom is there. I start cursing him from A to Z. My mother tells me to calm down. I tell myself, *This is a teaching hospital. They're learning.* I ask her to get me out of there immediately. We make some calls and get me a bed at North Shore University in Plainview. Another police escort and hero's welcome. The first doc I see there is waiting for me, wearing a big apron and a plastic face shield. That can't be good. He holds my foot and examines it; I can tell by the way he's talking to me that he's about to do something and needs to distract me. One by one, with a slurping sound, he pulls the pins out. This pea-soup fluid shoots out all over his bib like something out of *The Exorcist.* It's the second worst smell I've ever experienced, after Ground Zero itself. Getting the pins out hurts and feels so good at the same time.

"I'm not going to lie to you," he says, "it's going to be a bumpy road. We're going to do whatever we can."

I appreciate his straightforwardness. He tells me they're going to put me to sleep for a while so they can play with different medications to fight the gangrene.

Then it's lights-out for a couple of weeks.

When I come out of it, he tells me my system took a beating, but I'm out of the woods gangrene-wise.

"You're not going to lose your leg," the doctor says.

"I'm not losing anything" is my response.

"Well, we're working on that. But I gotta be honest with you. From what I can see, all I can tell you is you're at least not going to lose your leg below your knee."

"I don't know if you heard me; I'm not losing anything."

"John, I'm really trying."

Finally, they decide to amputate half my foot. I figure everything I've been through so far will prepare me for what that feels like. Not even close. And there will be no strong pain meds for me. Through this ordeal, I find out I'm allergic to morphine in an incident that requires lifesaving measures.

"What did you do that for?" I say when I come to after the surgery. "I have a DNR [do not resuscitate]; you were supposed to let me die."

At this point, the doc gets my sick sense of humor, and he just smiles. From here on out, all my surgeries and recoveries are without opioids—which is probably a blessing in disguise, this being the early 2000s and the eve of the opioid epidemic. My foot hangs, elevated over my bed. I can feel my toes, but they're not there. I can see the stump because they have to leave it exposed. My mother is there but I don't say a word. People come and go. I count the ceiling panels and the floor tiles; I count objects in the room. The counting becomes a mantra—I will learn that counting, like prayer, is a survival mechanism shown to have positive outcomes. The counting is how I pass the time, and I have enough time to become good at it. When we go to DC and I'm counting votes and memorizing phone numbers, the guys will nickname me "Rain Man."

The day after surgery, the doctors come in to say they need to take another half inch off my foot because they didn't get it all. Based on how I react to that news, they send in a shrink who diagnoses me as post-traumatic for the first time. After round two, it's time to graft and construct something I can walk on out of what's left down there. Someone I haven't seen before comes in. He introduces himself as my plastic surgeon. He sizes up the foot and says, "It looks like you won't be going dancing anytime soon."

"Excuse me?" I grab him by the tie, and that's when I notice for the first time how weak I've become. I can barely close my fist. My mom screams.

"I guess you won't be my doctor anymore," I tell him. "Get the fuck out of my sight."

A couple of hours later, there's a light tap on the door.

"Mr. Feal, is it alright if I come in? I'm your new doctor. I'm going to take a skin graft off your hip and wrap it around your foot."

"So, another surgery."

"I'm afraid so."

They do the surgery. It hurts. A couple of days go by. I keep my room dark. Nobody's allowed near me but Mom and my sister.

The doc comes back. "Can you walk for me?"

"No."

But the truth is, I have been walking. At night, I get out of bed and walk around the room using my IV stand as a crutch. It's agonizing, but I treat it like the mandatory road march in the army. In the morning, my dressings are all bloody and the nurses can't figure out why. If anything, I'm walking too much. I just won't walk *for* anyone. And I need practice. Toes are like suction cups that keep your foot from rolling to one side. You don't realize that until you lose your toes.

They keep coming back: "John, you got to walk for us."

They send cute young nurses: "Mr. Feal, it's your therapy time." That makes it worse. It's not about walking; I just don't want people to see how weak and broken I am. I came into the hospital 180 pounds. I'm down to 120.

Finally, the doc tells me I'm not leaving the hospital unless he sees me walk. "Can you at least stand up?"

When I'm on my feet, he shoves me without warning to test my balance. I shove him back, hard, like I'm starting a fight.

"What was that for?"

"Sorry, doctor, just force of habit."

"I think you're going to be fine."

Four hours later, Mom wheels me out of the hospital, with applause from the doctors and nurses, and out into the bright, cool, autumn sunshine. The first thing I notice is all the flags everywhere.

A few weeks after I'm released, I buy like $300 worth of cookies and flowers for all the doctors and nurses to say sorry for being such a pain in the ass. At one point, a nurse calls my mother to see how I'm doing, and Mom sets me up on a date with her. It's awkward. I feel like a freak. I don't want the attention for being brave or injured or resilient or whatever. I want to be left alone. I tell my mom to ignore her if she ever calls again. I don't want to see anyone but family and old hometown friends who know how to make me laugh.

Walking is clumsy and painful, and I have to wear special shoes molded for my feet, which I refuse to wear because they make me look and feel like a freak. I keep rolling my ankle. Finally, Dr. Decicco comes up with something: a surgery I can get excited about for a change. He proposes an experimental procedure where he takes the tendons on either side of my foot and crisscrosses them to support the foot and keep it from rolling. The surgery takes seven hours. But it works. My foot never rolls again.

In 2002, I get back on the golf course. The friends who couldn't beat me before 9/11 still can't beat me. Dr. Decicco had tried to manage my expectations: He said surgery could make walking easier and less painful, but I shouldn't get my hopes up about golf. I beat him by eight strokes when we play at his country club in Cold Spring Harbor. I tell him I'm going easy on him because he saved my foot and all.

Out in the world I keep counting: the trees, the billboards, the number of books on a shelf, so many flags, the dollars in my checking account. The insurance companies and hospital accountants don't give me the papal treatment I got from the docs. It cost a fortune to save my foot, and none of it is covered. I wasn't working in any official capacity besides being a credentialed volunteer with a badge.

I got hurt ninety-six hours into the cleanup; the cutoff for VCF (Victim Compensation Fund) claims is ninety hours. The Red Cross sends me a letter saying they've got $50,000 with my name on it. They follow up with a letter rescinding the payout because of the ninety-six-hour rule. When I go to the VCF to make a claim, I don't need affidavits. They know me because of my injury. But I got hurt six hours too late for a VCF claim. With no other options, I sell my house, I sell my cars and my Harley, my TV and my sofa. Eventually, I'll get workman's comp and Social Security, but only after I've sold everything but my boots. At every hearing dealing with the courts and the banks, I let them know I got hurt on the Pile, not because I think I deserve special treatment or pity or anything like that. I just want them to know. *Daily News* columnist Mike McAuliff will call what I went through "a miserable bureaucratic experience."

Meanwhile, Mom is worried, not about my physical or financial situation. She sees where I'm really hurting. One morning, hanging out at her place, she says to me, "You're going to therapy."

At first I don't know what she's talking about. I tell her I'm doing my PT exercises. That's not the kind of therapy she has in mind. I resist. It's not something I would ever have seen myself doing. But I also know she's right. Now it's her turn to save me. I have my doubts about therapy, but I'll go for Mom. I find these groups in Suffolk County through a 9/11 community newsletter. The format is like an AA meeting; we sit around and talk about what we're going through. From the get-go, it's clear that what we saw and did or didn't do at the Pile isn't the main source of our suffering. Like me, a lot of folks are dealing with financial difficulty, all of which compounds the memories of fire and dust and body parts. Guys are losing boats, losing cars, losing houses. They can't pay for their kid's college tuition anymore. PTSD is claiming marriages. Fucked-up dads are raising fucked-up kids. Responders have kids with drug problems as a result of living in the shadow of the towers.

Sharing my story and hearing theirs, it's clear I have stuff to process besides just my injury and my time at the Pile. I go through a bunch of therapists before I find a woman who's perfect. She has me doing EMDR (eye movement desensitization and reprocessing therapy) and working through everything, from the injury through childhood and back again.

Back in the group sessions, people stop coming. They're dying; they're going into hospice. We lose a guy named Tim Keller—he and I had been close. Tim would sit in meetings and fall asleep, which would get a laugh, like, "Are we boring you, Tim?" He had such bad upper respiratory problems, his heart just gave out. He's the first person I lose, but I know he isn't going to be the last, just based on everything I'm hearing in these groups and what common sense tells me about the dust.

I use my Rain Man skills to memorize everybody's phone numbers. I get the word out that I'm putting something together to do something about all this sickness and the red tape around it. People start calling. They keep calling, and I keep answering. I get a reputation as a guy you can call. I don't know what to do yet, but I'm listening.

I start sleeping with my phone on.

ACTION FOR ACTIVISTS: FIND YOUR MINIMUM VIABLE ACTIVISM AND TAKE THAT FIRST STEP

"What if I never walk again?" is a question that will defeat you. People can get lost facing big issues. Effective activism always finds a way, even when progress is slow and setbacks are frequent.

Challenge yourself to take just one step. Then take another. Find your "minimum viable activism" and take that first step.

Everything will feel more manageable when you break the work down into chunks, prioritize, and keep your focus on doing the next right thing. In the early stages of a movement, this could be as simple as making yourself reachable. Listening is a powerful form of action, and it's probably the best place to start if your goal is to speak for a community. When I started taking calls from people who were getting sick and their families, I hadn't made any promises or set any goals; I had no idea that someone like me could just go to DC and get a bill passed. All they knew is that if they called, I would answer and I would listen to them. So far, nobody had been listening.

Testimony

MICHAEL BARASCH

It was a nice day, so we had the windows open in our office. We're on Park Place, just two blocks from the World Trade Center. There's a hole in our view now, clear sky where we used to see the towers. When the first plane hit, we didn't know what to make of it. The hole looked too big to have been made by a small plane. It was more interesting than frightening, as awful as that sounds. When the second plane hit, I ordered everybody out. There were fifteen people working for me at the time, but four of us stayed in the office. We stood in the windows, frozen, watching people jump. At one point, my wife called, screaming, telling us to get out of there.

I told her, "They're not going to attack Eleven Park Place. We're safe here."

Just as I was saying that, the first tower started to fall; we all ran out of the office and down the stairs. When we got to the street, we met the cloud of dust and all the people running away. The cops and firefighters were running the other way—into the dust.

Michael Barasch is a managing partner at Barasch & McGarry, a law firm that represents 9/11 responders and survivors.

Before 9/11, I was already working with the FDNY as a personal injury lawyer representing firefighters who get injured in the line of duty. Our offices were closed for a few weeks after the attack because we had no electricity, so I spent the time visiting firehouses. There were few injuries from the collapse and the cleanup, but at every firehouse, we kept hearing people cough. The firefighters were calling it the World Trade Center cough. A cough is a symptom, the underlying cause was something serious: reactive airway disease, which is like asthma or chronic bronchitis. We were all told the air was safe to breathe. It certainly was not. Eventually, NIOSH (the National Institute for Occupational Health and Safety) would link 9/11 toxins to sixty-nine cancers and scores of gastro illnesses. But at that point, all we knew was that everyone had this cough. So, what I did was file all these notice claims to preserve the rights of six hundred or so firefighters who were suffering from these coughs in case, God forbid, it got worse and they couldn't go back to work. You can work as a lawyer with asthma, but as a firefighter, it's a career-ending disability. So, I filed these notices that have to be filed within ninety days to preserve the rights of these claimants, and the press crushed me, saying this lawyer sued the city.

A little while later, at Christmas, I took my family to Jamaica. We were in a bar watching the New York Giants play the Washington Redskins. There were three American kids in the bar rooting for the Redskins, so we all got talking. It turns out these were Ken Feinberg's kids. Feinberg had just been named the special master of the first 9/11 Victim Compensation Fund (VCF). I arranged to have breakfast with Ken the next day, on Christmas morning. I had called my secretary and asked her to fax me medical reports to bring to Feinberg. Like everyone else, he wanted to know why I had filed these notices of claims, given that there was now a VCF. The problem, I explained, was that a VCF award was contingent upon recipients waiving their right to sue over their illness or injury. But at the time, the rules said that only applied if the recipient went to a doctor within seventy-two hours of developing symptoms. Well, no responder was going to get off the Pile to go to a doctor to complain about a cough while there was a chance people were still alive under the debris. Everyone was coughing. Everyone sucked it up and did their jobs. So, Mr. Feinberg agreed to do away with the seventy-two-hour rule if we would drop all pending lawsuits against the city. That conversation changed everything. We had taken the first step on a long road. After we got back from Jamaica, I went to his office with three firefighters and a pulmonologist who explained how the cough was just the tip of the iceberg. We were going to see a lot of these latent respiratory illnesses, and the VCF was going to have to be prepared for that. We weren't even thinking of cancer at the time.

We were back in our offices on Park Place around October 10th. The National Guard was parked outside. There was a chain-link fence set up around Ground Zero. Inside, our offices were full of dust because the windows had been open during the collapse. We cleaned the surfaces, but the vents in the building were still recirculating the dust. As we got to work on the legal side of representing 9/11 illness, we started getting sick too. My secretary, already a breast cancer survivor, was lucky to catch a new cancer early after a fall in City Hall Park that required an x-ray. My paralegal died of breast cancer at age forty-seven. Another paralegal, also forty-seven, died of kidney cancer. Barry, our partner at the firm, has skin cancer; Dana, another partner, has sinus issues and lost her sense of smell. Of the fifteen of us who were in the office on 9/11 and during the cleanup, more than half have died or gotten sick.

I have the two most common 9/11 cancers in men: skin cancer and prostate cancer. And I only caught them because I get checked every year through the World Trade Center Health Program. The skin cancer was a speck of discoloration under a fingernail. The prostate cancer can be watched aggressively and doesn't require radiation or surgery yet. My doc says with any luck, I will die with it, not of it. I share this only to spread the word about the program. The outcome would have been very different if the doctors weren't already monitoring me closely. Causation is presumed in my case, as it is for anyone with a cancer known to be linked to 9/11 dust exposure. It doesn't matter if you smoked, which I never did, or have a family history, which I don't. The cause is presumed because the data shows that the 9/11 community is significantly more likely to get sixty-nine different cancers than the general public. The biggest challenge is that so many nonresponders don't know about these programs. Right now, 85 percent of cops and firemen who were there are in the program, but less than 10 percent of eligible civilians are enrolled. So, I hope that by sharing my story, I can change that.

If you were there, sign up today. You won't be taking anything away from responders or someone you think is more deserving. Quite the opposite: Your checkups, which could save your life the way they saved mine, will also help the doctors and scientists who advise the WTC Health Program and VCF get a better picture of the long-term health impacts of 9/11 and the needs of your fellow responders and survivors.

The fact is, September 11th never ended for us. And neither did the response.

Four

DO YOUR HOMEWORK

From the day I start giving out my number, the phone keeps ringing. The calls come in from everywhere because responders came from everywhere. Of the 435 congressional districts, 431 sent responders or had someone at the World Trade Center. Now they're getting sick everywhere. New Yorkers are lucky to have our community, and when someone gets sick, they usually know others in the same situation. The environmental fallout is obvious from Suffolk, Nassau, and the five boroughs. Less so in a small Northern California town that sent a couple of their woodland firefighters.

I never switch the phone off. I never sleep through a call. They keep calling. The busy signal beeps with one sick responder on hold while a widow is on the line. Up until now, there hasn't been much organizing or community action on the part of responders. I intend to change that. I don't know what I'm going to do, but I'm going to do something. I don't see anyone else stepping up.

I'm not a counselor, a lawyer, or a lobbyist. I'm just the guy you can call, jobless, broke, with nothing to offer these people but a kind ear and a good memory. And the phone keeps ringing. I get a reputation as the person to call to take down your story and connect you with others in the same situation. At the same time, I start gathering all available information on the dust and the legal and public health response. I clip, and I print. My room is barracks tidy. I spread the file folders neatly on the floor and on the bed when I'm awake—which is twenty hours out of the day.

I become like an obsessed detective with his corkboard and red yarn. I'm chasing a killer, but I may one day become another victim. I am angry, I am frightened, and I am becoming very well informed. I have no letters before or after my name; my IQ hovers around room temperature. I have to read everything six or seven times to understand it. If you feed me caviar, I'm going to shit hamburgers. But I also know how simple the facts are. I make it simple for myself so it can be simple for the people whom we will need to convince. From what I come to understand, the science backs up some simple, proven truths that we will recite in countless meetings, press conferences, and morning show appearances. It becomes like our Nicene Creed, as much a statement of who we are as what happened to us:

> *We no longer have to prove 9/11 made us sick. You have to prove 9/11 didn't make us sick.*
>
> *We worked there, we ate there, we slept there, we cried there.*
>
> *We were exposed 24/7 through the nose, mouth, and skin.*
>
> *We were told repeatedly by city, state, and federal officials that the air was safe to breathe. We know now, and the science proves, that it wasn't.*

Now, in retelling what I learned and am continuing to learn about the dust, I am going to jump around—from the results of the first sampling of the dust in late September 2001, through two decades of research, up to present day and what doctors are saying about the future of 9/11 illness. I'm covering the whole history of 9/11 illness here because it's important to know what the experts knew when they knew it and what the latest science has to say. In this chapter, I will borrow heavily from the writing of Paul Lioy and studies from the NIH, NIOSH, and the EPA, as well as clinical observations and opinions from Dr. Marc Wilkenfeld and his colleagues at the WTC Health Program. To not interrupt the flow, I have not cited these the way you would in a textbook or academic paper. For a list of sources and further information about the science behind 9/11 illness, see the "Sources and Further Reading" section at the back of the book.

To this day, everyone's first question is: "What was in the dust?" The short answer is *everything*. The scientist Paul J. Lioy put it more poetically when he spoke to the media, saying it contained "everything that we hold near and dear to us." Everything that's in an office building, everything that building is made of.

Two towers, 110 stories each with four sides, equals 880 stories of thick, floor-to-ceiling windows. Only one window survived the collapse. Over 24,000 gallons of jet fuel, some of which did not combust, lending its carcinogenic essence to the dust. The component parts of thousands of computers and phones and TV sets. Computer monitors and TVs of early-2000s vintage contain trace amounts of lead and are made of glass. Furniture, human flesh, bone and hair, cotton and dyes from clothing, a bunch of bizarre stuff you wouldn't think would be in an office building . . .

But because the whole scene was on fire, you also had new chemicals being synthesized by the heat and combustion. There were no probes in the plume or at Ground Zero at the moment of collapse, so we will never know what exactly was in there.

Some of the substances are harmless on their own but toxic when burned. Others, like the cellulose in paper or gypsum in construction materials, become irritants when inhaled. There isn't a lot of mercury in a fluorescent lightbulb, but two million lightbulbs contain a fuckload of mercury. There were fibers from carpeting and ceiling panels. Miles of carpet captured decades of hair shed by visitors to the towers and employees, something that would further complicate the search for DNA identification of victims since there was DNA from business travelers and commuters who left hair or skin cells when there for a meeting in the '90s and were now safely back in Stamford or Zurich. At the same time, the fire burned so hot and for so long that it degraded the DNA of many of the victims and, with it, their families' hope of closure.

Responders and survivors inhaled and absorbed cremated and pulverized flesh and bone. A survivor of the Nazi concentration camps living in Brooklyn was reminded of the smoke from the ovens. He told historians he "knew that ash."

In chemistry, they say "The dose makes the poison"—there were plenty of substances present that might have been benign in smaller quantities, but trace elements aren't so "trace" when you're covered in them, and they're drifting like snow all around, and you've got a mouthful. Early tests showed that some of the trace elements were no more prevalent than they would be in dust bunnies around your house. But you would never fill your mouth with dust bunnies or be so thickly covered in household dust that your skin color is unrecognizable. In the interest of making it simple for folks like me to understand, Dr. Wilkenfeld, an associate clinical professor at NYU Long Island School of Medicine, explains it this way: The chair you're sitting in, the coffee table in front of you, the airline seat if you're reading this on a plane, is probably full of all sorts of things that could give you cancer. But you're not burning the coffee table and huffing the fumes. You're not crushing your reading chair to coarse dust and clogging your sinuses with it. Early reports that the dust contained no more than 1 percent asbestos were seen as encouraging. But as Paul Lioy writes, that figure does not take into account the quantity of dust: "It was not just the concentration of the material in each gram of dust, it was the total amount present on the surface."

The main ingredient of the dust, and the buildings themselves, was concrete, crushed to the consistency of sand, making up 50 percent of the mass of WTC dust. On its own, if it were sand from a beach or a desert, the texture and consistency would make it a coarse irritant. But concrete contains lye, which is very basic on the pH scale, making the dust roughly as alkaline as Drano. This made it even more of an irritant to skin and respiratory tissue. It also made the water from fire hoses, burst mains, and the rain on Friday, September 15, an alkaline solution. Jet fuel also contains alkaline hydrocarbons, which leached into the water and clung to the dust.

Polychlorinated biphenyls (PCBs), so-called forever chemicals, are present in the coolants and lubricants of transformers and electrical equipment made before 1977, when they were banned due to their links to liver cancer and low birth weight among infants whose mothers had been exposed to them. PCBs and their alternatives, PFAS (which have been banned in the EU), are present in the dust. Their most useful property is being flame-retardant, so they were not consumed by the fires. These and other chemicals are found in the Pile in concentrations equivalent to untreated sewage. The main sources are the flame-retardant foam that coated structural surfaces in the towers and the foam in office furniture.

Plastics, when burned, release a range of carcinogens. Plastics are everywhere.

Finely ground glass and glass fibers made the dust jagged down to the microscopic level. Coarse glass fibers acted as an irritant and contributed to the immediate respiratory, nasal, and eye symptoms. The microscopic structure of these fibers pierce cells in the tissues they contact, contributing to autoimmune responses and cancer.

The color of the dust was pinkish at first and turned gray over time. Scientists think this indicates a "physical transformation," as Lioy writes.

The size of the particles was an important factor. The components of the dust ranged in size from gravel down to particles just a few molecules across and only visible under the microscope. This means that they could be absorbed in different ways by different tissues. Smaller particles make their way deeper into the lungs, while coarser particles will deposit farther up the airway, in the bronchia and nasal passages.

So-called supercoarse particles are not typically suspended in the air the way World Trade Center dust was and are therefore not studied or regulated the way finer particles, like exhaust fumes, are.

We know much of this thanks to a team of scientists from NYU led by the aforementioned Paul J. Lioy, who went to Ground Zero to sample the dust. They spent months testing and examining these samples. His book, *Dust,* explains the science that proves the severity of our exposure beyond a doubt and contradicts statements from OSHA, the EPA, and others who claimed the air was safe to breathe. Because Lioy was leading the science, he knew all there was to know at a given time. So when OSHA made what Lioy calls "the unbelievably naive comment" that indoor air quality in Lower Manhattan was within their standards for asbestos, he knew they had no data to back that up. Unfortunately, when the asbestos lie hit the press, the focus turned to the question of how much asbestos was in the air, not the real question, which is, *What else are they lying to the public about?* Lioy's dust findings were available to the relevant agencies as early as September 27. That's the earliest the authorities could have made educated statements, at which point they would have known for sure that we were being poisoned.

The medical and legal experts categorize us in a few different ways. We are broadly split into two groups: responders and survivors. A responder is anyone, civilian or EMS, involved in the search, recovery, or demolition work either directly or in a supporting role. Basically, a responder is someone whose job required they be down there. We are fire, EMS, police, federal agents, construction, trades, sanitation, and journalists. A survivor is pretty much anyone who was in Lower Manhattan on 9/11 or during the cleanup. This includes students, stockbrokers, office workers of all kinds, street vendors, homeless people, inmates at the Manhattan Detention Complex ("The Tombs"), and residents of one of the wealthiest zip codes in America. They call it "democratic dust." It is no respecter of class, job title, or status. Over the years, we will need "proof of presence" to establish our eligibility for the VCF and WTC Health Program.

Responders generally have no problem providing these. The folks who have the hardest time are commuters, taxi drivers, and bystanders who were in the wrong place at the wrong time. Like Chernobyl, for someone who is close enough, early enough in the disaster, a few minutes in the dust puts you in the highest category of exposure.

The scientists break down the exposure timing into five exposure periods:

Exposure period 1: The first few hours after the collapse. This was when the dust and smoke were the thickest, and the fires burned hottest. Dust particles in the air are estimated to be well over 5,000 $\mu g/m^3$ of air vs. 40–50 $\mu g/m^3$ on a "high pollution" day in NYC. This is science's way of saying what survivors report: "It was like breathing sand" . . . "Imagine filling your mouth and nose with flour." (Source: *The Only Plane in the Sky* by Garrett Graff)

Exposure period 2: September 11–13. Dust is still suspended in the air. Responders inhale and ingest it. Fires continue to release gas particles. Luckily, civilians are out of harm's way at this point, and exposure is limited to responders. Lioy and his team collect the first samples of settled dust.

Exposure period 3: September 14–25. Fires still burn under the Pile, but they are more isolated and produce less smoke. Dust is resuspended in the air from demolition work, but there is less inhalation exposure than in the first two periods. On the 17th, residents and office workers return and are exposed indoors in contaminated apartments and office buildings. Dust is recirculated in air-conditioning systems. On the 18th, the EPA makes their infamous statement that the air is safe to breath, but they won't conduct sampling until the 21st, as Lioy writes in *Dust*. Lioy and his team will have their initial results on the 27th.

Exposure period 4: September 25–December 20. On September 25th, rain falls on the Pile, followed by weeks of dry weather. The last fire burns out on December 20th. No more smoke. Dust is resuspended in the air and coats surfaces and clothing at Fresh Kills Landfill, where responders and investigators sort through the debris, exposing them in the process.

Exposure period 5: 9/11–2003. Long-term indoor exposure continues for residents, students, and office workers while the EPA develops guidelines for testing and cleanup. The end date for this period is 2003 because that's when the EPA concluded their testing program. (Source: *Dust* by Paul Lioy)

Geography becomes an important question and one that is still debated by the experts. For some exposure, the line is Houston Street; for responders, it's Canal Street. But like borders between nations, these are imaginary lines drawn arbitrarily by men in offices. While the concentration was less the farther you got from Ground Zero, and a light offshore breeze carried much of the plume out to sea, the dust knew no hard borders, and inches of it were found on cars north of Canal Street. They had to draw the line somewhere, but we will never know all the places touched by the dust. Lila Nordstrom's family lives in a building well north of even the most generous estimates for significant exposure, but every dog in her building that was alive on 9/11 died of cancer in the years that followed. As Congressman Jerry Nadler (D-NY) put it, "It wasn't as if there was a force field at Canal Street."

The respiratory harm ranges from asthma to fibrosis to lung cancer. Glass fibers and coarser particles do structural damage, causing scar tissue to build up in the lungs. A number of lobectomies and lung transplants among responders have been due to this physical irritation, not cancer.

Asbestos and other fibers are believed to cause cancer in one of two ways: by impaling themselves through the nucleus of a cell, disturbing the reproduction of that cell, or by lodging themselves in the tissue of the cell and causing the body to react against itself. The medical community continues to debate whether asbestos causes cancer, or if it causes a reaction that causes cancer.

Because of their function in oxygenating blood for the entire body, complications with the lungs can lead to all sorts of other cardiovascular and circulatory issues. The first friend I lost to the dust died of a heart attack from the strain of severe asthma.

The skin is the body's largest organ. Many of the toxins found in samples of the dust are readily absorbed through the skin. Female office workers had more skin exposure because of the difference in how men and women dress for work. They were also more likely to take their shoes off, rather than flee from the collapse in heels.

The alkalinity of the dust caused chemical burns in our sinuses, throats, and lungs. It burns the stomach and causes GERD (gastroesophageal reflux disease), which is severe acid reflux and the most common 9/11 illness.

The body's natural mechanisms to fight off foreign substances are kicked into overdrive by the dust and its toxic components; this causes immediate issues like allergies and asthma and worsening of these conditions when they are already present, but it also contributes to autoimmune response that can become chronic and irreversible. Some, like sarcoidosis and systemic autoimmune disease (SAD), are already linked to 9/11 dust exposure. Others, like multiple sclerosis (MS), have well-established links to environmental exposure, and doctors wouldn't be surprised to see the 9/11 community come down with these at higher rates.

All of these illnesses follow a grim timeline. All we can do is wait. The cough and eye irritation are immediate, blood cancers and lymphomas start showing up after about eighteen months. Solid cancers and filter cancers, like kidney cancer, after about four years. In the early years of the health program, the rules are strict concerning the timing of diagnosis. Many people have their claims rejected because their tumors showed up "too early." This penalizes people for getting screened early and forces some to wait until their cancer spreads to be eligible. Now, there are latency guidelines that make more sense and are informed by science rather than politics.

With all cancers, thanks to better screening and better drugs, the survivability covers up the true impact, in the same way medical advances on the battlefield mean soldiers who would have died in previous wars can now live as multi-amputees. The hallmark of all 9/11 cancers is how aggressive they are, and science doesn't yet know why this is. Another calling card of these cancers is that they are often age and gender inappropriate. Men get breast cancer. School kids develop cancers in their early twenties, like ovarian cancer, you would expect to see in older populations.

There are now sixty-nine cancer types and counting linked to 9/11 dust exposure, as of 2024.

The latency for mesothelioma from asbestos is twenty to thirty years. It was one of the first things the EPA tested for, and they claimed the amounts were within a safe range. We'll just be finding out now whether they were lying or not. Considering they made this statement before any testing had been done, I'm not . . . holding my breath.

Dr. Wilkenfeld is starting to see patients with tingling in their fingers—a sign of neuropathy, nerve damage. The condition is not yet covered by the World Trade Center Health Program as of this writing. He recently did an experiment on nerve cells using a sample of dust, the same way they test chemotherapy drugs for their neurological effects. The nerves went crazy in his test. He has no doubt there is a 9/11 link to neuropathy, and this study may lead to an understanding of a connection to other neurological ailments.

New studies, not 9/11 related, show a clear link between ambient toxic exposure and a higher risk of developing ALS, Lou Gehrig's disease. The study looked at a number of toxins, all shown individually to increase the risk. Many, if not all, of those toxins were in the dust and the smoke. There's no study on the risk of ALS in persons exposed to all of the above, but it can't be good.

A study published in *The Journal of the American Medical Association* in 2024 found a significant increase in early-onset dementia among 9/11 responders compared with the general population. The study found increased exposure to the dust translated to increased dementia risk.

We know there were 187 pregnant women in the area at the time of the collapse. We don't know how many children were conceived shortly after by parents who were exposed or whose mothers were exposed to dust while pregnant. Based on everything we know about environmental health and pregnancy and the presence of teratogens (substances linked to birth defects) in the dust, there's reason for concern here. But at present, exposure during pregnancy would only qualify the mother's health for World Trade Center Health Program coverage. The baby would need to have been present on 9/11 or during the cleanup to be eligible for the program. Anthony Flammia, an NYPD highway cop and 9/11 responder who went with us to Washington, has a child who was born with severe special needs. He is part of an ongoing cohort study of the children of responders, looking for a link to birth defects and other heritable conditions.

Women's health is woefully understudied in relation to 9/11, given that the overwhelming majority of responders were male, as were most of the tradespeople who responded and most office workers in the financial district. The ratio of men to women killed on 9/11 is three to one. This, combined with the way women's healthcare is overlooked generally, means there is less data on 9/11 illness among women. Uterine cancer was only recently added to the list. Breast cancer, especially when it recurred among survivors of a pre-9/11 cancer, was often dismissed.

Post-traumatic stress disorder (PTSD) is the most insidious 9/11 illness because of how underestimated and misunderstood it is. PTSD is more than a mental health issue, though its psychological effects can be devastating. If you want to learn more about the psychological toll of PTSD, keep reading this book. But there's a physical side too. As the name suggests, it's a disorder of the body and mind's natural stress response. This can lead to depression, anxiety, a general sense of restlessness and irritability, all of which can contribute to substance abuse (which is also recognized as a 9/11 illness). Make no mistake, PTSD kills. It kills by suicide, overdose, and misadventure. This we've known for a long time. Now, thanks in part to studies of veterans of the wars that started on 9/11, science is revealing PTSD's link to cancer and other illnesses. Besides the knock-on effects of sleep problems, high blood pressure, and elevated stress hormones, there is evidence to suggest an epigenetic effect where stress hormones actually cause changes in cells that can lead to cancer.

Dr. Wilkenfeld has his medical opinion, which confirms so much of what we, who were made sick by the Pile, have known all along. But his personal opinion is that he shouldn't have to testify to what we say about our own illnesses. In his view, whether or not to treat us shouldn't even be a question. He lives in a world of science, where proof is everything. But when Dr. Wilkenfeld talks about proof, he doesn't refer to peer-reviewed journals or double-blind studies. He relates an encounter with one responder he'll never forget:

> *Paul (Lioy) and I were on the EPA technical advisory committee together, and we were there to speak about cancer and this study and that study. It's all about proof . . . One guy came in, this emaciated guy with no hair, and he stood up during the public comment period:*
>
> *"I'm a responder," he said, "I was down there, and now I have leukemia. And it's very nice that you're studying this and all. But I don't*

have insurance, I don't know if I'm going to survive, and I don't know what's going to happen to my kids when I'm gone."

What do you say to that? This man is a hero. Let's start there. Why not give him the benefit of the doubt? Why not ask these people what they need? I'm a doctor. I don't set policies, but I'm going to keep doing everything I can to provide the people who do with the proof they need because I guess the word of a hero isn't enough.

There's another mantra I will say again and again in meetings over the years:

"Science finally caught up to us and validated what we already knew."

The Pile was killing us, and eventually science started to prove it. A 2008 study in the *Journal of Urban Health* has this to say two years before the Zadroga bill (which we'll talk more about): "3800 and 12,600 adults experienced newly diagnosed asthma, and 34,600–70,200 adults experienced post-traumatic stress disorder (PTSD)" (Farfel et al. 2008). It will be another four years before cancers are included in the VCF.

The doctors and scientists have their studies and data. We have our stories. Our illnesses and our deaths are our proof. Each one tells one part of the story of how the Pile is making us sick and killing us.

Bobby Beckwith, the retired FDNY firefighter who George W. Bush has his arm around during his speech through the bullhorn at Ground Zero, died of 9/11 cancer in February 2024.

Ellie Engler, an industrial hygienist in charge of health and safety for the United Federation of Teachers, who went into every school in Lower Manhattan to assess their safety, developed asthma from her exposure and had her breast cancer return after she had been in remission since 1985.

A podiatrist, Dr. Arthur Gudeon, "Dr. Artie," worked out of St. Paul's Chapel, across the street from the World Trade Center, which was used as a rest area and aid station. He cared for the feet of the responders, unlacing and lacing boots all day, getting the dust all over himself.

He and his wife both got cancer.

He lives. She died.

She did his laundry every day when he got home from the Pile. He insists his dusty clothes killed her.

Marcy Borders, aka "the Dust Lady," whose thousand-yard stare was captured by Agence France-Presse photographer Stan Honda and reprinted in papers all over the world, was a twenty-eight-year-old legal assistant working at Bank of America on the eighty-first floor of the North Tower. Following the attack, Borders turned to booze and drugs. She lost her job, lost her partner, and lost custody of her kids. She finally found recovery, getting sober on the day Bin Laden was killed. She was diagnosed with stomach cancer in 2014. Her illness put her $190,000 in debt, and she was unable to afford further treatment. She died in 2015.

Dr. Mike Brown had been working an overnight shift in a Las Vegas emergency room when the attack in New York came on the TV after 6 AM local time. With flights grounded, he got in his car and drove 2,5000 miles to the Pile, where he searched the rubble for his brother, Captain Patrick "Paddy" Brown, FDNY. Mike illegally planted a memorial tree one night in Central Park, with the help of some firefighters, "ninja gardeners," in the words of journalist Michael Daly, as the NYPD turned a blind eye, in a place where Paddy liked to stop and admire the city skyline on his jogs. Dr. Brown died in 2020 of an aggressive prostate cancer linked to 9/11 dust exposure.

Of all the many thousands of illness compensation claims and folded flags, there is one whose diagnosis will be remembered as an act of service to the entire community. Detective James Zadroga, for whom the 9/11 health bill is named, is a saint among 9/11 responders. Not in the sense of saintly goodness, but in the way saints are often tortured, humiliated, mocked, and dragged over the coals, and in suffering, bear witness to truth and justice. He went through hell for our salvation. Zadroga, a decorated narcotics cop, spent over 450 hours on the Pile. He developed a chronic cough and breathing trouble, headaches, and acid reflux, all of which he reported to the NYPD in 2002. But his claim of line-of-duty injury was denied. He was soon bedridden and required an oxygen tank and was eventually granted a disability pension. In 2003, he was diagnosed with black lung disease and pulmonary fibrosis. In 2006, he suffocated to death at the age of thirty-four. He left behind an orphaned four-year-old daughter, whose mother died two years before James.

Following Zadroga's autopsy, a New Jersey medical examiner told *The New York Times*: "It is felt with a reasonable degree of medical certainty that the cause of death in this case was directly related to the 9/11 incident."

They found "unidentified foreign materials" in his lungs but did not compare them to dust samples from the Pile. In a separate finding, a New York medical examiner claimed that Zadroga had been crushing and injecting pain pills, and this was not only the cause of his death but the cause of his lung disease. This was all the skeptics needed to cast doubt on his illness and 9/11 illness in general. Speaking at a Harvard symposium on public health, in October 2007, Mayor Bloomberg said:

"There are plenty of heroes. It's just, in this case, science says that this [Zadroga] was not a hero."

Outrage follows. Protesters outside city hall chant, "Zadroga is a hero, Bloomberg is a ZERO," as reported by CBS. Michael Barasch, a lawyer for the 9/11 community, asks for a meeting with the mayor immediately after he makes those remarks. With incredible patience and tact, he gives the mayor the benefit of the doubt and takes the time to talk him through the realities of environmental exposure that have consumed his work life and waking hours for the past five years. The mayor does an about-face, the first step toward becoming a crucial ally to the 9/11 community.

The family seeks a third opinion from a forensic pathologist for the New York State Police who backs the original autopsy results. Examining Zadroga's lung tissue, they find asbestos, lead, benzine, and glass fibers from the World Trade Center.

The family gets their apology from the mayor, and we have more proof of what we already know.

We worked there, we ate there, we slept there, we cried there . . .

We were exposed 24/7 through the nose, mouth, and skin.

We were told repeatedly that the air was safe to breathe and the water was safe to drink.

We know now, and the science proves that it wasn't.

It's 2006, we've carried the proof in our bodies and in our hearts for five frustrating years. It's time to take our proof to Washington.

ACTION FOR ACTIVISTS: ARM YOURSELF WITH FACTS, HARD EVIDENCE, AND TRUE STORIES

This is something activists tend to get wrong these days, relying on frothy emotional appeal or elaborate conspiracy theories rather than documenting reality and letting the truth speak for itself. Some people will treat feelings like facts, while others say "fuck your feelings." The truth is, you need facts *and* feelings, but feelings are nothing without facts and vice versa. If you can back up your feelings and convictions and sense of justice with facts and evidence, you will be much more powerful than if you're all passion. And this can be easier said than done in situations that understandably arouse passion. At the same time, beware of the delusion that the facts will speak for themselves and that public officials will listen to reason and be swayed by evidence. Stories, rhetoric, and emotional appeals can give you another way in and connect your facts with real people. Just be sure the stories are vetted and verified. Rehearse your stories and be intentional about how and when you weave them into your message.

I often say that immense tragedies, like 9/11, give those affected a choice: embrace conspiracy theories or become an activist. Notice how, with 9/11 illness, we put our trust in the scientists and experts.

We looked for instances where leading experts could back up what we were saying. We avoided jumping to conclusions without evidence or embracing unfounded alternative explanations or crackpot theories. Conspiratorial thinking is tempting when you find yourself on the receiving end of injustice with nobody listening, but it's a dead end. More often than not, the folks who cook up those crackpot theories are opportunists and hucksters, hoping to make a name for themselves or sell snake oil on the back of your tragedy. You need to decide to be better than that. You must commit to telling the truth and facing reality. And where science and evidence contradict your feelings, you must favor the evidence. One lie, exaggeration, or omission is enough to discredit you and your mission. So don't lie. Don't tell tall tales while you're waiting for your proof.

Factfinding is often a passive process of documentation and record-keeping. Activists, by definition, want to engage and stay in motion, but it's important to remember that listening, recording, and collecting are all forms of action. It helps to get organized and have systems in place. Start putting together your book to keep all your facts in one place. Take notes. Record. Film. Besides giving you data and information, these acts of bearing witnesses will supply you with material for social media and awareness campaigns.

I kept two books. One, "the bible," was everything we knew about the dust, 9/11 illness, and the individual cases of the people who were getting sick. The other book, "the Burn Book" was about human intelligence and opposition research. I'll have more to say about that later. Basically, we collected every tweet and every public statement related to 9/11, first responders, etc., from the members of Congress and senators who we were lobbying. Every "#NeverForget." Every "Back the Blue." This gave us ammunition with which to shame individual members of Congress, and it also helped us establish a pattern: The party that publicly aligned itself with troops and cops and first responders and the legacy of 9/11 and was the most loudly patriotic was also the party doing the most to stand in the way of our healthcare. This wasn't partisanship. It was just the facts.

When you've done your homework, it's your job to inform and educate. You can't fault the general public for what they don't know. Education is a big part of activism. In our case, we were up against some public officials and institutions whose ignorance was intentional or at least convenient, but most of the general public simply wasn't aware that 9/11 was still killing, or that the environmental and healthcare consequences were still unfolding years later. Mayor Bloomberg's comments about Detective Zadroga were regrettable and ugly, but they came from a place of ignorance and a lack of awareness. Public shaming and protest may have helped urge him to do the right thing, but the more effective action was the sit-down with Michael Barasch, who educated him on the reality of 9/11 illness and what his constituents had been going through for half a decade. It takes patience and discipline to be like that, and it's worth working on yourself to cultivate those qualities if you don't already have them.

Testimony

JAMES RYDER

The first thing you need to know about the personal effects we recovered is that we didn't find anything larger than an attaché case, and most of it was much smaller than that. We're talking a belt buckle, pieces of a credit card, a whole wallet if we were lucky. A lot of it wasn't very sentimental. A credit card isn't exactly a family heirloom, but it means something when you have nothing, and your loved one is just gone.

James Ryder, aka "Wheels," is a retired NYPD Highway Patrol Officer with Highway 03 in Queens who worked on DNA identification and returning personal effects after 9/11.

I was a "steal" as they call it after 9/11. That means I was still assigned to my command, but I was temporarily transferred to a different command, which in my case was the Office of Management and Planning. These are the brainiacs of the police department who scored first on their sergeant's tests and lieutenant's tests. I had computer skills at a time when not everyone in the department could type. I had done some web development for a captain and was building websites as a side gig, so they pulled me out of Highway. My wife was happy about this, because the job was indoors, and the hours were regular at a time when everyone else was on the Pile crazy hours. She would always know where I was, and it was basically a desk job. I was excited because I would be doing what I love—working with computers—and doing it for the right reasons. I got to work on building the spreadsheets used for the initial DNA identification program. I also helped with a lot of the back end, including getting us unlimited licenses from a German antivirus company when our system got hit with a virus that almost wiped out our network.

We set up on Pier 94, on the Upper West Side, with stations for DNA collection over an area the size of two football fields. We asked families to come with anything that might have DNA of their missing loved one: a toothbrush, a comb, dirty underwear, all of that got tested and logged in the system. We were the last station—we digitalized all that info. We didn't meet the families; we met with the DNA team. And that's how we built the DNA database. The site where we worked had these temporary Sheetrock walls just to make it look presentable. Those got covered with flyers from families looking for people. They preserved some of those Sheetrock walls and put them in the 9/11 museum. The database has lived on as a template for other disasters. It got used again right away with that plane crash in Far Rockaway.

There's a lot about the recovery of bodies and personal effects that the public just doesn't know about. FEMA has a team called D-Mort, disaster mortician response, made up of some of the most impressive people I've ever met. They're all morticians and funeral home owners, and a lot of them are big business people because it's a huge industry. We stayed friends with a lot of them.

All through the recovery and cleanup, we kept finding body parts, evidence, and personal property. I'm proud to say that by the time I retired in 2005, we had returned 92 percent of that property. It was a real problem in the beginning because we had no system to identify the owner. We couldn't show people the property because that could have led to all sorts of problems. We ended up asking for a photograph of the person with the object, in the case of objects. Things like ID cards were more straightforward; you just find the person [in the records]. One of the first items we found was a framed photograph of a man and woman, which had miraculously survived on one of the floors where the plane hit, with no damage other than a broken frame. We had a picture of the man in our files, which we confirmed is the guy in the photo. So, we called his wife and told her with great happiness that we'd found a photo of her husband that must have been on his desk . . . I'm sure you already know where this is going. So, the woman showed up and waited for close to an hour outside the building before working up the courage to come in and face this final piece of reality that her husband is gone. Luckily, I saw her waiting. I knew right away this wasn't the woman in the picture. I don't know who the woman in the picture is: his sister, his girlfriend, the neighbor. We didn't want to run the risk of causing her further anguish and delivering the news in such an awful way. So, we told her we made a mistake; it wasn't her husband. We lied to her, and we never returned the photo.

That experience taught us that we needed a system for dealing with what were bound to be highly emotional encounters. We noticed that nobody could just get their property back and leave, they all ended up lingering. So, what we did was set up this room that was like the size of a big closet. We put a small couch in there and a coffee table with an American flag and a box of tissues. We would sit you down and go get the item in an envelope, then give you all the time you needed. The average amount of time people were in there was about two hours.

I had the honor of visiting groups that represented the families. They had set themselves up by location: Tower 1, Tower 2, Cantor Fitzgerald. Rockville Centre, Long Island, a commuter town that lost thirty-two of its residents. We would keep these folks updated about the program and the percentage of items we had returned so far. We would describe some of the items we had been unable to match with a person. We couldn't show the items because that would be a violation of privacy. Anybody could attend these groups, and there was this woman who kept showing up to all the groups looking for her husband's belt. It was unique because it had etchings on it her children had made. When we did find a belt matching her description, she couldn't accept that there was nothing else left of him. She was so angry. After about four years, we found her husband's wedding band. We called her and said we'd like to talk to her, if she wouldn't mind coming in. We sat her in the room, cut the envelope, and walked out. She sat with the ring a long time, and when she finally came out, she said:

"It feels like you found my husband."

That was very emotional for all of us. And that's when I decided I had had enough and I could retire.

In total, we recovered over thirteen thousand employee ID cards and three thousand photographs, but nothing larger than a small briefcase.

We had to clean each item of personal property before we returned it to the family. So we were washing toxins off these items. We used a high-pressure washer and a wire cage with a fan to pull all the water and any remaining residue off it. The fan had an exhaust with nowhere to go. We worked in a basement at police headquarters with no ventilation. So, we were exposed to these toxins all day. My dear friend, Tom O'Neill, who was down there with me, died of sinus cancer.

Five

DON'T TAKE NO FOR AN ANSWER

The original purpose of the September 11th Victim Compensation Fund was to protect the airline industry from lawsuits and present an alternative to litigation for the families of the victims. Through an act of Congress in the immediate aftermath of the attack, the VCF was set up much like a class action settlement, where families can sign up and get their compensation in exchange for waiving their rights to sue the airlines, the government, or whoever. But for the fund to do its job, at least 80 percent of eligible families needed to sign up, and so the terms had to be seen as fair and reasonable by everyone involved. Anyone familiar with these kinds of mass compensation cases would know there's only one man for the job.

Ken Feinberg built his career as someone who can untangle wicked problems of wrong done and compensation owed to come up with solutions everyone can live with. Before 9/11, his best-known case was compensation for service members who had been poisoned by Agent Orange during the Vietnam War. In that case, the funds had come from Monsanto and Dow Chemical, the parties responsible for the poisoning. What makes the 9/11 VCF unique is that the funding is public money, appropriated by Congress, which was feeling generous, compassionate, and patriotic at the time. The funding is also unlimited. The statute gives no advice as to how the program should be designed, who gets the money, or how much they should get. As the newly appointed special master of the fund, Feinberg's unenviable task was to "design and administer the program," and that means deciding who's eligible and compensating them in a way that everyone can agree is fair. Doing that requires assigning a dollar value to each human life lost, which, like it or not, is going to be different for a dishwasher at Windows on the World vs. a fireman vs. a hedge-fund guy. Feinberg and his team recognized that to do this right meant looking at each life as more than a lost source of income. He wanted to give the families a chance to be heard, which for many of them was more meaningful than the fund's "blood money." So, his team made themselves available to any family member or claimant to meet privately and be heard. Ken conducted about 950 of these hearings, and his colleagues did another three to four hundred. He credits these tough conversations with the ultimate success of the fund. Very few want to talk about money.

Ken remembers: "Most came to vent about life's unfairness and to validate the memory of a lost loved one."

The conversations will leave an impression and, in some cases, haunt the special master.

A lady sobbed through her entire hearing. Her husband was a fireman who rescued twenty people, went back inside, and rescued twenty more. He was running across the World Trade Center Plaza to safety and was killed when someone jumping from the 103rd floor hit him like a missile, killing them both instantly. If he had taken one step in either direction, he would be alive today.

"Don't tell me there is a God, Mr. Feinberg," she said. "No God would ever let my husband die that way."

Feinberg remembers how he handled his role as witness to all this pain and sorrow. He told me: "The number of times I kept it together in a hearing, totally professional, and then grieved in private with tears afterward . . . Unless you have a heart of stone, you are going to be impacted, and you learn there is no immunity from that emotional impact."

One conversation about money does stand out. A twenty-six-year-old woman comes to see him and cuts right to the chase, as Ken remembers:

"Mr. Feinberg, I lost my husband at the World Trade Center. He was a fireman. Our children are six and four. Now, I need my three million dollars and I want it in thirty days."

"Okay," he says, "but why do you need it in thirty days?"

She tells him that she has terminal cancer (not 9/11 related), with ten weeks to live. The plan had been for her husband to survive her and look after the kids. Now she needs to set up a trust for the kids while she still has her faculties.

Ken accelerates the payment and gets her VCF payment to her in thirty days. Ten weeks after her hearing, she's dead.

The living are more complicated for the fund. The way the program is designed, it covers death and physical injury. Mental anguish and PTSD don't count. The statute says that the physical injury has to have occurred at the World Trade Center, the Pentagon, or Shanksville, or in the immediate vicinity. That's all straightforward at first. The temporal question, the one that I find myself on the wrong side of, is trickier. What do they do about the person who's coughing up blood a week after the attack? They have to draw a line somewhere, and for the first VCF, that line is seventy-two hours for civilians and ninety hours for responders. The ninety-hour cutoff is an extension based on Michael Barasch's recommendation that firefighters should be eligible to have their respiratory complaints covered, even if they don't report them within twenty-four hours of developing symptoms, which, of course, no responder would have stepped off the Pile to do. But they have to draw a line somewhere, and some of us are on the wrong side of it.

Years later, when I meet Ken Feinberg at a lunch, I will thank him for denying my VCF claim.

"It sucked at the time, but it made me who I am . . . maybe I would have taken the money and run. I'm glad I stayed and fought."

I didn't tell him this, but one important consequence of the path he set me on is getting a chance to meet people like him. Ken Feinberg is probably one of the smartest people in the world, and I can get him on the phone whenever to talk about anything. If this had never happened to me, there's no way I would get a chance to know somebody like that. Ditto Ben Chevat, ditto Jon Stewart.

To learn more about the original VCF and hear more of these heartbreaking and life-affirming stories from the hearings, check out Ken Feinberg's book *What Is Life Worth*, which was made into an excellent movie, *Worth,* staring Michael Keaton as Feinberg.

The fund is over in 2003, having used up all the money allotted and served its purpose of compensating the families of the deceased, with over 97 percent of eligible families coming to the program voluntarily. Around the same time, Detective Zadroga, sipping oxygen, is diagnosed with black lung disease. We're getting sick, we're dying, and we will have to find another way to be heard and helped.

I take my first trip to DC in 2005 with the Sierra Club. They extend an invitation after seeing me on TV in one of my early interviews, making noise about 9/11 illness. I'm coming off surgery, with my foot in a boot, and limping along with this group and the staff of friendly members of Congress, with a documentary film crew following us around. We're working on the first 9/11 health bill, introduced by Congresswoman Carolyn Maloney (D-NY). A member of her staff gives us an insider tip to look at the lapels of people's jackets in the halls. If they have a little pin, they're a member. So, with a little knowledge and a lot of pent-up passion, I hop along after anyone I see with a lapel pin and give them my canned sales pitch like I'm selling vacuum cleaners.

"Excuse me, Congressman, my name is John Feal, I was injured during the cleanup at Ground Zero following the September 11 attacks. I am here today representing the men and women who . . . blah blah blah."

That approach got me a lot of:

"John, thank you for your service. Now, if you'll excuse me, I'm running late for a meeting. God bless."

It's frustrating, ineffective, and humiliating. If there's one thing I can't stand, it's being brushed off. And as a lobbying force, we aren't getting anywhere. It seems like the members of Congress have their own script for dealing with irritating special interest groups crawling their halls. It pisses me off. It's called public *service* for a reason. It's their job to serve their constituents. And the reason we're even taking this issue to the Hill and not just the state House in Albany is because there's at least one 9/11 responder or survivor in every district but two. This is an American issue, we're Americans, and we're here to hold these reps accountable to their oath to serve us.

Finally, I go off script. I see a jerk with a lapel pin. He dodges our group and gets in an elevator. I limp after him, hold the door, and suggest he hear us out, saying: "How about I put my bad foot up your ass?"

Stunned silence. This is not how the Sierra Club operates. It's way outside of the "normal order" you're supposed to adhere to on the Hill. Any jackass can lose his temper; plenty of people think they have something to yell at Congress about. It's another thing to know when and how to vent frustration strategically. When I yell at this guy, I'm not being strategic or intentional, I'm just pissed off that we keep being ignored, but the strategic impact is not lost on me. For one thing, he listens, not to me but to our group. This is my first experience being the "bad cop" to open the door for my more reasonable colleagues. He suddenly has plenty of time for my tree-hugging friends if it means getting away from me and my boot.

On those early trips, my antics catch the attention of a man who will become my mentor and turn me into "FrankenFeal," a lobbying monster. Ben Chevat is Congresswoman Maloney's chief of staff at the time. He's already hard at work on the first 9/11 health and compensation bill when we meet. This bill will address the growing healthcare and toxic exposure crisis that the original authors of the VCF hadn't seen coming. Maloney is working with Congressman Nadler, who represented Lower Manhattan. Her connection to 9/11 healthcare was through Mount Sinai Hospital, which was in her district and is home to the environmental health monitoring program. She and Nadler are fighting for federal money from the Bush administration, which was anti-New York and spending every dime on two wars.

The Sierra Club's 2005 report, "Pollution and Deception at Ground Zero," is as damning as its name suggests. The subtitle spells it out in no uncertain terms: "How the Bush Administration's Reckless Disregard of 9/11 Toxic Hazards Poses Long-Term Threats for New York City and the Nation." The report makes it clear that the decision to reassure the public about air quality at Ground Zero came directly from the White House and was based on policy, not science. Early air quality data was deliberately misrepresented by the EPA, particularly with regard to asbestos, and, in the words of the report, "the EPA didn't find health hazards because it didn't look for them." These troubling findings point to questions at the heart of the whole mess: What did government officials at the city, state, and federal levels know about the health hazards at Ground Zero, and when did they know it? And more specifically, what did Mayor Giuliani know, and when did he know it? In 2007, *The New York Times* will report that the city was aware of the dangers from the beginning, in an article titled, "Ground Zero Illnesses Clouding Giuliani's Legacy." The *Times* quoted Wayne Barrett, author of *Grand Illusion: The Untold Story of Rudy Gulianni and 9/11*, who wrote that the former mayor "said all the right things, but did all the wrong things."

In the interest of a full and truthful account, Ben Chevat, Congresswoman Maloney, and others will spend two decades petitioning the city and filing Freedom of Information Act requests for documents indicating what Giuliani's administration knew and when they knew it. The city will stall, citing the risk liability and exposure to lawsuits (neither of which is grounds to deny an FOIA request). As of this writing, the first documents are finally being released, nearly a quarter-century after the fact.

From the sidelines, working in the House minority wilderness, Maloney had been sending a series of "Dear Colleagues" memos urging joint delegations to write to the president, urging him to look into the health impact of 9/11. These were ignored by the administration.

Nothing changes under Bloomberg's mayorship until his Zadroga sound bite provokes pressure from the *Daily News,* Michael Barasch, and other representatives of the 9/11 community.

Ben has books of his own. He helps me fill my "bible" with more health stats and studies and newly released records about what the city and government knew and when they knew it. I will become Ben Chevat's "break glass in case of filibuster" hired gun. His refrain through the years will be: "You didn't hear this from me, but . . ."

When I'm not in DC or at home with my folders, I'm taking turns with my sisters being with Mom. She had fainted at work one day in 2004. They rushed her to the hospital and we all met her there. A few hours later, we were told it was bone cancer. Not from 9/11, just regular, awful cancer. Not a day goes by the whole time she's sick that I don't wish that I could have it instead of her.

We still don't have a bill at this point; I'm still just a guy who you can call, collecting these thick files on every illness and every bureaucratic roadblock. Now that Mom is sick, I struggle to justify being away from her in the name of a project that still is so far from where it needs to be. I'm still in physical therapy, learning to walk again, and getting EMDR to learn how to think and feel again. It's a lot. I try to find little quiet moments when I can, between all the phone calls, Mom's chemo, my PT. It's funny what can happen in those moments when you're paying attention.

One afternoon, not long after my mom's diagnosis, early in her treatment, I'm on my way back from visiting her in the hospital, and I go into McDonald's for a cheeseburger and a Diet Coke. It's quiet. I've been in "poor me" mode all day, thinking *I suck, I'm jobless and crippled, Mom's sick, all my friends are sick, and I'm carrying all of them. It's a heavy load, and I'm tired.* I must have been sitting there for a half hour, staring at the burger wrapper, sipping the melted ice at the bottom of my cup, when in walks this guy with his two daughters. They look close in age, maybe ten, elevenish. One looks like a normal, healthy kid. The other is severely handicapped. She's noncommunicative, grunting, hand curled in on a limp wrist. The dad orders their Happy Meals, and I'm thinking, *Please don't sit next to me, please don't sit next to me, this place is empty, go sit over there.* I just don't have room to feel more.

They sit one table over from me.

The kids are putting the *happy* in Happy Meal; they're having the best day by the looks of it. The dad's got this joy in his eye. Like real joy. At McDonald's. He's helping the one girl with her food and her toy. She's struggling to get the straw in her mouth. Here's a kid who was born with no choice in life, and she's not complaining. And here I am, feeling sorry for myself, doing nothing but complaining. I get up and leave; I regret not going over and saying a kind word. But I make a promise to myself—I'm never going to complain again. If I am going to carry my mother, who was always so strong for me through everything, who I have never seen complain, if I'm going to carry this community, I don't have time to feel sorry for myself. On my way home, I get to a little parking lot for Blydenburgh County Park. I get out of my car and walk a little way into the woods where I scream at the top of my lungs. Then I just sit there and let it all out for about twenty minutes before driving home.

I'll never know if my mother made a similar promise to herself, but she will never complain. Even when it gets really bad, and the cancer spreads, and the pain must be something even I can't imagine, she doesn't complain, not once.

A couple of days before the end, while she's still lucid, she tells me:

"Keep doing what you're doing. You'll make a difference."

That's nice to hear; I'm not sure how much she even knows about what I'm doing . . . at this point . . . I've been on TV a couple of times, and in the papers . . . but she and I have always had more important things to talk about than my work. Then, a little while later, as she's starting to leave us, she starts whispering names:

"Keller . . . Fernandez . . . Borja . . ."

These are people who've died of 9/11 illness, people I was working with. I had no idea she was following that closely, or that she had taken an interest to the point where my dead friends would be on her mind in her last moments of consciousness. She had always been my hero. It had never occurred to me that I might be hers.

When Mom dies, I let out a scream that rattles her little apartment and echoes through the town. The coroner comes and I tell them to wait while I sit with her a little while longer. When I'm ready, I carry her out.

Mom died in April 2006, three months after Zadroga. That September, on the fifth anniversary of 9/11, Senator Hillary Rodham Clinton (D-NY) brings an amendment to a ports security bill looking to create a $1.9 billion program for 9/11 illnesses. Back in 2005, Congresswoman Carolyn Maloney introduced the Remember 9/11 Health Act, which died in committee, as a follow-up to her bill to extend the VCF in 2004. Up until this point, a team at Mount Sinai has been regularly checking up on the responders in what's called a "medical surveillance" program. They study what's wrong with us but offer no treatment. Around this time, a Mount Sinai study finds that 70 percent of us have some form of lung disease or damage, which the senator cites in her proposal.

In a statement on the anniversary, Clinton says:

> *If we don't take care of these people now and start putting up a system we can have in place for the next several years, we are going to betray a fundamental responsibility to those who we salute whenever it's convenient, whenever it's political.*

She goes on to perfectly sum up the anger and frustration our community has been feeling for half a decade: "They don't want our speeches, they don't want our flowery rhetoric. They want our help."

The help required amounts to at least $30 billion in losses, rebuilding costs, and anti-terrorism security measures, plus whatever 9/11 healthcare is going to add up to as more of us get sick. In a 2002 Rose Garden ceremony, President Bush pledged $21.4 billion in federal funding to New York, an amount that the federal government has treated as "a ceiling rather than a floor," according to Rep. Maloney. And so far, they've fallen short of even that sum.

On September 8, 2006, an international relations and national security subcommittee convenes a hearing on 9/11 illness. Among the witnesses is Joseph Zadroga, father of the late Detective James Zadroga.

He tells the committee:

We need our government to do the just and proper thing and help these heroes. We can't do anything for our son now, but we want to help make sure that other workers get the treatment they need when they get sick. They all deserve a real commitment from our representatives to provide for long-term monitoring and treatment.

Then he reads and enters into the record a list of recommendations for a 9/11 health program:

We must make the first priority the treatment of the heroes to improve their health and save their lives . . . Don't worry about what it will cost, spend the money that is needed to improve the health of the heroes. I can't understand how this country can place a value on a life . . .

New York Governor George Pataki signs legislation to expand the death benefits of responders who die of cancer and other illnesses.

Critically, this bill includes presumptive causation with regard to these illnesses—if you worked on the Pile or meet the criteria as a survivor, it is presumed that your 9/11-related illness was caused by your exposure. You don't have to "prove" that the dust made you sick. Science and the opinion of the medical community have already established the links between your type of illness and 9/11 dust exposure. Pataki signs the bill at Ground Zero on August 14, 2006 and mentions Zadroga in his speech.

But despite the rhetoric, Pataki opposes Clinton's bill, as does Giuliani. Both take issue with New York having to cover 10 percent of the healthcare costs in the bill.

The bill eventually dies in committee, like Maloney's earlier attempt.

In what will become a common theme in our long battle to finally get our bill, we have better luck attaching something we want to a larger vehicle for another cause. With the Walsh amendment to a bill related to disaster response for Hurricane Katrina, Clinton helps us get back $120 million in federal funding, plus an additional $5 million that had been allocated for workman's compensation for 9/11 responders only to be rescinded by the Bush administration. It's a small win in a year of getting crushed, in a year when we have a Democratic majority in the House and a tie in the Senate. This is our first lesson that you can't count on partisan mandates to get legislation through. We had Democratic heavies on our side, but the bill had lacked the ground game to generate the kind of support it needed from either side.

And on that front, I have work to do. With Ben Chevat calling the plays, it's time to get strategic. If we want co-sponsors and votes and political will when we try again next year, we're going to have to walk the halls and get them ourselves. I waste no time complaining, even to myself, about our tough luck in '06.

I lace up my boots and rally my troops.

ACTION FOR ACTIVISTS: A SLAMMING DOOR IS NOT THE END, IT'S AN INVITATION TO ACTION

So you've hit a wall, had a door slammed in your face. What now? Think of how you might use "no" as a rallying cry rather than a refusal.

In the first five years after 9/11, we all knew something needed to be done, and we were all starting to go to the Hill as a show of force. I was there with responders and survivors, so were the unions, fraternal orders of police, the law firms, and other special interest groups. We had Carolyn Maloney, Hillary Clinton, and Ted Kennedy on our side, to name a few, and they enjoyed a narrow majority in the House. We had sympathy from GOP members whose patriotism and respect for first responders could move them to care about what many considered a "New York issue." On paper, it looked like we had a lot to be hopeful for. But we got crushed. Both the House and Senate bills died in committee, and what we came away with pleased no one and left our urgent needs unaddressed. Looking back, the truth is, that refusal forced us to get organized, to regroup, and fight harder for something better. We didn't take no for an answer. That setback worked in our favor.

One thing to watch out for is toxic persistence. Don't hit your head against a wall, doing more of what isn't working. The key to effective persistence is to regroup when you get shut down. Learn from your setbacks and adjust your game plan. In our case, the door slammed when the bills didn't make it out of committee. We didn't have the support we needed. So our plan was to go get it, by going to the Hill and taking meetings to get the support we needed, one vote at a time.

Testimony

DAWNELE HOLBROOK

I've never been one to keep my mouth shut. As a woman in a big boys' club, that doesn't always go over well. But I wasn't going to be silenced about my illness, not when speaking up could mean saving lives. I wanted my colleagues and fellow responders to know that if you feel something is off, you should get it checked out, and you should know there's a connection between the work we were doing and all kinds of cancer.

Dawnele Holbrook, aka "Fed," is a retired FBI Special Agent and mother of two who worked in counterterrorism and was already involved in the hunt for Bin Laden before 9/11. She is a two-time cancer survivor who was made sick by toxic dust exposure while responding to the attack on the Pentagon and through her work with the Bureau's evidence labs.

I reached out to John because I could see there was so much more support for responders in New York. I wanted that support, and their movement could use a few more voices from DC. All these people were helping each other and fighting to be heard, and I had no one at the time. I was a single mom with a rare lymphoma. My colleague, Special Agent Tom Mohnal, had the same kind of lymphoma. When he first came to me to tell me that he was sick, I made sure he was aware of the WTC Health Program and the VCF. We were together constantly at work after that. If I wasn't checking in on him, he was checking in on me. We compared notes on chemo and the different treatment options our doctors recommended. The fear of what the future might hold, the fear of dying, was easier to deal with when I shared it with him. We always greeted each other with a big hug.

Going back to September 11th, I was in the office, on the counterterrorism desk, when the first plane hit the Twin Towers. My father was working as an FAA inspector at the time. He was in Vegas where the workday hadn't started yet, but I called him to try and see what they knew on the FAA side. When the second plane hit, we started setting up an internal command post, and when the Pentagon was hit, some of us were sent to respond directly to the scene. Tom, I would later learn, was in traffic right across from the Pentagon on his way home to pack a bag for New York, where his expertise was needed, when Flight 77 tore through the Pentagon. He called it in to Quantico and alerted the FBI before making a U-turn and responding to the scene.

We were responders first and investigators second. It was a hectic scene but nowhere near as complex as the World Trade Center. For one thing, there was a parking lot right there where EMS could stage their response. In the back of my mind was that I was also a counselor for the Employee Assistance Program (EAP) at work. That was a duty I took as seriously as my work as a responder or an investigator, and I made myself available to counsel the responders who had gone in. You go into "work mode" but it's hard. Nothing prepares you for that kind of destruction and horror. And it's the unexpected things that really get you. I expected to see bodies and burns and wreckage, but I wasn't ready to find little kids' clothing; there was a "princess shirt" and a boy's shirt with little airplanes on it. I had a little girl at the time, and seeing those things really affected me. Nobody prepares you for how eerie it is to see everyday objects and office supplies perfectly preserved in a ruined building that swallowed an entire passenger plane. These visuals would become even more poignant in my memory because my work with the evidence would eventually give me audio to go with the visuals. I would listen to the cockpit voice recorders and 9-1-1 transcripts. I would hear the hijackers and the passengers screaming. I saw so many of their faces because we were searching for IDs to compare to photos the families had provided and photos of the terrorists, who had been identified by the FBI not long after the attack. For months after, I worked on a lab team out of warehouses and forensics labs processing piles of evidence. We found some of the hijackers' passports and boarding passes. We found the box cutters. Everything we handled was covered in dust, and the dust hung in the air in the building where we handled evidence with little or no PPE and no information about the toxic nature of the dust. Even after everything that happened, I feel the same way many of my fellow responders did about this work: I was in the right place in the right time, and I wouldn't want to be doing anything else. This was the most important investigation in American history, and I collected crucial pieces of evidence.

I came alive in crisis mode, and I was the same way dealing with my diagnosis. The cancer came out of nowhere. There was no cancer in my family. At the time, my doctor, in Virginia, had no idea about all the 9/11-related cancers in New York. I kept him in the loop with my research and connection to that community. Sure enough, my cancer, follicular lymphoma, was one of the ones linked to dust exposure. To get into the health program, I had to get proof of presence from the Bureau, stating that I had been working in the labs where I said I worked. At the time I was so afraid they were going to deny that as retaliation for my disobeying their suggestion that I not mention 9/11 illness. Luckily, I was able to get in the program. I put my life in the hands of my doctor and of this community and got ready to fight like hell.

I got sick toward the end of the summer, going into a new school year. At the time, I had one daughter graduating from high school, which is a big year, and a daughter in second grade, which is so young and just the beginning of real school. My thought was nothing is going to change in their lives. I'm going to do everything the doctor says and go to chemo, and we are going to get through this. I'm not leaving my girls. Christmas is going to be the same as every year. I remember thinking about Christmas before I even asked about the prognosis. I ended up going overboard with presents that year. Amazon's free shipping and one-click checkout helped me make Christmas happen even though I was too unwell to go out and shop. But thanks to a lapse in short-term memory called "chemo brain," I did a little too much clicking and ordered the same presents multiple times. One of my girls got three of the same jacket. We all laugh looking back at that Christmas on chemo.

Later that year, they found a second cancer, not a spreading of the first cancer, but a new, simultaneous cancer. Having these two exact cancers at exactly the same time was further evidence of a link to 9/11 dust exposure. They put me on a treatment that's known as "the red devil" because it's literally a poison they put in your veins. My second grader had a field trip coming up and I had volunteered to be a chaperone. My hair started falling out right before her trip. So, I told her: "You know, it's okay if you don't want me to go on this one. I can go on the next one when my hair grows back. I don't want to embarrass you or draw too much attention to you."

This goes back to not wanting anything to change for my girls. I didn't want to put her in the position of being the girl whose mom has cancer; I wanted her to have a nice normal field trip.

"Mom," she said, "I don't care what you look like. I just want you to be there."

I completely lost it at that point.

I told her, "I will always be there." I told her my hair was falling out because of the poison that was going to kill "the ick," and my hair will grow back one day. And that's how it went for a while: I would drive her to school and go to chemo one day and work the next, fighting terrorism with no hair. Tom would be there with a big hug for me, and I would tell him the things I couldn't tell my daughters or my colleagues about my dance with the red devil. I went through two years of that and watched friends die along the way. I was determined to help as many people as I could, getting the word out, educating doctors in the DC area about 9/11 cancers, and eventually telling people at work to join the program if they were exposed. Tom and I started working with John and going to the Hill to tell our part of the story.

Tom would eventually have the opportunity to speak before a congressional subcommittee, in 2019, on a panel with Jon Stewart. I was there for that, a few rows back, listening to my dear friend tell the whole world about what we had been through. Tom died in 2021. Not a day goes by that I don't wish I could give him one more big hug.

My proudest moment from our trips to the Capitol was early in the fight for the bill, when I was still riddled with cancer, and we were a long way from getting what we needed from Congress. I was walking the halls with John and his guys. This young photographer named Faye was with us, documenting the whole thing. There were about a dozen of us in a conference room meeting with a congressional aide. The aide, this young woman, was horrible, she just gave us this rambling harangue about spending and all these smug devil's advocate arguments. We were getting nowhere. Finally, I interrupted her.

"Excuse me, that's all very interesting, but there's something I would like to show you. Here's what I'm dealing with."

I pulled up a picture on my phone of my latest scan. You didn't have to be an oncologist to know what you were looking at. It showed my chest was black all over with cancer in all my lymph nodes.

The room went silent. I was petrified I had done the wrong thing by going off script. I didn't want to embarrass John. It turns out it was the right move. Sometimes, people need visuals to cut through all the talk.

After a long pause, the aide spoke just above a whisper:

"Ummm . . . uhhhh . . . thank you for sharing that."

The floor was now ours.

Six

USE YOUR OPPONENT'S WEIGHT AGAINST THEM

You need a strong back to attend the State of the Union. The Capitol has these old wooden seats made for smaller people in simpler times. My local representative, Tim Bishop, invites me to Bush's last one, the first of three I will attend. The sitting is hard on the back and the ass, while the partisanship is an ab workout. You get up and clap, clap sitting down, stay down, and don't clap. Everybody's keeping score and clapping or not sitting or standing according to points the president's scoring; the score is kept by each member as a tally in their head. I'm sweating keeping up with the applause, and the heat in the balcony is brutal. After three of those, when I get invited back, I always pass the honor along to someone who doesn't know about the hardwood benches and the furnace, someone for whom it's still special.

It's 2005. At this point, I'm working with Chevat. He's coaching me ahead of the fight for the first healthcare bill. The key skill he teaches me, that I will teach my team leaders and everyone I take to DC through the years, is how to do a meeting. It's simple, and yet few get it right.

1. You come in, you sit down, you introduce your people, starting with those from the member's district.
2. Talk for five minutes. State your business.
3. SHUT THE FUCK UP.
4. Let them talk. Put them on the spot.

I have a whole chapter coming up on how we picked our teams, and way more to say about that. In our case, it helps to bring people who are sick and people in uniform, people from different affected groups. The visuals matter. But one thing that's vital is that you bring someone from the member's district. People make the mistake of going to the top, right to the Speaker, when you should always start with your representatives. When we meet with Seth Moulton, who represents Massachusetts' North Shore, we bring along a guy from Marblehead who was a high schooler on 9/11 and went to the Pile to volunteer with his friend. Now he's sick and ineligible for the VCF because there's no official record of him being there. And so, we can show this is a Massachusetts issue. As Speaker "Tip" O'Neill once said, "All politics is local." Moulton signs on as a co-sponsor.

The reason I emphasize "SHUT THE FUCK UP" is because, as we learned the hard way, if you show up with a sob story and spend the whole meeting lecturing them, you'll get the members' sympathy and a "thank you for your service" and then, with the time remaining, they'll brush you off with some nonsense about fiscal responsibility or whatever on their way out the door. You need to get them talking so you can expose the holes in their arguments. I start driving down to DC for these meetings, and some responders and survivors take the bus and meet me there. We get meetings, first with staff, then chiefs of staff, then members. And when I say we take meetings, I mean a lot of meetings; when we finally get organized, my teams are having fifteen, twenty meetings per day. Our record was fifty-five meetings in one day.

We come in polite. We shake hands. We let them know: "You're about to hear some passionate stories right now, and you're going to hear the cold, hard facts. Hear us out, listen to what we have to say, and if you're on the fence, we'll make another meeting. But we're not going anywhere. We'll be back with more stories, more facts, more statistics, but we're not going to let up. You're either with us or against us, and believe me, it's going to be a lot easier if you're with us. We've got facts on our side, and if all you have to go up against that is partisanship and ideology, I feel sorry for you."

To back it up, I have phone numbers for every local news channel and local paper in the districts where their member of Congress is against us or refusing to co-sponsor. We're in DC when they're in session, and responders from their districts are in their home offices when they're home. Those are some small offices. We make it crowded. The meetings are a courtesy call to let them know what's going to happen to them in the media if they stand in our way.

When we do talk to the media, we learn to keep it simple. More often than not, the people at home, on the other side of that broadcast, don't know anything about you or what you're about. So, whenever the cameras are on us, we start with our simple, sound-bite-friendly refrain: We're here today because hundreds of thousands of people are sick and dying from the aftermath of 9/11.

We take advantage of the duplicity we encounter at every turn. The members we're dealing with are often different people in a room alone or in a meeting than they are on the floor or when the cameras are rolling. They have constituents to please and images to maintain. Whenever possible, we try to give them an opportunity to follow through in public with promises made in private. Where they choose hypocrisy, we're quick to call that out. Sometimes, the smart move is for me to meet with a member alone and let them know they're free to spin it any way they like, and nobody has to know what we talked about or how we settled it.

The great Ray Pfeifer, whom you'll meet soon, used to say, "Do the right thing, even when no one's looking."

I used to argue with him, because I say, "How about do the right thing when *everyone* is looking."

As hard as we are on the officials and staff we meet with, we are ruthless with ourselves. Everything we are asking them to do has to come from our example. It isn't enough to rest on our hero credentials or what we had done years ago at Ground Zero. Those events, the loss of life, set a standard we have to live up to every day. We keep our side of the street clean, and that means putting aside union and professional rivalries and political differences; we can't afford to divide ourselves or put personal squabbles ahead of what we're trying to accomplish. We do our homework, and I teach others how to teach what they're learning so that I don't have to hold anybody's hand. We come to meetings prepared, with vital intelligence on the folks on the other side of the table. If you're giving me a meeting, I'm showing up knowing what you had for breakfast.

We have all your tweets, every #BacktheBlue, #SupportOurTroops, and #NeverForget. We know if you or someone in your family served or if you were a volunteer firefighter back home or if you are just a fire buff. We bring our books breaking down, by district, how many people are in the health program, how many people are sick, and how many have filed a VCF claim. I teach my guys to update this intel constantly and take notes on every meeting. Because you better believe we're coming in knowing exactly what you said to us last time. The way I know if everybody's paying attention in the meetings is when we debrief, if I get six people telling me the same thing, all with basically the same notes, I know they were all switched on. If I get six different versions, I know they weren't paying attention.

Everywhere we go, we're given the brush-off business cards, a galling reality of working the Hill that Jon Stewart will call out with devastating

Showing Senator Dan Sullivan (R-AK) one of his own tweets. #NeverForget is highlighted. (Photo/Faye Murman-Dorsey)

effect at the hearing in 2019. At some point, we develop an SOP for dealing with the business card brush-off. We give them a card in return: a funeral mass card from a 9/11 responder who has died from 9/11 illness. A prayer or a few lines of scripture on one side, and the beaming young firefighter or cop, usually in an official department portrait, on the other.

Here's Greg, Congressman, I held his hand in the hospital while he was dying. His last words to me were "Make sure my family's taken care of."

Are you going to help me keep that promise, to Greg, Congressman?

I'll take your card and you can have his.

Now the 9/11 Museum, in their display on post-9/11 illness, features a stack of congressional business cards beside a stack of prayer cards with a placard describing this practice.

Congress has seasons and a timeline. Cancer has a timeline of its own. Both stacks of cards keep getting higher.

Going into the 2010 bill, I get my first meeting with Congresswoman Nancy Pelosi (D-CA), and like many of my all-time great friendships, ours does not get off to a smooth start. She gives me seven minutes. I go in there with a workers' comp attorney and team member Sean Riordan. Something about a meeting at this level, I thought I needed an attorney present for some reason.

First thing I do is put my feet up on her desk.

"Young man, take your feet of my desk."

"No. I got seven minutes, so let me tell you what's going to happen. My team is going to be blowing up your phones, and Maloney's phones too. Now you're our allies, but you're also playing games, and if you're with us, you can't be playing politics with these people's lives. These people aren't going to be attached to a larger vehicle. These men and women are not pork."

Pretty soon, my seven minutes are up, with no indication of whether she got past the placement of my boots. I must have made an impression, because the next thing I know, she calls Maloney to say, "Tell Feal we're good."

At the press conference announcing the bill, Madame Speaker is standing shoulder to shoulder with me. In a quiet moment, I say, "Speaker, I am so sorry for my behavior. I hope you can forgive me. Please understand that I was acting out of concern for my people and their humanity, not my own ego, but that doesn't make it right to have treated you with such disrespect."

We're "John" and "Nancy" from that day forward.

When we're not on the Hill or in home districts taking meetings, we're keeping our promise to blow up their phones. We make it known: *In case you missed the press conference, we're getting the bill back.*

In the fight for the first bill, we lack the media attention and public interest that will later prove decisive, but we don't let that stop us. The key, as in wrestling, is to use our opponent's weight against them. Over the years, we will have plenty of frustrating interactions, but we rarely have to deal with the real extremists, because they will ultimately yield to the interest of their party. We're not weighed down by party machinery, indebted to a union, or persuaded by special interests. We're a motley crew of men and women from all walks of life who got sick in the course of our public service and survival and are now fighting to have our health needs taken care of. The cumbersome nature of government at the root of the problem can be turned to our advantage if we're smart about it.

The only people who ever give us trouble are the representatives themselves. We end up making fast friends and loyal followers with everyone else. One day, I'm coming out of a meeting in Chuck Schumer's office that did not go well. I walked out after about two minutes of him giving me a smug lecture about what I can and can't say in the press. I may have told him to "suck my dick." I may have said it loud enough that they could hear me out in the hall.

Leaving Schumer's office, I ran right into my guys, all holding hands in a circle. And these guys aren't the hand-holding types. There's a guy standing with them in the circle, a Black man with his head down and his eyes closed. It's none other than the Reverend Jesse Jackson. What he's doing there today, I have no idea.

"Let us pray for the 9/11 community, the FealGood Foundation, and all the righteous work you are all doing here today. In Jesus's name, we pray."

AMEN!

"Sorry for cursing, Rev."

We have God on our side; now we just need to get some more co-sponsors.

Congress, as a body, has some of the lowest approval of any part of the government. However, many individual members enjoy near-triple-digit approval among their constituents in polarized, uncontested districts. This is a recipe for persons of very little talent, intelligence, or decency to make it all the way to the halls of government and stay there.

Heading into the 2010 vote, as a Republican filibuster drags on into the night, a Rep. Barton from Texas, whose anti-science/pro-pollution remarks had recently been lampooned by *Time* magazine, tells me, "This is a game, boy, and we can play it all night."

It's late. I'm hungry. I don't have the energy to spar. I order up a bunch of pizzas to the Capitol and pretty soon, we've got Republicans and Democrats breaking bread.

With a mouth full of Dominos, I say to Barton:

"This is a game, and we can play it better than you can."

Congressmen from Texas can believe the Earth is flat if they want. My guys' politics is their business. But one thing we can't have is politics, particularly extremist politics, sowing division within the group. It starts with the Tea Party and birtherism in Obama's first term. In 2015–2016, you start to see this new right-wing Trumpism sneaking in. These people are uncompromising, angry, and completely out of touch with reality. In all my years in DC, I saw Republicans and Democrats getting drinks together after work, same with the reporters from CNN and Fox. No matter how heated things got, they behaved like colleagues and fellow countrymen. The slide into Trumpism introduced these bilious trolls and agitators who, to quote Churchill's definition of a fanatic, "can't change their minds and won't change the subject." Luckily, dealing with House members of this persuasion is easy because they all fall in line and do what their party tells them, even if they make a big stink about it. I don't have many Trumper stories from the Hill because we tended to go around these people and talk to the sane if frustrating party leaders they took their marching orders from.

Policing the politics within our movement was a bigger challenge. Palin's, and later Trump's, right-wing populism resonates with many first responders and disaffected union Democrats. It's understandable that

Trump's siren song of taking America back from leaders who screwed over working Americans would connect with some of these guys. Don't get me wrong, there's a derangement happening on the left as well around this time, with identity politics and victim culture crowding out the working-class values the Dems had always been so strong on. The issue in both cases is extremism and ideology. The way I see it, if you go too far to the left or to the right, you've got one ear up against a wall and it's harder for you to listen. The issues with left-wing radicalism are less of a problem in our group than the cult of Trump is. Nobody on my team was "self-identifying" as anything other than a cop, a firefighter, a responder, a soldier, or marine.

A lot of us who come to the Hill with strong opinions or a sense of party loyalty have those views challenged and some do a complete 180 when we see how the party of "law and order" actually treats cops. I end up with a bunch of Republicans who love Kirsten Gillibrand, who fought for the bill at a time when nobody on either side of the aisle wanted to touch it. And the guys have to grudgingly admit their appreciation of the New York senator who Gillibrand inherited the bill from: Hillary Clinton.

The main thing, at this critical juncture, is to put group unity above personal opinions and partisan politics. We have to operate that way, or fault lines will start to appear. This is where many movements go wrong.

Rich Palmer, one of my team leaders, and I and the other team leaders make one thing very clear, and we repeat it every morning on every trip. We don't care what you are, Republican or Democrat, when you go into a meeting, you are 9/11 responders and survivors. Period.

When we go after a member of Congress or a senator, we do so on the basis of the issue and their stance. It's not partisan. It's not even political. We don't use the words "Democrat" or "Republican."

We deal in facts and statistics. We're not here to peddle "alternative facts" or conspiracy bullshit. I tell the guys, if you don't know the statistics, if you don't know the facts, keep your fucking mouth shut. If you can't read from the book that's right in front of you, don't fucking read. If someone fucks up in a meeting, they get pulled into the hallway and told to never do that again. If they do, they're gone.

I conclude every briefing by saying:

"Nobody will fuck this up but me."

We're heading into the 2010 vote, trying to make it happen before the holiday recess, after which it might not happen at all. One day, around lunchtime, I get a phone call from Beth Shaw, Jon Stewart's assistant.

"Mr. Feal, Jon Stewart would like to talk to you. Can I put him through?"

"Yeah, go ahead."

I think lunchtime is when they start their day over at *The Daily Show*; they're working until like dinner and then it's time to get ready to air. I'm packing a bag for DC and the final push for the vote. He's catching me on my way out the door.

"John Feal, Jon Stewart here, check this out." I can hear him eating. "I've been watching you for the last couple of years. You're going to come on my show tonight. We'll make fun of Republicans, and we're going to help you get your bill passed."

"Wow, Mr. Stewart. I like the sound of that. But I can't come on your show tonight. I'm leaving for DC right now. We've got two days to get the bill passed, and I've got to go finish what we started. I have a meeting with Pelosi in the morning."

There's a long pause. I get the impression that people generally accept invitations to be on *The Daily Show*.

"Wow. A man of integrity, I like that. Alright, check this out. Give me four guys. I'm assuming you're worth four guys."

I send Kenny Specht, Chris Baumann, John Devlin, and Ken George. A fireman, a cop, an operating engineer, and a city Department of Transportation guy. The rest of us go to DC where I watch the show from my hotel room. It was beautiful. Funny but in a biting way that cuts right through to the hypocrisy and shamelessness we were up against. Stewart drops a hashtag #WorstResponders for Paul Ryan and the GOP leadership opposing the bill. As Jon points out on the show, McConnell had his own reasons for wanting to kick the vote down the road until after the holiday season, as Jon and I remember he gave this big weepy speech about wanting to be home for Christmas. And it was in response to these remarks that Kenny Specht brings down the house on *The Daily Show*. Before the cameras rolled, Stewart told Kenny about McConnell's "home for Christmas" sob story. *The Daily Show (the Book)* quotes Kenny's reply, "Oh, you know we always thought it was an honor to work on the holidays, to protect people's families."

Stewart decided *that* would be his ending for the show.

I'm on my feet, watching in my hotel room. They're devoting the whole show to us, and the guys are killing it. I can't believe how good it's going. Then Kenny drops that unforgettable line and it feels like we won—not the big game, because that's still two days away, but maybe we clinched the playoffs: "You won't find a single New York City firefighter who considers it a sign of disrespect to work in a New York firehouse on Christmas Day or Christmas Eve."

The next day, Shep Smith tells Fox viewers something they're not used to hearing: "Jon Stewart is right! No one's covering this. It is shameful!" Fox gives the issue what Stewart calls "the full Fox treatment," and Republicans start to sweat.

When you name a bill, you give it a heartbeat. Six days after we go on *The Daily Show,* Congress approves the first James Zadroga bill by unanimous consent with $4.3 billion to cover medical care for responders and survivors. I tell the press the bill gets a six out of ten. For one thing, it doesn't include cancer, and the geographic zone covered is too small. But the biggest issue is what Stewart calls a "devilish catch:"

The funding will expire in 2015.

That means we have five years to get it right.

ACTION FOR ACTIVISTS: DRILL YOUR MEETINGS

When you're in a stressful, high-stakes situation, you don't rise to the occasion, you sink to the level of your practice. Rehearse the situations before you're in them—and know when to shut the fuck up.

It's amazing what a small, disciplined, principled group of citizens can achieve in the face of a mighty system. Everything we've accomplished is a testament to that. Looking back, one thing we got right without even realizing that is not to get sucked into a "growth mindset." People love that word, in political movements, in business, startups, there's a cult of growth that often does more harm than good. Not everything is better when it's bigger. We learned that the hard way, as I'll get into in the next chapter, when we brought too many people back to DC and ended up with factions and a few people who weren't there for the right reasons threatening the group.

The writer Edward Abbey said, "Growth at any cost is the ideology of a cancer cell."

We didn't need growth. We'd had enough of cancer. Ideologies—theirs, not ours—were getting us killed. What we needed were small, decentralized, and highly effective teams. The Green Berets live by the principle that "special forces can't be mass-produced." I found the same to be true of guerilla lobbyists. Let Congress be big and bloated and wasteful. Let their members tie their own hands with partisan ideology.

We were gonna eat the elephant, one bite at a time.

Discipline isn't a set of rules or a rigid attitude; it's a way of operating and showing up. This is where you find out if you've done your homework. By the time you find yourself in a meeting on the Hill, it will be too late to figure out if you can run a meeting or if your talking points are clear and impactful. So my advice is to practice and drill and rehearse. "Red team" your arguments and practice defending them against anticipated objections. Seek out the strongest arguments against your position, not the easy, loaded questions that prove your point.

It's so easy to beat someone who's full of themselves. Arrogance—theirs, not yours—is your best friend.

At the end of the day, people like underdogs. History shows that size is often a weakness in governments, not a strength. If you're just getting started, and the forces you're up against seem truly overwhelming, think about it this way: Your biggest fear is probably that you'll get squashed by The Man. But even if that happens, and it probably won't, you still win, because squashing the scrappy underdog is a bad look. In all likelihood, your opponent knows this and will try to avoid looking like a bully, in which case, like us, you'll have to do something even harder: find a way to negotiate with Goliath.

Testimony

PHIL RIZZO

As a corrections officer, I know a thing or two about bullies. You might think a career at Riker's Island would have prepared me to deal with the absolute worst that humanity has to offer. The truth is nothing could have prepared me for the way Congress behaves.

Capt. Phil Rizzo, aka "Mellow," served in the Emergency Services Unit (ESU) at Riker's Island. Corrections responded to 9/11 and worked the Pile all through the cleanup. He was one of my team leaders in Washington.

I've seen these representatives give standing ovations and vote a bill down the next day. Where I worked, it's a different culture. There's a saying in jail, "your word is your bond." If you want to lie and make up stories you can, but in there you're going to get hurt. So you need to be a man of your word. If you're a man of your word and you give respect, you get respect, you survive, it's that simple. But these elected officials . . . I can't see them thriving in a jail environment, I'll put it that way.

How the Department of Corrections ended up working the Pile and how a lot of us ended up getting sick is a relatively unknown chapter in the 9/11 story. Our involvement makes sense in light of other things that were going on at the time. The fire department lost 343 guys when the towers fell. Everyone who wasn't at the Pile, or on duty providing the city's ordinary emergency services that had to continue through the cleanup, was busy with funerals for all their brothers. The NYPD, meanwhile, was busy with anthrax and all the new security measures. All that left a manpower shortage that Corrections stepped up to fill from day one. We brought our skills dealing with a high-stress, chaotic environment, and my ESU guys had most of the same training as NYPD ESU or fire rescue. New York City has fifteen jails. When I was there, Riker's had ten thousand corrections officers. I was one of eight hundred captains, and our specialized unit was two hundred strong. So, there were a lot of us. We deployed like a small army.

On 9/11, we locked down Riker's Island in minutes, and once everything was under control, my team led the way with all our gear, and we got to work, assisting first with the rescue, then the recovery, and eventually cleanup. With all the time I spent down there, it was no surprise when I got throat cancer. I was older than a lot of the guys, which maybe made me a little more safety conscious. I knew the dust was dangerous, how could it not be? I made a point of washing it off me at every opportunity, and I didn't eat at the Pile. I instructed my guys to do the same. It wasn't fashionable in those days right after the attack to distrust the government, but common sense told me that the air around us wasn't safe. And they knew it. I remember one day, OSHA came down and put meters on us. I asked them:

"Are you guys going to tell us what the meters come up with?"

"Yeah," they said.

At the end of the day, the guy from OSHA collected the meters and we never saw him again. I told my guys that was a bad sign. But what were we going to do? It was our job to be there, and someone had to do it. I only wish they had told us we were in danger. And when we started getting sick and dying, I wish they hadn't given us and our families such a hard time. That's all.

I started working with John when I got sick. He took me to a Mets game; my family started going to social events with the FealGood Foundation. At this point my kids have grown up with John and all the kids from the other responders and the guys we went to DC with. That's been great.

I started going to DC with John back when we were taking buses down and eating bagged lunches. I always felt a sense of loyalty to him, and he recognized that and my experience in leadership. But it wasn't something I actively sought out. I used to put my music on for those long bus rides. I would do what he needed me to do while we were in DC and put my music back on for the ride home and went back to being retired and trying to beat the cancer until it was time to go down again. As a former training captain and someone used to controlling groups of hundreds of inmates, I guess I had the skills he needed in a team leader. But I accepted the task reluctantly.

There was only one time where I drew a hard line with John. On one trip we had the *Daily News* with us. John was in another building, and we had just gotten word that the Capitol Police were on their way to our building. John shows up and says, "Don't worry, Ray is back in New York with bail money if they come and arrest us."

If it came to that, they were going to make sure the *Daily News* guy got everything, and we would be on Channel 5 news: Capitol Police Locks Up 9/11 Responders.

I turned to Montu and Rich Palmer, fellow corrections guys—Palmer was another of John's lieutenants—and the three of us said to each other, "If they're coming to arrest people, we're out of here. We don't know these people."

We've all been in intake, and we're not going there in our spare time.

I love John. I would die for John. But I wasn't about to get locked up for John. In the end, cooler heads prevailed and nobody got locked up.

Testimony

TYSON JONES

On September 11th, I was taking inmates to court, at the supreme court in Brooklyn. I was there with a busload of inmates down in a sally port in the basement of the building where we could load and unload them from the transport vehicles securely. It was taking an awful long time to get me and my prisoners in. They just had us waiting there, underground.

Tyson Jones, aka "Iron Mike," was a corrections officer at Riker's Island in the transportation unit.

Eventually, I stepped off the bus to get some information about what was going on. A court officer told me what had happened. I ended up going up to the rooftop, about fifteen stories high. Manhattan and the towers were right there, across the Brooklyn Bridge. Somebody made a comment that those buildings couldn't burn like that for long. Just as we were having that conversation, the first tower came down. All you could see was smoke. We heard a military plane flying low at one point. That caused a panic, and you had hundreds of people rushing for an elevator that could hold six or seven. Luckily it was the good guys.

Standing on the roof we could see people covered in dust walking over from Manhattan. Black, white, you couldn't tell, they were all the same color in the dust. They all had the same dazed look of disbelief. I still can't watch that TV show *The Walking Dead* because of how much the zombies remind me of all those people walking out of the dust cloud.

I tried calling my niece, who was working in Lower Manhattan, and couldn't get through to her. I managed to reach Riker's Island and was told to bring my prisoners back to the island so they could be secured. I was then dispatched to Ground Zero. Before I tell you about that, I'll say one thing about what it was like at Riker's in the aftermath of the attack that I think says a lot about how humans behave in a crisis. Everyone was on their best behavior. Violence, assaults, our use of force, inmate fights, every kind of incident was at its lowest rate probably in history, and they stayed that way for a long time. Everybody was on the same page, and nobody gave each other problems or hassle. The inmates weren't problematic in the way they normally would be. The inmate population experienced that same sense of "we're all in this together" that the whole country did.

Riker's is like a small city with everything it needs to be self-sustaining and highly secure. That means every type of emergency and transport vehicle available. Upon receiving our orders, we loaded up our vehicles and drove into Manhattan to make ourselves available to the rescue effort. They call us "New York's Boldest" because we work totally outnumbered and unarmed in the most violent place in the city. Chaos and an unsafe working environment is the norm for us, so we're the perfect people to send into chaos.

But nothing could have prepared me for what I was driving into. All I remember was saying, "Oh my God; oh my God" over and over.

Oh my God, you could still feel the heat from the buildings.

Oh my God, it was like a war zone.

We didn't wear personal protective gear. Our own health and safety were the last things on our minds. I did a lot of different things down there, going where I was needed. I worked in the makeshift morgue, I hauled supplies and transported people between the Pile and the Fresh Kills Landfill. It was nonstop until one day at Fresh Kills, they told me it was my last day. It was all over. There were no pieces left to pick up.

Seven

PICK YOUR A, B, AND C TEAMS

Lobbyists lie for a living; our job is to tell the truth. It turns out, lying is easier. The truth has to be fought for. Going back to the Hill, ahead of the renewal of the bill in 2015, we get organized. At this point, we already had our hard-won majority, but we didn't want the bill to get weighed down with amendments or attached to a larger vehicle or rolled up in an omnibus tax bill. The combination of our press coverage in 2010 and the growing ranks of sick and dying have attracted an army to these trips. We will learn by taking too many people in 2015 that thirty to forty is the ideal number to bring, roughly a platoon. I break down the groups of thirty to forty into teams, each with a team leader. The team leaders further break down the teams into squads. Everyone has a job, whether that's intel, note-taking, collecting business cards, or logistics. Each team leader, or lieutenant, can send their three squads of three or four into three separate meetings, which is the ideal number for a civil, productive, or friendly meeting. We don't always get those, so when a meeting calls for an intimidation factor, the team leader sends two squads or the whole team, putting six to twelve of us in the room. And there are times when all thirty or forty of us go, to really make a show of force. Breaking things up this way allows us to be everywhere all at once and seem bigger than we are. Thirty guys in a hallway is congestion, ten groups of three in every building on the Hill is a tidal wave. The office buildings would call each other, and say:

"Mr. Rizzo is here with those guys again."

"Really? We just saw them."

"They're in Longworth."

"Now they're in Cannon."

"They're here in Rayburn."

"Now they're in Russell, and they're coming down the hall like Vikings."

We call this approach "shock and awe," to borrow a phrase from Bush's war on terror.

The three teams—A, B, and C—are assigned based on skill and experience. No favoritism or special treatment.

The C team is my fluff team. Their job mostly is to shake hands and pose for pictures with friendly members and certain "yes" votes. But they are versed in all the same intel and procedures as my other teams, and they make a point to always conclude a meeting by asking the kind member to please speak to their colleagues for us.

The B team takes the most meetings and works the hardest. They work the people who are on the fence, meeting with the same member five or six times to secure verbal commitments to "yes" votes and, if they're lucky, co-sponsorship.

My A team is the best of the best. They take meetings that were definitely a "no" and work the hard cases and lost causes. When they do get a "yes" or the rare co-sponsorship, it's a real victory.

Over time, I rotate some of the guys within the teams, like rotating men off the line in war, so A team members can get a break and see friendly faces for a change and C team members can learn what it's like to live on a steady diet of busy signals and slammed doors.

I float between the groups, going where I am needed. I take meetings with Congress members and chiefs of staff who were strongly against us or have an issue with the bill but can be swayed, or with those who were threatening to get in the way of the bill or do something shady.

One element I am brutally honest about is the need for "eye candy." These are the folks whose physical appearance speaks volumes about what the responders have been going through and what the dust has done to our bodies. As people get sicker, I have no shortage of candidates to send into meetings hairless, on oxygen, in wheelchairs, just skin and bones. It's hard for anyone but the most shameless politician to look a dying man in the eye, check their watch, and say they have somewhere more important to be. Shame is a weapon, and we put it to good use.

Diversity is important, too, not because of fairness or equality but because we need to show the broad, democratic impact of 9/11 illness. As Detective Lou Alvarez will later point out to the subcommittee, his life isn't worth more or less than the next person who gets sick. We take meetings with officials who romanticize 9/11 as a time when Americans of all backgrounds and beliefs were united. We're there to show them that's still the case among responders and survivors.

The presence of women is vital. For one thing there aren't many of them—two-thirds of all 9/11 victims were male, as are something like 90 percent of responders. Women like Dawnele Holbrook can tell different cancer stories than the guys. Back to the shaming effect, even Republicans from Kentucky have mothers, and hearing from one who's dying hits home in a way that the story of an old, sick man might not. We also find that women have a mellowing effect on the group; boys are less likely to be boys in their presence, and the Capitol Police are less likely to see us as a physical threat when we show up in mixed company.

One time, we're getting tailed in the hall by two guys in plain clothes, dressed just like us, who fall in with our group. I confront them:

"Who are you guys? You're not with us."

They're Capitol Police, fans of what we were doing, as it turns out.

"We're just making sure you guys are behaving. We have no complaints. We love you guys."

We end up taking selfies and exchanging challenge coins and patches. Eventually, they show their support by providing us with escorts from our hotels.

We have our experts. We use them, and they use us. When we need more than pathos, spectacle, and street smarts, we deputize Ben Chevat, and Suzy Ballantyne of the AFL-CIO & 9/11 Health Watch, my most graceful team leader, to lead meetings, bringing their legal expertise. Ben is fond of adding, "By way, I wrote the bill" when he makes his opening remarks. Ben and Suzy, the unions, and the law offices we end up working with use us to say and do things they can't. We become a back channel and a fifth column of alternative lobbying when the brainiacs need muscle. Working together this way for nearly two decades allows Ben and me to do things we never could have on our own, and we become great friends in the process, though I will always consider him a teacher and mentor first.

The army has Delta Force, NYPD has ESU, FDNY has rescue units. We have our "hit squad," a team that floats around like me and shows up as needed to go after hard-case members and get impossible meetings.

We send in the hit squad when we start hearing lame excuses like:

"Sorry, that person doesn't work here . . ."

"We never got that message . . ."

I teach these guys to be ready to run a meeting on the spot, because sometimes, the element of surprise and their intensity get them a meeting right away, and they need to be ready for that.

The mindfuckery and psychological warfare starts within the teams, and it gets to where I take a sick pleasure in weaponizing hardship and antagonism to get my guys fired up. We take buses to DC. Eventually, law firms handling VCF claims will put up our streamlined teams in nice hotels and shuttle us around. But ahead of the 2015 vote, I'm the one selecting our accommodation, and I make sure to pick the sleaziest, most roach-infested, by-the-hour motels in town. And since I'm the one handing out room keys, I make roommate selections strategically. Who can't you stand? That's who you're rooming with. Cops with firemen, bleeding-heart liberals with gun-nut Republicans. I don't want anyone in a good mood when we go talk to Congress in the morning.

The cheap hotels all blend together, as I'm sure they must for a struggling rock band on tour. But one hotel does stand out: the Days Inn on New York Avenue. We get in late, and there are sixty of us, so that's thirty-one rooms, with everyone sharing but me. I get my own room for the same reason a company commander doesn't dig his own foxhole. I have a battle to plan, and I need the second bed to spread out all my files and folders.

So, we get to the Days Inn, and the man behind the desk says, "Mr. Feal, we're one room short."

"What do you mean?" It's late. I'm tired. We're about to go take on Congress, and we're in no mood to let some clerical glitch be our problem. We've booked the whole damn hotel, and we expect to be taken care of. I can let somebody have the extra bed in my room and put the files on the floor, but that still leaves us one room short. We need that room.

But this isn't some double-booking accident. The man leans in and lowers his voice: "Umm . . . We had a little incident last night."

"What kind of incident, what are you talking about?"

"Mr. Feal, somebody was murdered in the room."

Turns out some woman shot her husband in the head after following him to the motel and catching him with a prostitute.

I turn back to my guys crowding the small lobby and spilling out into the parking lot, many of them no strangers to crime scenes and gore.

"Well," I say, "can we see the room?"

Reluctantly, the manager agrees. It's no longer an active crime scene, the cops and forensics people are done in there, but it hasn't been cleaned up either. He slides the key card and switches on the light, and we all poke our heads in, like kids checking out some overripe roadkill. It's pretty bad. The chalk line is still on the floor. There's blood everywhere and chunks of brain and skull on the rug.

Charlie Kay, who worked for the Department of Design and Construction, just an old-school tough guy, shrugs and says, "I don't mind."

"You sure?"

"It's cool. I'll stay in this room."

"Charlie, you're a team player, bro."

These trips become like our work on the Pile. We cry together, we laugh, and we set aside politics, race, creed, and personal differences. Even though we're once again in a situation none of us would ask to be in, we wouldn't want to be anywhere else in the world.

Not everyone is a team player. Some people just don't fit with what we're trying to do, and I'm quick to send them home. Nobody's special. Nobody's bigger than the work. Prima donnas have to go. Anyone with a personal agenda is out. Coming from jobs that are overwhelmingly male, some of the guys didn't know how to work with women. There was a line, and anyone who crossed it was out. Fortunately, this was rare, and the positive side of these hypermasculine jobs is that they attract men with a strong protective streak. Lila Nordstrom, an advocate for her fellow student-survivors—you read her words before chapter 1 of this book—experiences this when the group shields her from a guy who is being a creep.

The sad cases were the ones where I had to cut good people whose illness had made them too sick or too erratic to make the trip. One guy gets sent home after I find him wandering a motel parking lot barefoot in his underwear. There's another guy who I have to send packing, and it breaks my heart. The problem is he falls asleep in every meeting—whether it's five minutes or twenty, he nods off. We can't have that.

All the wrangling and babysitting is one thing, and by 2015, everyone more or less knows how to behave so I'm less of a nanny than I was on our early trips. The hard part, the part that I carry with me always, is the burden of taking care of the sick and the dying. Their wives and mothers, whose job it is at home, all tell me, "Make sure he takes his meds on time." "Don't let my husband die."

We never lose one on these trips, but the fact remains that time in DC is time away from families in the final weeks and months of these guys' lives. It's their choice; they want to be here. But if I'm going to call myself a leader, I have to put the responsibility on my shoulders and mine alone. No legislation will ever give these families time back with their loved ones, and that's on me for dragging them down there. If we had been successful in 2010, the guys who come with me in 2015 could have been at home instead. If we got what we needed in 2015, the guys who come in 2019 would have been spared their ordeal. That's on me. I failed them.

As their leader, I have more responsibility with no additional privileges. I get my own room only so I can use the second bed and the extra space to spread out my file folders. I'm up before everyone else, and I go to bed last. I will never ask my guys to do anything I wouldn't do.

We "stand to" at dawn, like an army, "up before the enemy." Our days start with a meeting over breakfast with my team leaders. By 2015, two of my three lieutenants are from the Department of Corrections: Phil Rizzo, aka "Mellow," a captain in ESU at Rikers, and Rich Palmer, aka "Angry Bird," a warden. These two are tough and soft-spoken. Rich is our HR department, he polices any bullshit and is quick to send people packing. I trust them both totally, and by 2015, they don't really need me. We plan each trip for weeks ahead of time, and the purpose of these breakfast meetings is just to run through the plays and drill the plan for the day ahead.

Leaders aren't leaders without anybody following them. An army needs soldiers. It needs more soldiers than leaders. Ray Pfeifer is a good soldier. He starts coming down in 2015, riddled with bone cancer, walking the halls in unimaginable pain, never complaining, totally devoted to the mission and the people he serves. Ray retired at the rank of firefighter, having committed himself to the work of saving lives and fighting fires with no regard for promotion, status, or salary. It's something else to see someone with those values staring down an elected official whose whole existence revolves around chasing status and power at any cost and who probably thinks they're doing so much better in the game of life than the Rays of the world. As Stewart remembers in his book, "He's [Ray's] going down there to try and get these people to look him in the eye."

We always let the media know we're coming, so our work ends up on the news, and we get to make our case on Fox and CNN. For all their partisanship and bias, Fox loves us, and I go on there every chance I get. A documentary film crew from Canada working on *No Responders Left Behind* follows us for years. Ray's personal motto, as I've mentioned, the words that they will put on his memorial T-shirt when his time comes, is "Do the right thing even when no one is looking." I get that. But I always say to him, "Do the right thing when everyone is looking."

As the 2015 vote approaches, we get invited back on *The Daily Show*. At this point, Stewart has left the show, and Trevor Noah is hosting. This episode is Stewart's return as a special, surprise guest. They start with a bit about whose show it is, followed by a super cut of Ray and Stewart getting shown the door, handed business cards, and otherwise brushed off by Senator Rand Paul and other opponents of the bill.

Stewart tells receptionists and aides that he's available whenever because "I'm unemployed now."

An aide, dressed like a slutty prairie wife, shoos them out, saying: "You can't film in the office. You can film in the hallway."

"Why," says Stewart, "the acoustics?"

Noah wants to re-create the panel from our first appearance, but sadly that's not possible. Of the four responders who were on with Stewart in 2010, one is dead from cancer, one is too far gone with PTSD to be in front of the cameras, and a third is too sick to travel.

We send Kenny to do the show again, this time flanked by three empty chairs.

ACTION FOR ACTIVISTS: NO PLAYING FAVORITES

Take some time to be brutally honest about the roles in your team. For the sake of your cause, this has to be 100 percent merit based and utilitarian—no pity or playing favorites. Don't be shy about optics and "eye candy." Remember that everyone is replaceable. Make sure your teammates all know that. Egos must be checked at the door. Principles come before personalities.

If you're working alone, get honest about your own strengths and weaknesses and where you might benefit from outside help.

Building your team starts with accepting that you can't do it all yourself. It helps to have company and support. You may think you can go it alone, or that your work is somehow too important to delegate, but you have to accept that every task you don't have a person assigned to becomes your job and yours alone. If you have no one, you have to do everything. If assembling a team and dealing with people isn't your strong suit, then that might be the first thing you delegate. Or if it is your thing, maybe you find someone to do the other stuff while you focus on the human element.

By 2015, we were getting major media attention, and this attracted fans, followers, hangers-on, and people who wanted to help or, in some cases, attach themselves to our cause for selfish reasons. The urgency and importance of our mission had taken us from "doing the right thing even when no one is looking," as Ray would have it, to doing the right thing and occasionally fucking up in front of a global audience. It became more critical than ever to make sure everyone was squared away and there for the right reasons. It became clear that we were rolling too heavy, and we would eventually scale back the teams on later trips. Cancer made its own cuts, too, of course, taking some of our best guys.

The big takeaway when assembling your teams is quality over quantity. You can always fake size by sending out small teams in all directions when you need overwhelming presence, but you can't fake quality. Keep your core teams and leadership small: three or four leaders with teams of three to twelve each. This core group will be a force multiplier, with a disproportionate impact for their size. When you do need to expand or merge with other groups, your teams can branch out and lead teams of their own, scaling your mission without sacrificing quality or going off script.

Doing this right means empowering your people at every level. Have each team member learn the other jobs within the team. If you organize A, B, and C teams, rotate them so that everyone can learn from the group's collective experience.

Don't underestimate the team-building power of a crappy night's sleep in a sketchy motel. Stripping away frills and comfort will weed out the people who are there for the wrong reasons and motivate the right people.

Testimony

TOM WILSON

I'm sure a lot of people who had been to war had all sorts of memories come flooding back on 9/11. War was a foreign experience for most New Yorkers to be under attack like that, but not for everybody. In my case, my job on 9/11 was exactly the same as one of my missions when I was deployed to Bosnia-Herzegovina as a young MP (military policeman) in the '90s.

Tom Wilson, aka "Shrek" was an NYPD sergeant on the burglary squad in Williamsburg and Bushwick, Brooklyn. Tom is the father of five kids: Tommy, Ryan, Lewis, Connor, and Katie. He lost his tongue to 9/11 cancer.

They had us secure a bridge across the Sava River that could support heavy armor. It had been blown up and rebuilt, and it was our job to secure it and prevent an armored column from advancing across it. We were critically undermanned and undergunned and were lucky that the attack never came.

After the army, I joined the NYPD and worked burglaries in

Williamsburg back when it was still pretty rough. The morning of 9/11 was primary election day, so all my guys were assigned to polling locations. I was following up on a burglary from the previous night at the home of an elderly couple. My radio started to blow up with chatter, something about a plane hitting the World Trade Center. I told the couple I would be back. I never got back to them.

Instinctively, I went to the Williamsburg Bridge, just to police traffic and make sure emergency vehicles could get across. At this point only one plane had hit. When the second plane hit, I crossed to the Manhattan side, at Delancey and Clinton, and secured that side of the bridge while anti-crime sergeant Richie Payton secured the Brooklyn side. Our first mission was to get emergency vehicles across. Our second mission was security. Our third mission was to facilitate the mass exodus from the island—all those people covered in dust, walking like zombies. We didn't know what was going to happen; there were rumors that turned out to be just rumors that there were terrorists in armored cars driving around shooting people. We didn't know if the bridge was a target. It was just me and Richie. Like in Bosnia, we would have been in trouble if anything had happened to the bridge, but nothing did, and we went home to our families after spending September 11th babysitting an on-ramp.

The next day, the 12th, was my first day on the Pile. I worked down there and at Fresh Kills Landfill. A lot of detectives and sergeants were reassigned to Ground Zero. Property crime and burglaries were down citywide during the aftermath, so they could spare some manpower for the cleanup. I ended up working down there for about three months. Later, in 2002, I left the NYPD to work for the Suffolk County Police Department, out on Long Island. I started to get sick around that time. I had the World Trade Center cough that never went away, and by 2002–2003, I started getting more serious respiratory and sinus issues, which all seems minor compared to what was coming.

In 2008, I was diagnosed with very aggressive tongue cancer. This was early days for the 9/11 health program, and cancers weren't covered because they were just starting to present themselves among responders. I went for major surgery and had my tongue cut out. They cut some flesh from my arm to make a new tongue and removed an artery and transplanted it in my neck to supply blood to it, then they grafted skin from my leg to fill in what they had taken from my wrist. Then I had another surgery where they took out thirty-nine lymph nodes. The cancer spread to the skeletal muscles. They followed up with radiation. I'm still dealing with the long-term effects of that. My grafted tongue is better than no tongue, but it hurts all the time, and I can't talk for more than a half hour. It's sore now, but telling my story is cathartic, so I'll keep going until I can't anymore.

Dr. Eric Genden at Mount Sinai saved my life. He was recommended to me by the early 9/11 health program. He was one of the first people to understand the aggressiveness that is the hallmark of 9/11 cancers and proceeded with aggressive treatment and monitoring. I was out of work for four months. About a month after I got back on the job, I got run over and crushed by a car at the scene of a major vehicle accident. I was rushed to Stony Brook Hospital. At that point, I had already used all my sick leave and then some, dealing with my cancer treatment, because none of these cancers were certified yet, so they weren't considered line-of-duty. The NYPD gives you unlimited sick time, but not Suffolk County. I called my unions, and they said there's nothing you can do. That just didn't sit right with me. I started googling, and I found a foundation that helps 9/11 responders called the FealGood Foundation, run by John Feal. So, I sent him an email.

John put me in touch with Anthony Flammia, who was his law enforcement liaison. Flammia told me there was still nothing they could do about the sick time and certification, but he and John asked if I wanted to come to work with them and help with some legislation that might get cancers covered by the bill. My first trip was in 2009. We went to a fireman's union hall up in Boston. I made a couple of trips to

DC after that. I really got involved in 2015, heading into the fight for the permanent bill, and I ended up making like sixty trips.

What immediately struck me about John and really resonated with my experience in the army and as a police sergeant was his organizational skill. The folders, the business cards, the books of every #NeverForget tweet and every statement about 9/11 from the members. And it was so personally satisfying to have a chance to call out that hypocrisy directly to an elected official's face, instead of just grumbling about it at home watching Fox. I'm going into your office and I'm going to read you back your words with my reconstructed tongue.

There were a few times where we got to do real police work, like the office was a crime scene. One time, we went in there for a scheduled meeting and got told the congressperson had been called away on business, and they would give us some staffer to talk to instead. But then I looked around and saw a steaming cup of coffee on the desk and the bathroom door slightly ajar. It was like a war movie, where they go into a Vietcong hooch and the rice is still warm.

After a while, that kind of conduct really gets to you. We took every opportunity to call out hypocrisy where we saw it and throw it back in their faces. There was one time heading into the 2019 vote where we took that a little too far, and John ended up having to do damage control. I was walking the hall with Rob Serra, who was rolling beside me in a chair that had belonged to Ray Pfeifer. We saw Congressman Dan Crenshaw walking with another congressman, and did what John had trained us to do when we see a member—we stopped him in the hall, respectfully. I said:

"Sir, we understand you're not a co-sponsor of the bill. Congressman, I'm a veteran; you're a veteran. I am a lifelong Republican. You and I probably agree on just about everything, and I appreciate everything you're doing . . ."

Now at this time, Crenshaw had been publicly butting heads with Congresswoman Ilhan Omar (D-MN), a Somali-born, Muslim

American who wore a hijab on the house floor, over controversial comments she had made about 9/11.

"What I don't understand is: How come Congresswoman Omar is a co-sponsor of the bill and you're not?"

Gotcha!

"Ummm . . . uhhh . . . I'll have to look into it."

They always "have to look into it." Unfortunately, the *Daily News* got wind of our confrontation and ran with it, in response to coverage about Crenshaw's attacks on Omar over the legacy of 9/11:

"FDNY firefighter who survived 9/11 says Republican criticizing Ilhan Omar told him he was 'too busy' to talk victim benefits"

John was irate, because we had blown our opportunity by attracting press before Crenshaw had a chance to respond. Dragging his name through the papers would have been the move AFTER he came out against the bill or tried to hold us up, but it was a tactical blunder and poor sportsmanship to go after him publicly before he had a chance to change his mind. The upside was that John got a personal audience with Crenshaw a few days later. He came to apologize to the congressman, and by the end of their meeting, we had a new co-sponsor.

Going back to 9/11 . . . As a sergeant, you're the lowest-ranking supervisor in the police force. A chief can call up a level-four mobilization, a thousand officers, if needed. A sergeant, I can call up a level-one mobilization of about ten officers. Standing on that on-ramp, looking at the vast roadway reaching over the water to Brooklyn, all I could see was one big target and no way to stop a vehicle headed into Manhattan with bad intentions. I made requests for more personnel on the bridge and was denied because there were no personnel available. But pretty soon, they started showing up. Guys and gals came from off duty, in uniform shirts and blue jeans. They spread out across the bridge until probably a couple hundred officers were there, one every five or ten feet. Nobody ordered this or told them to be there. They just came, because we all knew the bridges would need to be held.

I took a lot of pride in being a part of that. I was proud to sift through rubble at Ground Zero and look for little parts of people on the conveyor belt at Fresh Kills Landfill. And I was proud to walk the halls with John and the guys. I don't know how to explain what those trips to DC meant to me except to say there wasn't anyone to save on September 12th. After all that sifting on the conveyor belt for the smallest fragments, something like 1,100 people are still missing without a trace. If you were down there, you left behind pieces of yourself at the Pile. Helping people, being around guys like Lou and Ray, it makes you feel whole again.

Eight

BUY A TREADMILL

Marble is an unforgiving surface. After a decade of walking the halls, my body is breaking down. I don't complain in front of the guys, but I'm hurting. Over the years, I get both knees done, both hips, both heels, ankles, tendons, plantar fasciitis, I get my jaw reconstructed, but the most painful procedure of all is a hernia repair. Phantom limb syndrome tickles and burns constantly. I don't take pain meds. I won't ever. I get back in the gym as soon as possible after each operation, working my upper body with my leg in a boot. I try to stay ahead of further breakdown and old age as the years drag on with no sign that I will ever be able to retire.

I estimate my total driving miles to get this bill done as roughly three laps around the earth. Rich Palmer, one of my team leaders, wears a Fitbit and finds that we average twelve miles of walking every day on these trips. On the first day of a trip, we've got the energy of a bunch of eight-year-olds. The first night, we get together for dinner and have a beer, and we're all in bed by ten o'clock. Day 2 is when it's clear these are a bunch of sick people. On the second night, we're all asleep by eight.

One time, outside Longworth, Jon Stewart needs to sit down. We're both tired and battered from days of walking.

"Welcome to my world," I say.

"Your world sucks."

My cartilage and tendons aren't the only parts strained and torn by long miles in the halls of government and nights away on the road. Eventually, the work claims my marriage of seven years. Marzena and I became like roommates, and there was just no room in my life with all the space taken up by the bill, the trips, and the constant grieving. At the time, neither one of us knew enough about the effects of PTSD to see what it was doing to my relationships. Sleep is to rest my eyes between meetings. The bed is for spreading out files and paperwork. Treating this like a military operation is effective, but there's a lot of collateral damage.

I remind my teams constantly that everyone is expendable for the sake of what we're trying to accomplish, and I have to accept that the same is true for my own personal relationships. It's a credit to her commitment and character that she stays involved with the movement after we go our separate ways and remains on the board of the park in Long Island that we built to honor the responders. I'm okay with being a shitty husband, but I will never allow myself to be a shitty friend.

Everybody hurts. We all make sacrifices. We're all going to die someday. But you don't dare complain about these things or let in the fear when you're lucky enough to know a man like Ray Pfeifer. Because if he has no complaints, how could you?

As the cancer eats his leg, he starts walking with a cane. Agony with every step.

"Can't complain" is all he ever says when you ask how he's doing.

"It's okay, Ray," Stewart will insist, "you can complain."

He lags a little behind the group as the disease progresses. The doctors put a steel rod in his leg. The cancer grows and puts so much pressure on the medical-grade steel that the rod snaps. If that hurt, Ray never says so. The only thing that bothers him is that he's slowing down the group. But cancer is no respecter of attitude or willpower. It will kill him the same way it kills the people who moan about it. As the disease eats his bones, Ray takes to an electric scooter that is given to him by Sandra McGee, whose husband, John, died of 9/11 brain cancer. The wheelchair is my idea. Ray doesn't want it. He's determined to keep walking, no matter how slowly or painfully. But he's starting to make us late. He's missing the tight turnarounds between meetings. He isn't going to make any allowances for his own comfort or welfare, but he cares deeply about the group. It's his thoughts of us that keep him going.

"Ray," I tell him, "you have to get in the scooter; you're slowing us down."

"John, I'm embarrassed. I can walk; I'm just slow."

"Then you can't go to DC. We can't wait up for you, and we can't be responsible if something happens. Right now, you're hurting us."

He's devastated, but he doesn't realize the scooter is a promotion.

"Ray, I want to make you the face of this movement. When people see you coming down the hallway in a scooter, on oxygen, with stage four cancer . . . You're going to make them blink. They'll show us who they really are. You're going to move mountains."

He eats that up.

And that's exactly what happens. Ray was always phenomenal, but in the chair he's a force to be reckoned with. A man of simple tastes, Ray has only one demand: All he wants is for these representatives to look him in the eye. He buzzes down the hall in his scooter, dressed in FDNY Class A's, and when he encounters a member of Congress, he won't let them pass until they look him in the eye.

Jon Stewart is his frequent sidekick. I paired them up. In one memorable encounter, captured by the film crew making *No Responders Left Behind,* Stewart chases Deb Fischer of Nebraska down the hall into an ABC camera crew, and then, as he put it, Ray comes around the corner in his chair "like John Wayne riding in on a horse."

In his eulogy to Ray, Stewart remembers what it was like to be the Tonto to his Lone Ranger.

> *We played "good cop/ bad cop" . . . I was the bad cop because I couldn't believe the disrespect that was being shown to this man and to the other heroes of 9/11. We would go office to office, to senators who would tweet out "#NeverForget, the heroes of 9/11." And yet, here was this man who was suffering from a stage 4 cancer because of that day, and they wouldn't look him in the eye. They wouldn't be in the office. And I was losing my mind. But Ray just sat, resolute. He knew that in this situation, he was in the right, and he didn't have to show histrionics, he didn't have to yell, he didn't have to scream. He sat, his body becoming as big as a boulder. People wouldn't get by until they looked him in the eye. And it was magic.*

The physical toll is one thing. Physical wounds heal. The suffering of terminal illness mercifully comes to an end. But disrespect festers. Not knees or ankles or steel pins or bones breaking down or relationships ending. Disrespect, being brushed off and ignored. That's the part that goes on hurting. That's what tests our resolve and pushes us to the brink. And we use it to our advantage. It's the dirty-burning fuel that keeps us going. But it's exhausting to keep coming back. We're all tired from chasing our own apology.

You might think the representatives who are against us engage in blustery debate or use meetings as a chance to grandstand. But their go-to move is to run and hide. We get good at chasing. We put guys at back doors and learn where the secret exits are. We linger outside bathrooms. We pretend we don't hear aides who tell us to try calling next time.

We have a meeting with Darrell Issa (R-CA). He decides not to show, so we go to his office. They say he's not here. But we know he's in the office, so I split the team and send guys three doors down to wait while the others stay in the lobby. When Darrell tries to sneak out the back door of his office, he walks right into us.

John Feal training in the 101st Airborne, c. 1986. (Photo/Courtesy of John Feal)

John Feal at The Pile. (Photo/Courtesy of John Feal)

The Pile. (FEMA Photo/Andrea Booker)

A responder takes a breather among the twisted steel. (FEMA Photo/Andrea Booker)

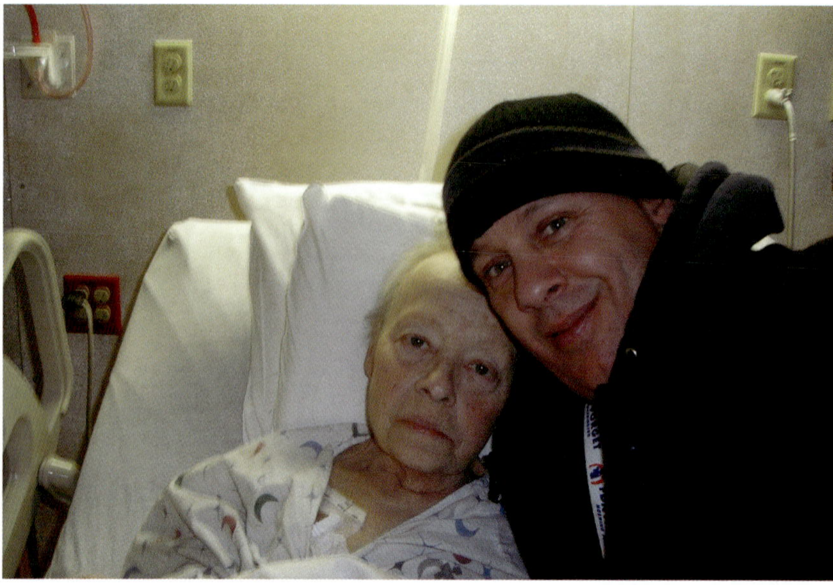

With Mom in her final days. (Photo/Courtesy of John Feal)

Portrait of Ivonne Sanchez, 2002.
(Photo/Joel Meyerowitz)

Goofing around with Ray.
(Photo/Courtesy of John Feal)

Rich Roeill sucks oxygen outside the Capitol.
(Photo/Faye Murman-Dorsey)

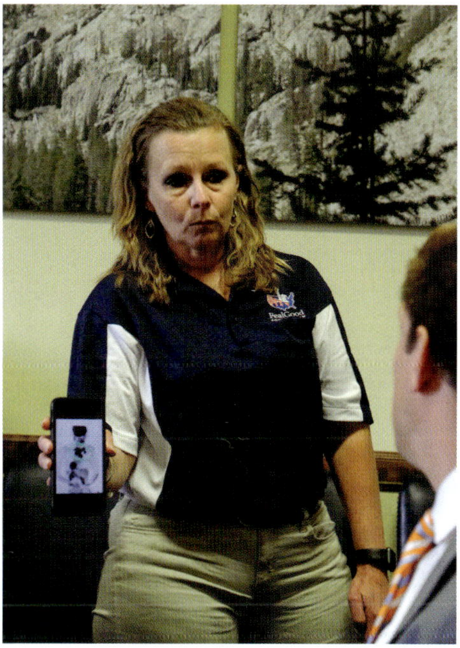

Dawnele Holbrook, FBI, shows a Congressman a recent scan showing cancer all over her body.
(Photo/Faye Murman-Dorsey)

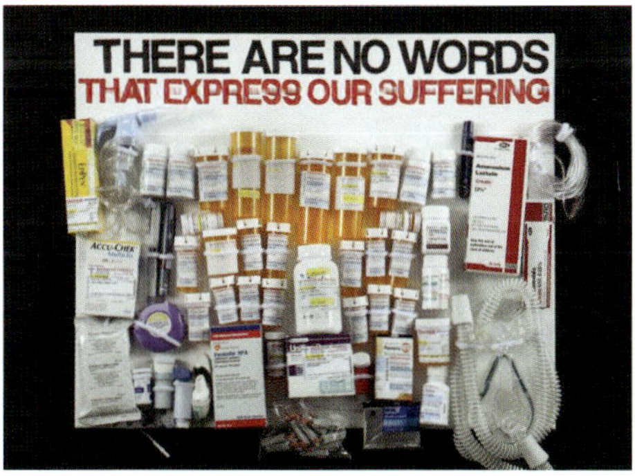

Left: Medications, inhalers, and breathing devices prescribed to paramedic Freddie Noboa, which he fashioned into a protest sign.
(Collection of 9/11 Memorial Museum)
Right: With Ray at Arlington, on our way to the Tomb of the Unknown Soldier.
(Photo/Courtesy of John Feal)

On our way to meet with Senator McConnell. (L-R) Kenny Specht, John Feal, Rich Palmer, Matt McCauley. (Photo/Courtesy of John Feal)

Meeting with Congressman Dan Crenshaw, burying the hatchet. (Photo/Faye Murman-Dorsey)

Preparing for the hearing. (Photo/Faye Murman-Dorsey)

In a meeting with Kenny Specht (on my left). (Photo/Faye Murman-Dorsey)

Swearing in at the Congressional subcommittee hearing. (L-R) Michael McConnell, Lou Alvarez, and Jon Stewart. (Photo/Faye Murman-Dorsey)

Coaching Stewart. (Photo/Faye Murman-Dorsey)

Lou did good. I love this photo. (Photo/Faye Murman-Dorsey)

Jon Stewart holds up Ray's bunker coat before the hearing and says, "We're gonna do it today. Not just for Ray, but for all you guys and for everyone Ray was fighting for." (Photo/Faye Murman-Dorsey)

Ray's empty chair in the White House Rose Garden for the signing of the bill. It is now on display at the 9/11 Memorial Museum. (Photo/Faye Murman-Dorsey)

Stewart and I break down in each other's arms following his remarks to the Congressional subcommittee. (Photo/Getty Images Zach Gibson)

Stewart and I have a cry after he read my note. (Photo/Faye Murman-Dorsey)

Hanging out on the marble steps of the Capitol (L-R) Jon Stewart, John Feal, Rich Palmer, Kenny Specht, Michael O'Connell. O'Connell wears a "343" hat for the FDNY's death toll on 9/11. (Photo/Courtesy of John Feal)

Meanwhile in Iraq . . . (LOGISTICS SUPPORT AREA ANACONDA, Balad, Iraq) Smoke billows in from all sides as Sgt. Richard Ganske, 84th Combat Engineer Battalion, pushes the bulldozer deep into the flames of the burn pit. (Photo/U.S. Army)

A firefighter pays his respects at the reading of the names event at the 911 Responders Remembered Park. (Photo/Faye Murman-Dorsey)

The A-Team. (L-R) John Feal, Michael O'Connell, Jon Stewart, Rich Palmer, Ray Pfeifer, Kenny Specht, Anthony Flammia, Keith Delmar. (Photo/Courtesy of John Feal)

Victory! (Photo/Faye Murman-Dorsey)

I say, "Hey, Dee, what's up, bro? How've you been."

"Errr . . . Uhhh . . . I'm really busy."

"No. You're a coward."

Back when we were fighting for the first bill, in 2010, Scott Brown (R-MA/NH) tried to duck us while he was with his wife. I reminded the guys to leave her out of it; she had nothing to do with it. Brown was surrounded. I introduced myself.

"I don't like the bill," he said.

"What don't you like about it?"

"It's just . . . well, the thing is, I'm about to introduce my own bill."

"Really? That's terrific, Senator, I'd love to see it. How about we sit down tomorrow."

"Ummm . . . Sure . . . now, if you'll excuse me."

Brown did not have his own bill. Here was a grown man who had been elected to help govern the greatest democracy in the world acting like a kid caught with his hand in the cookie jar. Exchanges like that were a reminder that as frustrating and fatiguing as this whole thing is, we're not dealing with good vs. evil. More like good vs. incompetent or good vs. cowardly and self-serving. In many ways, those qualities are harder to deal with.

We learn to get it on the record. Give them a chance to get on board and trap them with their own hypocrisy if they're against us. This is where it helps to have guys like Rich Palmer on your side. Before he was one of my team leaders, Richie was a warden with the Department of Corrections. His ringtone is the theme song from *The Godfather.* He's leading a meeting with Ivonne Sanchez. "Angry Bird" and "Miss America," a full foot height difference between them, making a show of force in the office of a congressman who won't meet with them without an appointment and won't give them an appointment. The congressman loses his temper and starts wagging a finger in Ivonne's face.

"Miss, why should the gov'ment pay for you to buy another pair of shoes."

She's about ready to knock this creep out. Richie and the guys step in. They don't use physical intimidation, and they hold Ivonne back. They quietly remind the gentleman that we're going to mention his remarks to the news crews we're about to speak with. He can't swallow his words fast enough. He starts stuttering an apology. Then, something amazing happens. He suddenly wants to talk about the bill. His issue, it turns out, is a simple one.

"I just don't think there's anybody from my district affected is all."

Richie and his team have the stats on hand and are ready to educate the congressman on the spot. They refer to our "bible." It turns out there are many responders from his district: some construction workers and Red Cross volunteers.

After about five minutes, we have a new co-sponsor.

Ray's scooter becomes a machine that scoops up co-sponsors. He and Stewart run and roll after a member who tries to dodge them. Ray asks him why he's not supporting the bill.

"Well . . . You know . . . financially, I'm a numbers guy."

Ray, undaunted, looks up and says, "So, tell me about the numbers."

"Well, um, uh." He's got nothing.

They carry on like that for fifteen minutes, and at the end of their conversation, he signs on to the bill.

Time and time again, we're reminded that "All politics is local." Everything we do is based on the nationwide relevance of this issue. You don't have to like us; you don't have to care about New York or agree with Jon Stewart's politics. But you better care about the people in your district, and if you didn't already know, there are 9/11 responders and survivors among them. On each trip, I spent about $1,400 at Staples making copies of "the bible" so that everyone will have these stats in their hands: the science, the numbers of illnesses in each district and the number of VCF claims, the local news clips from every district. The book worked, and I know this because we had members tell us they were a "no" until they read it. (For folks who want to play along at home, Ben Chevat built a fantastic website—911healthwatch.org—with a fun little tool that takes the intel in "the bible" and makes it interactive. Visitors can type in their zip code and see how their representative has voted on this issue, and how they have tweeted about 9/11 and first responders through the years.)

What we're fighting for in 2015 is permanent reauthorization of the bill, with cancers added this time, and funding for a health program that will inform future eligibility and the scientific understanding of 9/11 illness. What we want is to not ever come back. We want to go home, knowing our families will be taken care of. We want our medical care in the hands of doctors, not politicians. We want our elected officials to stop playing politics with our lives.

On April 14, 2015, the House introduces HR 1786 and the "James Zadroga 9/11 Health and Compensation Reauthorization Act" of 2015 to renew the health and compensation program and make it permanent. The legislation is introduced by Carolyn Maloney (D-NY), Jerry Nadler (D-NY), and Peter King (R-NY) with forty-nine bipartisan co-sponsors

What we're up against isn't outright opposition to the bill or what it stands for. We could face that head-on. It's not that they want to stop us; they want to use us. They want to attach our bill to a larger vehicle and use it to get things they want. Nobody does this more brazenly than Senator Mitch McConnell (R-KY). In 2010, McConnell used the original bill as a "political football," in Stewart's words, to make sure President Bush's tax cuts would be permanent. Now, he wants to include the 2015 renewal in a transportation bill that will get him a nice little kickback from the oil lobby, as reported in the *Daily News* and elsewhere.

We have a deal and Mitch pulls it off the table in November so he can get a payday from an import tax on oil or some such nonsense. That means we have to wait 'til the end of the year to get it done, and we're looking at a neutered version of the bill attached to Mitch's transport grift.

I want a meeting. We stage a sit-in outside the senator's office, bad-mouthing him and talking about the bill with everyone who goes in or out. At last, he grants us a meeting. Per his conditions, I can take three guys. I bring Kenny Specht, Anthony Flammia, and Rich Palmer. We are escorted by Capitol Police with AR-15s: a firefighter, a cop, and a corrections officer being treated like a security threat. Kind of backhanded compliment to what they think we're capable of.

While we wait for the senator, we spend about twenty or thirty minutes with his staff. These are smarter than the usual brush-off brigade, but we hold our own, presenting them with the facts from "the bible" and the votes we've counted in our favor in both chambers.

The first words out of the senator's mouth are all about him. I would expect nothing less. "I suppose you feel good about yourself, beating me up in the media. But I can take it."

"Sir, you haven't seen anything yet. You, sir, are a colossal douchebag."

Flammia speaks up: "John!"

I turn my wrath in his direction. "Pipe down or you're out of here."

I turn back to the senator. "Who the fuck do you think you are? You're here because your constituents put you here. Your duty is to them. This is a courtesy call to let you know it's fucking game time."

"Look," he says after a long pause. "I promise you'll get this done by the end of the year."

"You're lying. Because if you had any intention of keeping that promise, you wouldn't have squashed the bill when we were this close to getting it passed with more co-sponsors on both sides than we know what to do with. Now you're getting everything you want, and you're still whining like a little bitch."

Something about the way he is just sitting there, taking it, makes me lose more respect for the guy, if that's even possible.

Then, a girl walks in with a piece of paper. He unfolds it and says, "Oh, uh, I gotta go."

I lean over and peek at the piece of paper.

"Oh my God, that's the oldest trick in the book. A blank piece of paper. You fucking douche."

This continues for another half hour or so. We leave it on shaky ground: We're getting it done with or without him. And he gets the message that life will be easier if he gets out of our way.

After that, it's more meetings and press conferences. We make the rounds on Fox, MSNBC, and CNN.

As always, Comedy Central's satirical newsmen, John Oliver, Trevor Noah, Stephen Colbert, and Stewart, can be counted on for reports that are more truthful than the "real" news. They devote episodes to our bill and bring out the hashtag #WorstResponders in reference to the congressmen and senators standing in our way.

In a special return to *The Daily Show*, Stewart talks about McConnell's obstruction of the bill: "So far, he has been an enormous obstacle, unwilling to move the bill forward for purely political reasons . . . He's not nice."

McConnell's staff tells Politico that the senator "always intended to back the bill, regardless of Stewart."

Senator Schumer enters the fray, saying, "the lives of our first responders is not a bargaining chip."

Then, in a twist nobody had on their 2015 bingo card, we lose the support of the New York delegation. We had fought all year to get our bill rolled into the omnibus—the president's budget at the end of the year. Now, the New York delegation is voting against the budget because hurricane relief for Puerto Rico has been left out, angering many of their constituents who have roots on the island. I've already sent my team home, thinking our work here is done. So Senator Schumer has me go office to office on a Friday night to claw back those votes. There's a leak in my hotel room causing a massive puddle on the floor. On my way out the door to the Capitol, I step in it. My shoes and socks are soaked, and it's like ten degrees outside. I'm cranky. I'm pissed. I'm raging with a fear of failure, fear that we won't get this done and that will be on me. We technically have the votes we need, even without the support we had counted on from

New York, but Schumer wants me to whip all of them. Normally, he has a problem with me being me, but in this case, he's all for it. I knock on doors, say unprintable things, and fight like a man possessed.

All the while, Ray is texting me, calling me:

You got this.

It's all on you.

I get it done at that late hour in soggy shoes.

We have our bill, just a few hours before the 2010 legislation is set to expire. It's folded up into an omnibus, so the only way we know who was for our bill specifically is by who co-sponsored: that is 272 in the House, 80 Republicans and all 192 Democrats; and 69 in the Senate, 23 Republicans and all 46 Democrats. That's our beachhead to get a better piece of legislation next time. As Stewart points out every time they bring up the money, nobody has to fight like this or justify spending for corn or soybeans or weapons. But we have to play the game and chase our own survival.

The bipartisan will we generated this time around speaks for itself and leads President Obama to sign a law making the VCF and health program permanent and extending funding until 2020.

We'll be back in five years . . . some of us.

One night, on one of our last trips before the vote, we're back at the hotel, and I'm making the rounds to get everybody in their rooms. Ray has his door open. He hears me pacing and saying my goodnights. He must sense that I'm flustered and anxious. Lights-out is the worst part of these trips because all I can think about are the wives in my ear saying:

"Don't let my husband die."

"Be sure he takes his meds with a full stomach."

"Be sure he changes his oxygen tank."

You want to go into battle with your best soldiers. My best soldiers are sick and dying.

When I get to his room, I lean in and say, "Good night, Ray."

He's washing down his medication with two fingers of Johnnie Walker. "Johnny, Johnny, Johnny"—he's the only person in the world who can call me that—"come back."

"What's up, Ray?"

"Listen, I know you're stressed, and you need to make sure everybody's in their rooms. Don't worry. These guys are all grown men. Sit down, have a drink with me."

"Nah, man, we're getting up early."

"Come on, just two fingers." Ray can talk me into anything. He can call me "Johnny," he can make me drink Johnnie Walker, which I think tastes like ass.

"Let's make it three tonight."

So, we're drinking, and he goes:

"I gotta show you something."

"What?"

He's lying on his side, wearing these really loose gray shorts, and he pulls his testicles out. They're absurdly swollen as a side effect of his treatment. Each one is the size of a grapefruit.

"What do you think of that?"

"Ray, that's impressive."

We're both laughing so hard we can barely breathe.

"See, Johnny. It's not that bad. You're calm now."

ACTION FOR ACTIVISTS: BUY A TREADMILL

The time to develop a physical and mental self-care routine is BEFORE you have a breakdown. The same goes for the collective well-being of the group. Insist on singleness of purpose and don't let outside issues, personal opinions, or egos divide the group.

Let nothing fester.

Own your shit and deal with problems as they arise.

Prepare to be in it for the long haul.

After every trip, the first thing I did when I got home was take a long shower. I did the same while working on this book. It's my pressure valve, the place I go to wash off what I'm going through. That's my thing, a "self-care ritual," if you want to call it that. Yours can be anything, but it helps to keep it simple; that will always be there for you.

The American author and environmentalist Edward Abbey had some practical advice:

"Do not burn yourselves out . . . keep your brain in your head and your head firmly attached to the body, the body active and alive."

You are no good to anyone if you're burned out and broken down from your activism. So, self-care is vital. Take care of your physical and mental health. Develop good habits and cut out bad ones before you're in a situation where your movement relies on your levelheadedness. Prehab is better than rehab. It is so much easier to maintain health and fitness than it is to nurse yourself back from a breakdown.

I tell activists who ask for my advice to "buy a treadmill," and I mean that literally and figuratively. Everything we accomplished in DC, we did on our feet. We got our bipartisan support by walking office to office and coming back hundreds of times over the course of a decade. This took two types of endurance. The first kind was measured in years: five years to get the first Zadroga Act and another five for the renewal. By the nature of what we were fighting for, not everyone was going to live to see the spoils of victory, and that sad fact was part of what we had to endure. The second type of endurance was the stamina to get through a day on the Hill, doing it our way. We didn't come down to just take a meeting here and a meeting there. Each team took dozens of meetings every day, 2,400 in total. Our record was fifty-five in one day. This meant long days and long years, hearing "no" a lot, getting lied to and ignored, and coming back for more every time.

Testimony

BRIDGET GORMLEY

My father was just the sort of person who is always going to help somebody out. Obviously, that's what firefighters do, right? But he didn't leave that attitude at work; helping was who he was. That's the example that will live on with me and my brothers. The homeless guy in the street gets a dollar, or someone to talk to. If you can fix something, fix it. If you can help someone, help them. Try to make things better. Not in a cheesy, do-gooder, Hallmark way, but because it's the right thing to do. That's what it meant to be a man and a good person, in his eyes.

A lot of young women who've lost their fathers talk about his looming absence at their wedding day, that old cliché, "He won't be there to walk me down the aisle." And while, yeah, that's true in my case, and it would be nice to have him around, he already gave me the only lesson I need in that department: Masculinity is about helping and fixing and giving. You don't see that a lot these days. My kids will never meet him, but I'll be sure to teach them what he taught me. They'll watch the documentary. They'll know how he died.

The other thing about my father . . . He was funny. He was funny as hell right up to the end. He used to tell me, "You can laugh, or you can cry, Bridge, and where does crying get you?"

Bridget Gormley is the daughter of FDNY firefighter Billy Gormley, who died of 9/11 cancer in 2017. She channeled her grief into a documentary, *Dust: the Lingering Legacy of 9/11*.

The whole time he was dying, all these firemen kept coming to see him, and they would all sit around telling stories and cracking jokes. It was a living wake. He refused to let visiting hours turn into a pity party, even if that meant joking at someone else's expense. I'll never forget the time he told my fat aunt she was blocking the fire exit.

He kept quoting that line from Jimmy Stewart in *It's a Wonderful Life*; he would say:

"Bridget, I'm the richest man in town."

He would repeat that line so often, it got obnoxious.

I wanted to hit him at the time, but now I get it: He was showing us how to die, just like he had always set the example of how to live. One time, when they were getting ready to transfer him to hospice care, I told him it's okay to be sad that you're dying. It's okay to admit you're in pain.

"Bridget," he said, "the children's wing is right above me. There's kids with what I have. I'm good. I have a family. I have kids. I lived my life."

You have moments like that where it's really beautiful, and you're so aware that this will be one of the most poignant memories in your life, and then you'll have these moments where it just hits you that he isn't going to be here next week. We didn't get into God and life after this one and those big questions. I know he was more open-minded about that stuff than you might assume an Irish Catholic boy of his generation from Brooklyn would be. I got him into doing yoga, for example; he asked if I would go with him, so we went together to some classes, and I brought along college friends. From what I could tell, he approached these big ideas like faith and hope the way he approached everything in life: with motion and action. He knew there is something else after this. He told me he had a dog and some buddies he was looking forward to seeing again.

A line-of-duty death is ritualized. They carried my father in a flag-draped casket on the back of an old-timey fire engine. Our family followed behind—"chauffeured" in fire department parlance by a special FDNY SUV. Bagpipes played "Going Home" as we moved at a walking pace down a street lined with white-gloved probie [probationary] firefighters whose attendance is mandatory.

Afterward, we drank. And the firemen all chanted "Gormley, Gormley, Gormley."

The quiet and relief that it was all over didn't last long. Mike McGinn, one of my father's closest friends, had been noticeably absent from my father's wake and funeral. When I asked around, I was told he had just checked into hospice care.

He died two weeks later of 9/11 cancer. And the bagpipes played "Going Home."

Mike Duffy, who was at Dad's funeral, died three weeks after of 9/11 cancer. And the bagpipes played "Going Home."

A little while after the funeral, an old captain sent me an email about my father. He wrote, "I think of him often, this is just a small story I wanted you to have." Attached was a citation for bravery he had written up in the summer of 2001 describing my father's actions in a recent three-story house fire with numerous people trapped inside. In an upstairs back bedroom, three unconscious victims were sprawled on the floor. The fire was approaching, and the hoses were unable to stop the fire from spreading to the bedroom. My father worked to remove the victims, who were tangled in bedding, shutting the door to keep the flames out. In the words of the citation:

> *FF. Gormley committed himself to a dangerous position without the benefit of a charged hoseline throughout the time needed to untangle the*

(3) victims, as well as during the removal of the first two victims, thus placing himself in jeopardy . . . it is therefore respectfully requested that the Board of Merit consider the efforts of FF. Gormley.

That's the kind of man my father was; that's what he was doing on a summer night in 2001, a story he never told us, an act of merit that was never officially recognized, lost in the shuffle with all the merit and all the sacrifice of that September. It's the kind of thing Fire Chief Ed Croker was talking about in his eulogy for five New York City firefighters who died in the line of duty in 1908:

Firemen are going to get killed. When they join the fire department, they face that fact. When a man becomes a fireman his greatest act of bravery has been accomplished. What he does after that is all in the line of work.

Two of my triplet brothers have taken that "greatest act of bravery" and joined the FDNY: Billy is an EMT waiting to take the promotion exam, and Raymond just graduated the academy. He is now at Ladder 174, my father's old firehouse, where the guys showing him the ropes were once probies under our father's guidance. Kevin works at a law firm that handles VCF and WTC Health Program claims.

Firemen are going to get killed, and daughters are going to miss them. I've tried to keep moving mentally, physically, and spiritual. A therapist told me people either keep moving or they stop and can't get out of bed, they go catatonic in front of the TV, they get bitter. You gotta move. I run a lot; I go to the gym. Some of my best workouts come from just trying to get all the hurt out. I don't care if it's self-medicating. It's what my father would have done. My other coping strategy was to pick up a camera and capture their stories, while they're still here to tell them.

Nine

LIVE IN THE LINE OF DUTY

One day Stewart asks me for a nickname. Wilson is "Shrek," Rizzo is "Mellow," Orozco is "Preacher." But Stewart has always been just "Stewart."

"Come on, all the other guys have a nickname, I want one too."

"You're Jon Fucking Stewart; you don't need a nickname."

The truth is he doesn't need a nickname because he isn't dying. The nicknames are my way of putting a little distance between myself and guys who aren't going to be here too much longer. With Jon, the same logic applies in reverse. I don't ever want to think about him dying, so I don't dare nickname him.

"Come on. Come on. I want a nickname."

"Alright . . . You can be 'Colbert.'"

He shakes his head and kicks me in the shin. He's the one guy I would let do that and not kick him back. Ray can call me "Johnny" and Stewart can kick me.

I never had a brother until I got to know Stewart. We spend more time together outside of our work; we get together to watch Warriors games.

I'll text him things like:

I just rewatched BIG DADDY, forgot how much your acting sucks.

And he'll reply:

Whatever, I'll always be taller than you.

As I go on TV more and start to get a little more recognition, I learn that if you're kinda famous and you want to be invisible, stand next to someone more famous. We're out having pizza one day in Georgetown, I order a slice, he orders two. Before we get to our seats, someone comes over and asks for a selfie with him. Someone else comes over just as we're taking our first bites. Then, another fan. Pretty soon, I've finished my slice and one of his before he's had any. He tells me he's used to it, but I don't know how.

One day, I'm walking in Lower Manhattan wearing one of the hoodies we wore to DC. This girl comes up to me and says, "Oh my God, you're John Feal, right?"

"Yeah."

"Will you tell Jon Stewart, thank you for everything he's doing?"

"Sure thing."

Jon becomes a true friend to the guys, and that means more to me than even our friendship. Lou Alvarez's widow will call him "my liberal friend." He talks to Ray every day. He has so much admiration for their service, and we're all in awe of this guy who has millions in the bank, can do anything he wants or nothing at all, and decides to roll up his sleeves and work with us. No entourage, no cameras. He drives himself to DC, wears a T-shirt and a ball cap, and walks the halls with the guys, asking our elected officials why they're not helping us.

Stewart doesn't care about fame; watching his experience of it makes me not want it either. But our work and the TV cameras end up attracting some limelight and shenanigans that the guys have a lot of fun with. We get to hang out with the cast of *SNL*. Bret Michaels, lead singer of

Poison, reaches out to me, and we hit it off. He puts together a benefit concert outside of Fox's studios. I bring Jen McNamara, whose husband died in 2009, and Ray and Karen Pfeifer who are die-hard Bret Michaels fans. That night, he brings us along to hang out backstage and has some of my guys come out during his set.

We get Ray into a New York Giants practice where he catches a pass from Eli Manning.

The WWE awards me a championship belt, and I bring the guys along for that. They're coming with me or I'm not going. We take up three tables when I'm recognized with Jon at the Nassau County Firefighters Museum. Jon brings me and some of the guys to the Emmys. I joke that he has fifteen of these things—can't I just have one? All night, people are offering me their Emmys. The New York State Police give me an award. The statue is a bronze Stetson hat. I keep my speech short and to the point, like I'm getting pulled over:

"Can I put this on my dashboard? Have a good night."

When Jon Stewart is presented the Mark Twain Prize at the

Ray, at the ceremony where he donated his key to the city to the 9/11 Museum. (Photo/Courtesy of John Feal)

Kennedy Center, I present him the award with the help of a soldier who survived an IED and was badly burned.

As soon as we pass the bill in 2015, I start telling the press that the City of New York ought to give Ray the key to the city. I say it every chance I get, no context, "Oh, and by the way, give Ray the key." Sometimes that's my whole speech. In January 2016 Mayor de Blasio gives him the key in a ceremony at City Hall. A couple of months later, in a ceremony at the 9/11 Museum, Ray donates his key to their collection. I donate the red bomber jacket I wore to DC, which they display in an exhibit on 9/11 illness.

There's a sadness behind these antics. These are "Make a Wish Foundation moments" for some of the guys. The real joy in it has nothing to do with getting close to fame, going up on stage, or being ushered behind velvet ropes and into green rooms. There's a delight for me in seeing the guys enjoy themselves. I like seeing the way an evening with Ray Pfeifer rubs off on these VIPs. He's someone who makes you a better person by being in your life. In my experience, those people are rare. When you meet one, my advice is to never let them go.

As Ray gets sicker and needs more care, my guys are there for anything he needs. In typical humble fashion, he's embarrassed by the attention and oblivious to his own charisma. It's not that these guys' idea of a fun weekend in our nation's capital is chauffeuring a wheelchair-bound cancer patient, it's just that it's an absolute pleasure to spend time with him and an honor to help him with anything he needs.

Mike O'Connell is Ray's "chauffeur." They live about ten minutes from each other on Long Island. Mike picks him up in a van we got donated to his family. The wheelchair goes in the back. Ray sits up front.

Mike remembers, "He would tell the greatest stories ever all the way to DC. I've never met a storyteller like him. He was a legend in the fire department."

Ray's fond of saying: "I'm a lucky guy. I'm still here." He isn't just putting a brave face on a dire diagnosis. On September 11, he lost his whole firehouse and was the lucky survivor because it was his day off. In the aftermath, he took over the house and looked after widows and families. He got a call from President Bush who was having all the FDNY widows come down to DC. Before he met with them, he had Ray come to the Oval Office. The president poured him a glass of scotch and promised that his brothers will not have died in vain. Ray must really believe that because he never once loses his temper or gets discouraged when we're working on the Hill. He knows we will prevail, and his work will honor their memory.

As the trappings of moderate fame and media fanfare come our way, my tendency is to use the attention we need for our cause and pass along all the perks and starfucking to my guys. I tend to give away my actual trophies and accolades. I'm not going to give an acceptance speech if I can't get a table for my guys. I don't drink or gamble or sleep around. My addiction, if you want to call it that, is helping. Getting our bills passed gives me a taste, and I want more.

Back in 2005, I started the FealGood Foundation, a 501(c)(3) nonprofit. I knew I wanted to help my fellow responders and survivors. I wanted to help at scale and give back more than I could on my own. It was a long process, and I had to learn a lot and file mountains of paperwork. The foundation got its name when I was wrestling with tax forms. I needed an EIN to open a bank account and get a business license. Helping me with all of that was an elderly part-time employee, this tiny woman with the sweetest voice. As she went through the paperwork, she caught a big omission: "Honey, you have everything but the title of the organization. It needs a name. I can't process this until you fill it out completely."

"Well, what do you think I should call it? My problem is all these organizations to do with 9/11 have '9/11' in the name. And when people think 9/11, they think tragedy. I want what I'm doing to be about solving problems and making a difference. I want to make people feel good."

"Hmmm . . . It says here, your last name is 'Feal,' is that how you pronounce it, like 'feel'?"

"Yeah."

"Honey, you're the Feel Good Foundation."

"That's not bad. But can I spell it 'F-e-a-l' Good? And maybe make it one word with a capital 'G.'"

"It's your foundation; spell it any way you want."

It started as a way to help out the families of people who were getting sick with all the things insurance doesn't cover (even if you have insurance). We would help out with gas cards and gift cards. I would go to houses and fill refrigerators with groceries. We helped with utility bills. We helped pay for funerals.

On the DC trips we wore FealGood Foundation T-shirts, hoodies, and polos so we were all matching and looked more like an army. One year we wore red, for the firefighters, another year we wore blue for the cops. Black one year for the fallen.

Through the foundation, I build a park on one acre of land, bordering a dangerous intersection, sold to me by the Town of Nesconset on Long Island, for one dollar. The 911 Responders Remembered Park is the first of its kind, dedicated to responders who died of 9/11 illness. While the names of those killed in the attack line the perimeter of the pools at Ground Zero, and there are many memorials to cops and firefighters, there's nothing to memorialize the far greater number who have died since the attack. There is no nonunion volunteer construction workers memorial or one for citizen responders. I built a park in their memory. The centerpiece are marble slabs bearing hundreds, and eventually thousands, of names. There is no division on the wall between departments of emergency services, no distinction between first responders and civilian responders. The wall is flanked by a flagpole, complete with statues of a miniature Marine Corps honor guard. Down a winding path to the other side of the park are statues representing the branches of the armed forces and first responders, including service dogs. There is a piece of World Trade Center steel, which I filed the bolts off so they wouldn't snag kids who play on the steel.

If you were at the Pile or in Lower Manhattan, if you were made sick by the dust and died from your illness, your name goes on the wall. Occasionally, this criteria has dragged us into the fray with families who are fighting for recognition of their loved one's cause of death. Judy Simmons, who is now president of the park, was married to a firefighter, Marty, who would win natural (i.e., no steroid) bodybuilding competitions before he got sick. This real-life Adonis was killed by shortness of breath, drowning while playing with his kids in shallow water while on vacation in Lake Tahoe. Judy had to fight like hell to have her husband's drowning linked to his 9/11 illness, arguing that it wouldn't have happened if his respiratory system wasn't compromised. The medical experts agreed and ruled that his death was 9/11 related. So, his name goes on the wall.

Occasionally I have tough conversations with surviving relatives of responders who suffered horribly from their illness but didn't die from it and are therefore ineligible. One woman calls me, in hysterics, demanding that her husband, who had 9/11 cancer but died in a motorcycle accident, go on the wall. Finally, I say to her, "His girlfriend was on the back of the bike. Should she go on the wall too?"

That may sound harsh, but I have to protect the integrity of the park in the name of everyone on that wall. When my time comes, if I die in some unrelated way, I want no mention of me in the park. I wouldn't deserve it. If I die from a 9/11 illness, my name can go somewhere on the wall with all the others. No special treatment.

Every year, on the first Saturday after 9/11, we have a reading-of-the-names ceremony. One year, Bridget Gormley reads with two daughters of fallen NYPD officers. Each of them reads 120 names, 360 that year.

Letting them know I'm sorry we failed. These panels at the 911 Responders Remembered Park at are now full. (Photo/Bridget Gormley)

On the legislative side of things, there's work to be done. We don't waste time bemoaning the imperfection of the statute or the five-year holding pattern. We go to Albany and get legislation passed at the state level to address shortcomings and loopholes in the federal legislation. While we're at it, we pass a bill in Albany to ban puppy mills. Nothing to do with responders or 9/11, but I will throw my weight around for man's best friend any day.

In 2011, we use the momentum from the Zadroga bill to hold our government accountable to a recommendation of the 9/11 Commission Report: interoperability among first responders and law enforcement. The bill that we helped pass allocated funds to improve communications between emergency services. Before 9/11, fire and police were on different radio frequencies, and departments in different states often couldn't talk to each other without picking up a phone or meeting at the state line and rolling down the windows of their patrol cars. Those comms failures, compounded by problems with the FDNY's internal radios, caused confusion and loss of life on 9/11. By 2011, little had been done to improve this gap in our nation's emergency preparedness. At a press conference in support of the interoperability bill around this time, I tear up a copy of the report, saying why not tear it up if we're not going to follow it. Then I get on the phone, making bipartisan introductions to members who want to get this done.

I get a call from a group of firefighters and their families in Michigan who are fighting for their own bill to address environmental cancers, with language about presumed causation modeled on the 9/11 health bill. They ask me what I charge. I tell them my per diem is a bottle of water. I fly out and meet them at the state House. I tell them, "Stay here and hold hands around the building, nobody gets in or out. I'm going inside to get your legislation passed."

I go in, talk to the governor, tell him I didn't think much of the way he handled the water crisis in Flint. When I come back out, the firefighters have their bill.

As Ray gets sicker, whatever he wants, I make sure he gets.

I only fail him one time.

There comes a day when I have to drive out to his house on Long Island to tell him he's too sick to come back to DC with us. When I get there, I sit in his driveway for a long time, watching the flag outside his front door flap on the breeze, thinking about my friend and all the good times we had, seeing him the way I will always see him, a big man with a big smile, so full of life. No wasting, no wheelchair. My friend who shook the halls of government.

I get out of the car and head inside for the worst conversation I will ever have.

"Ray, Karen doesn't want me letting you go to DC anymore. I have to respect her wishes."

"Johnny, it's my life. I know I'm dying. I have the chair. I can keep up."

"Ray, I'm not going to live with that the rest of my life if something were to happen to you."

"Johnny, I can go. I won't slow you down, please."

"Ray, I'm sorry, you can't. You've done enough."

I drive home. I spend all afternoon in the shower.

In 2016, we get our long-overdue apology from Christine Todd Whitman. She told *The Guardian*:

> *I'm very sorry that people are sick. I'm very sorry people are dying and if the EPA and I in any way contributed to that, I'm sorry. We did the very best we could at the time with the knowledge we had . . . Every time it comes around to the anniversary I cringe because I know people will bring up my name, they blame me, they say that I lied and that people died because I lied, people died because I made a mistake.*

News outlets around the world are right to print her apology alongside her previous statements:

"I am glad to reassure the people of New York . . . that their air is safe to breathe, and their water is safe to drink." (A week after the attack.)

"The good news continues to be that air samples we have taken have all been at levels that cause no concern." (Three days after the attack.)

When asked for a statement, I say if she had been sincere, she could have gone with me to any one of the 154 funerals I've attended at this point. She could have sat down with Ray or any one of the dying responders. She could have come to the park and faced a thousand names on the wall at that point. She could have come on the first Saturday after September 11 to hear us read the names that are going on the wall this year and ring the bell for each one.

Ray's last wish was to lay a wreath at the Tomb of the Unknown Soldier at Arlington National Cemetery. I get on the phone to Gillibrand's office and say he's got a few months to live, and we need to make this happen.

She says, "Done deal."

The waiting list for that is normally about nine months. We get it done in time. Stewart and I go down there with him. The ceremony on its own, the playing of "Taps," the precision of the honor guard, gives you chills. But to see Ray do it, to know how seriously he takes it, and how in his view, it's not about him but about paying respect to the fallen and the nation . . .

I go to see him every day toward the end. I buy him every color of Johnnie Walker and we have "two fingers." Right up to the end, we argue over his life philosophy; he says, "Do the right thing, even when no one is looking." And I insist it's just as important to do the right thing when *everybody's* looking. Do the right thing and inspire others to do the same. But for Ray, just to do the right thing was enough. He could care less about credit or a following or the spotlight. To do right was enough.

Jon Stewart remembers his last call with Ray:

> *I was in Upstate New York with my daughter. She used to like driving around looking at old houses and farms. The phone rings, it's Ray calling from hospice.*
>
> *I say, "Ray, how's it going."*
>
> *"Can't complain."*
>
> *That's the kind of dude you're dealing with. It's insane. He was calling to ask if I would say a few words at his funeral.*
>
> *We were pulled over. I was trying to keep it together. I could barely get the words out.*
>
> *"Anything you want, brother. Whatever you need."*
>
> *It was heartbreaking. All I kept thinking as we were driving is how none of this ever should have happened. It was so heartbreaking and unnecessary.*

Ray dies on May 28. A vintage fire truck carries his casket through Hicksville, Long Island. Bagpipes play the wistful Irish love song "On Raglan Road." His honor guard includes members of the FDNY and the East Meadow Fire Department, where his life of service began as a teenage volunteer. Hundreds pay their respects at Holy Family Church, including Mayor de Blasio.

Jon Stewart says a few words:

It's almost like he didn't know how special he was . . .

I don't know where he got his strength from, but I think I can see it now: It was the people he loved and the people who loved him.

Make no mistake, Ray Pfeifer died in the line of duty, because of illness from the terrible terrorist attacks of 9/11. But more importantly, Ray Pfeifer LIVED in the line of duty, now and forever.

That's what I remember most about him . . . It wasn't about him, it was about service to others. ALWAYS. Always do the right thing.

I remember at the end of our lobbying efforts, down in DC, I felt beaten. I was disgusted by what I had witnessed and what had been done, and all I was getting was business cards.

I said to Ray, "If I get another business card, I'm going to scream. I'm going to lose my mind."

Ray said, "I'm okay."

I said, "How, Ray? How can you maintain your cool in all this?"

He patted his chest, and he reached in.

[Jon blinks away tears and takes a deep breath.]

And he pulled out prayer cards, hundreds, and said, "I got all the cards I need."

[Jon reaches into his suit and pulls out Ray's mass card and holds it up.]

And now, Raymond, I got one. And it's going to teach me how to do right.

Ray's flag-draped casket is carried out to "Going Home" on the bagpipes. A lone bugle plays "Taps," after our friend is loaded back onto the truck, a dalmatian at his side. A moment of silence, then a fire chief presents Ray's helmet to his widow. He is carried off on the vintage fire truck to "The Minstrel Boy," an Irish rebel ballad, on the bagpipes. The motorcade turns a corner, the white-capped firefighters stand at ease, and the people Ray loved and who loved him are left with an ache no ceremony or flag-waving or sad Irish songs or long showers will ever soothe.

Every death is hard. Each one makes the next one a little harder. Ray's not the first, nor the last, but he's the most painful. I can feel my soul leave my body. I numb it all out. The only person I show my emotions to is Jon. He and I were close before, but sharing the pain of this loss, hugging, and crying together brings us even closer. He might say otherwise, but Jon never *had to* be there. He chose to get close enough to Ray that it would mean losing a part of himself when this sad, inevitable day came.

In the last conversation we ever have, before he slips out of coherency and out of my life forever, Ray gives me a final piece of advice:

"See it through to the end."

ACTION FOR ACTIVISTS: WHO DO YOU LOVE?

Put the notepad down. Go for a walk or find someplace quiet. Spend some time thinking about a person or people you love more than you love yourself.

Then get to work. Do it for them. Don't stop. Like Ray said to me, "See it through to the end."

When the going gets tough, the only thing that will keep you going are the people you love and the people who love you.

When in doubt, center everything you do around people. Not ideas, or sentiments, bold statements about right and wrong. There's a time and a place for big ideas, but they're meaningless without human connection. Most movements get off track and end up doing great harm in the name of some supposed virtue when they choose ideology over humanity. That's the story of every revolution that turned tyrannical and every despot who promised utopia.

But even the word "humanity" is too big and amorphous and abstract. You're better off focusing on one person or a core group. When you need to convey an idea or communicate your purpose, have a spokesperson or face of your movement. This is why bills and laws tend to have names. Ray was one man in a wheelchair who forced Congress to pay attention to thousands of men and women suffering from 9/11 illness. Fifteen minutes with Ray, the man, meeting his gaze, communicated what we were going through better than any slide deck or well-rehearsed talking points.

Ray's empty chair at the Capitol.
(Photo/Faye Murman-Dorsey)

Testimony

GLEN KLEIN

When civilians need help, they call 9-1-1. When first responders need help, they call us.

> Glen Klein, aka "Tackleberry," is a retired NYPD detective with ESU (SWAT/Rescue) and a NYPD Combat Cross recipient with expertise as a rescue diver, heavy weapons armorer, and hazmat specialist. He also served on the FEMA Urban Search & Rescue Task Force, and now trains instructors on civilian response to active-shooter events.

We do it all: high-angle rescue, with ropes and harnesses to get jumpers off buildings and bridges; we're trained in SCUBA, rescue diving, vehicle extractions, even radiation detection and working with hazardous materials. In movies and TV, we're probably best known for the SWAT team, kicking down doors and saving hostages, and we do that, but there's a rescue component too. Everything we do is about saving lives and keeping New York City safe. Staying current with these skills

Glen Klein's thousand-yard stare.
(Photo/Steve Spak)

means we're constantly training; even if you've been on the job fifteen years, you never stop learning.

I joined the NYPD in January of 1983 and was assigned to the 107 Precinct out of the academy. I spent about five years there before I got into ESU. I was one of four officers who trained the rest of ESU in SCUBA, which wasn't one of our capabilities at the time, but it was something I had experience with outside of the job. We spent about a year in the Police Academy pool teaching guys to dive on the midnight shift. Before we got everybody dive qualified, ESU had a small dive unit that required a helicopter ride to wherever they were needed—not ideal in a rescue diving situation where victims might be running out of air. By

SCUBA qualifying the mobile ESU units in all five boroughs, we could get to incidents faster and save lives.

My normal shift was midnight to 8 AM, but in September 2001, I was serving as a PBA delegate for the union, so I had meetings with my commanding officer every couple of months. On 9/11, instead of working the night before, I had switched to the afternoon shift to accommodate one of those meetings. So, I was home when the towers were hit. If I had been working my normal shift, I would have just gotten off, and I probably would have been a few blocks away from the precinct and turned around when the plane hit. I was having a cup of coffee, looking out my window and thinking *what a beautiful day*. The phone rang. It was my friend Brad, a photographer who covered the area where I worked. He would show up and photograph accidents.

I was used to him joking around and being the clown and pulling shenanigans to lighten the mood. So, when he told me a plane had crashed into the World Trade Center, I said, "Get the fuck outta here. Not on a day like today, good try."

"No. I'm serious. I'm not fucking playing. Put the TV on."

I watched a replay of the first plane hit, got dressed, and headed into Queens. I was on the Northern State Parkway going 100 mph when I passed a state trooper. He put his lights on, I showed him my badge, and he escorted me the rest of the way. I called up my command from the car to see if any of the guys were still there. He said he was with a couple of guys getting ready to go. I told him to hold up, I'd be about ten minutes. I told him to load the vehicles with extra gear in case we needed it. I was senior at the time, so they listened. We were fully loaded when I got there: ropes and harnesses, Scott Air-Paks like firefighters wear, cutting torches, all the toys. People were cheering us down the streets. We made our way over the Brooklyn Bridge into Manhattan. The first tower had just collapsed, and it was so dusty we couldn't see where we were going, even with the windshield wipers on. We picked up an injured police officer who was having trouble breathing and put him on oxygen in the vehicle with the AC on. Then we made our way toward the meetup point on Broadway. On the way there, the second tower started coming down. We ran into the Woolworth Building, which saved our lives. We got on the radio, trying to figure out our plan of action. My lieutenant came over and he said . . . He said we had seven guys from ESU in each tower, and we hadn't heard from them. He didn't think they made it out. We lost fourteen guys that morning. I spent eight months down at Ground Zero looking for them. We only found the remains of three out of the fourteen. The others were evaporated. Those were fourteen guys I worked with every day. They were closer than brothers to me. The man who welcomed me to ESU, who was my sergeant for sixteen years at ESU. A good man.

9/11 destroyed me. It destroyed a lot of people, mentally and physically. Since then, I've lost fifteen to twenty other friends that I worked with. The dying hasn't stopped yet. I've suffered post-traumatic stress and major depression. What I went through on 9/11 was compounded by a plane crash in the Rockaways that November. An American Airlines flight went down shortly after takeoff. At the time, everyone assumed terrorism, but it ended up being a catastrophic mechanical failure. I was there with my guys at the crash site, putting bodies and body parts in body bags all day. I felt something soft in the wreckage and did some digging and found an infant still strapped into a car seat strapped to the plane seat, burned to a crisp. That fucked me up on top of everything else.

I was having vivid nightmares every night. I started drinking. Heavily. When I would get in a fight with my wife or get angry with my kids, I'd punch a hole in a wall. Eventually there were holes all over the house. It was no way to live, no way for my kids to grow up. I started googling support groups for 9/11 responders. I thought about starting one if there wasn't already something out there. That's when I found John and got into the health program. I went with him to DC, and John suggested that going to speak to police officers around the country might be good therapy for me. I started speaking about PTSD and resilience. I remind

people that it's a natural response to an incident, and it doesn't make you any less of a man or any less brave. Admitting that you're struggling, and dealing with it, THAT takes real courage. I remind them and remind myself that I'm still here.

I stopped punching walls. One day, John came over and patched up all the holes.

Ten

PUT YOUR SPEECH AWAY

Jon Stewart's pen is legendary. Every show began with him furiously marking up pages moments before his opener. He would wag his pen for emphasis, fidget with it while finding his train of thought mid-monologue. He closed each episode by flinging it into the audience.

It's June 2019. The 9/11 health and compensation funds are broke. I've been trying to get Stewart to put his pen away all week and go off script at the upcoming House Judiciary Subcommittee hearing to address these shortfalls and their consequences for the families for whom the fund and the health program are a lifeline. We don't need what comes out of Jon's pen, clever and brilliant as it is. We need him to get pissed and to articulate how weary we all are of having to come back to Washington, hats in hand, every five years. More of us are sick, fewer of us are still walking.

By 2018, the VCF was on track to run out of money before the expiry in 2020. This was due to high demand from what Congressman King called the "latent and aggressive" nature of 9/11 illnesses. To balance the budget, the fund automatically cut awards. If you were supposed to get $100,000, now you might get $50,000 or as little as $10,000. On average, awards were cut by 77 percent. Many of these recipients had waited years for their claims and were already financially ruined. Getting their full claims would just mean paying back creditors and, hopefully, getting their heads above water. Not some lush payday. Fiscal responsibility had doomed the 9/11 responders and survivors to be broke as well as sick.

My phone keeps ringing. I take calls from desperate, heartbroken families. As I listen, I see my own Corvette and Explorer backing out of my driveway and my furniture hauled away all those years ago, as the rot that first took my foot came for my financial security. I cry with these people and remember pleading with a judge to keep my house, trembling inside, feeling a pain worse than any physical injury as my modest dream of home ownership was taken from me. I risked contempt in open court because I needed him to know that broke and broken though I was, the man standing in his courtroom had been made that way by the Pile. No liens could take away the work my friends and I had done, or what the work had done to us.

Rich and I start taking small groups to the Hill in the fall of 2018, before there's a bill. The community blows up the phone lines. In February, 2019, Gillibrand introduces legislation to renew the VCF and fund it through 2090, just like the 9/11 healthcare program. The same guys who had been telling us "no" through the years had similar bills in their districts. Coal miners in Mitch McConnell's Kentucky have their permanent bill. Lindsey Graham has a submarine bill for South Carolina. These are much more localized than the 9/11 community.

Gradually, as the bill picks up momentum, we change our tone from "suck my dick" to "who's coming with us?"

We start collecting co-sponsors like jellybeans.

By March/April, we have enough votes for our bill if we attach it to something larger and maybe weigh it down with amendments. Even our allies want us to wait and take this safer approach.

I put forward the idea of pushing for a vote now as a standalone bill, put to the floor on its merits. No larger vehicle. No pork. Permanent so we would never have to come back. I want the bill to go out undefeated like Rocky Marciano.

Back in 2010, a looming recess had worked against us and threatened to kill the bill. Now, in June 2019, we're going to use the time crunch of an upcoming summer recess to get this thing done.

The House Judiciary Committee convenes a hearing on June 11 to recommend this legislation for a floor vote. The hearing won't be our Super Bowl, it's more like the Eastern Conference Final. It took relentless effort to get this far. This will be our chance to testify to the merits of the bill and to prove there has been no waste or fraud. It's also an opportunity to let them know how fucking exhausted we all are and how none of us want to keep coming back.

I work with Ben Chevat and staffers from Nadler's, Maloney's, and Gillibrand's offices to assemble a panel for the hearing. We try to capture the diversity of the survivors and responders: police, fire, trades, men, women, Black, white, all ages. All volunteers. As I reach out to folks who have already received their VCF claims, something powerful happens. They all say yes. They all step up even though none of them have to. They want to pay it forward for future recipients who will never know their names. Rich and I spend hours selecting the speakers and the order of the panel. But there's no debate over who will be our closer.

Jon Stewart will be speaking not as a witness but as a man of rhetoric who has been with us for a decade, chastising the system and verbalizing what we've been carrying in our hearts for fifteen years. The task humbles and terrifies him. He keeps saying he's afraid of letting down the guys and fucking it all up. So, he does what a man of his intellect and verbal gifts does when intimidated: He takes refuge in his words and his thoughts. He writes. He rewrites and polishes. But that is not what we need from him. We need Stewart raw and unfiltered, like he has been in so many meetings. We need the committee to know what Ray's friendship meant to him.

I get to work coaching him and getting in his head while he works with bright, young Hill staffers to hone his talking points on the page.

All week, Jon sends me drafts I refuse to read. We text nonstop as the hearing looms.

Stewart: I made a change, wanna hear it?

Me: Eat a dick.

Stewart: What do you think about this sentence . . .

Me: Dude, I already gave you my opinion. Put it away.

I get where he's coming from. But he's the greatest sit-down comedian of his generation, and he's limiting his powers by speaking in refined talking points out of misplaced fear and imposter syndrome.

The day before the hearing, the team leaders and I meet at a turnpike rest stop like we have on so many of these trips. I drive alone. Stewart is going to meet us down there. Lila Nordstrom is staying with friends in Georgetown. Already this trip feels different. Nobody's goofing around or talking shit. We just stand around watching cars pass on the highway. We're tired. We're ready. Nobody says so, but this feels like going into battle. This time, it feels like something big is going to happen. We get back in our cars and drive to the Beltway.

At the hotel, I get a room to myself, as always, so I can spread all the paperwork out on the second bed. We're met by Faye, a photographer I've hired to document these trips, and two documentary crews. *No Responders Left Behind* is a Canadian production that's been shadowing us for a while. *Dust* is Bridget Gormley's tribute to her father, Billy, an FDNY firefighter who died of 9/11 cancer in 2017. We take over a restaurant that evening. I eat with my team leaders. Normally I give a big speech the night before and tell everyone to be on their best behavior. But we're a machine at this point, and nobody needs scolding. I don't babysit this time or tell anybody they can't drink. Just like I want

Stewart to have the courage to put away his prepared remarks, I know I can ease up, too, because the team leaders and their teams know what to do. We all know we're getting this done. We didn't come here to lose. No bedtimes because nobody's going to get much sleep.

At breakfast in the hotel, I go from table to table checking in and being social. Finally, I sit down with Lou Alvarez. Lou was a detective on the NYPD bomb squad, a post he took later in his career because it was less stressful than his previous work as an undercover narcotics detective. Before that he was a boy from Cuba whose parents came here so he could have a better life. He repaid a debt of gratitude with a life of service, starting when he joined the US Marine Corps at eighteen, and now ending in agonizing illness contracted in the line of duty, having one of his last breakfasts in a business hotel in DC on the morning of his final act of service. Lou used to walk around at 190 pounds before cancer wasted him to 120. Just yesterday, he went through his sixty-eighth round of chemo. He's scheduled for his sixty-ninth. Lou is speaking on the panel today. But he's also eye candy. Anyone who wants to talk deficits and fiscal responsibility is invited to look into Lou's sunken, jaundiced eyes and say it to his face.

I don't want him to be here. He shouldn't have to be here. But like Ray, he wants to be here to the end. Sitting across from him, my heart is breaking because my friend is dying and because I'm overwhelmed with gratitude to know such a man and to share this work. As with Ray and the 170+ whose cards I carry with me, I'm jealous that Lou won't have to watch more of his friends die. Like Stewart says, "You make friends, and you watch them disappear."

I drink black coffee and pick at the dry scrambled eggs Lou isn't eating. I bust his balls so I don't break down.

"Big day today, Lou, you nervous?"

"No."

"Well, I'm nervous. But you got this, man, it's like you're batting cleanup."

I get to the Rayburn House Office Building early. It's time to take my coaching and mindfucking up a notch. Yesterday there was a charity golf outing in memory of Ray Pfeifer, where one of the items for auction was Ray's bunker coat. I phoned in my $7,000 winning bid and paid some dude $1,200 to drive it to DC immediately. As people start showing up, I get them to sign the coat. When I see Lila, I press a FealGood Foundation challenge coin into her palm.

Stewart shows up and the cameras are all over us. I ask for them to give us a minute.

I've never seen Jon this nervous.

He says, "I don't want to let everybody down."

Stewart's got his pages; he tries to show them to me and I don't even look.

"Will you put that away. I have something for *you* to read."

I hand him a note.

Dear Jon,

This is my first "Dear John" letter in 53 years on this planet.
I miss and love Ray dearly.
I miss and love my mother dearly.
Don't ever make me miss you,
because I love you dearly.

-John

We hug, we cry, then we go inside where everyone is waiting for us in the hallway. Kenny Specht, firefighter and cancer survivor, steps out of the crowd and presents Ray's bunker coat to Stewart, signed by every one of us.

Jon holds up the coat and speaks to the crowd and the cameras, choking back tears.

"We're gonna do it today. Not just for Ray, but for all you guys and for everyone Ray was fighting for."

It's go time.

The panelists, the film crews, and about forty of us make our way into the committee room, where it's standing room only. Many others, including unions and other groups with interest in the bill, go to watch the hearing remotely in an overflow room. It's like a gathering of the Avengers.

I stop our Iron Man on the way in, who's still marking up his pages.

"I'm serious. Put that fucking speech away."

"Enough. I get it. I understand."

Inside the committee room, Stewart turns to firefighter and fellow panelist Michael O'Connell, dressed in Class A's, looking like a recruiting poster.

"Mike, I'm nervous, I don't want to fuck this up is all."

"Remember, we're the ones who are right. They're the ones who should be nervous."

The survivors and responders are facing a small fraction of the forty-one members of the committee. Some file in and out, to put their perfunctory attendance on the record. I lean in and speak to Stewart:

"Can you believe the disrespect? All these people are sick and dying and these motherfuckers can't even be bothered to show up. What disrespect."

Representatives King and Maloney, one Republican, one Democrat, make their opening statements, Maloney wearing an FDNY bunker coat. Jerry Nadler states the lofty purpose of the Zadroga bill, in the words of Abe Lincoln, as immortalized in the motto of the Veterans Administration:

"To care for him who shall have borne the battle and for his widow and his orphan."

During the opening remarks I turn to Michael O'Connell and say, "Be authentic, be yourself . . . and don't look back because everyone here is relying on you, and I don't want you to get nervous."

Then I look up and see the Pile. It's being projected on big screens in the gallery, that smoking awful place that made us all sick. My jaw hangs open. I'm there again. I'm smelling it. And I realize that all this coaching and mindfucking, it's my way of coping. It's the only way I know how to live with the constant reminders of all my friends disappearing and the dread that when things get quiet, I will be alone with visions of that awful Pile and all the suffering that followed.

Nadler continues: " . . . for our panel of witnesses today and for many people in the audience, 9/11 never ended. We live every day with the events of that morning and the impact of the decisions made by the federal government in the aftermath."

He's got that right.

First up, we have our experts:

Rupa Bhattacharyya, special master of the VCF, testifies that there is no fraud, despite the accusations. She points out that the current state of the fund is a simple numbers game: more cancer, more death.

Dr. Jacqueline Moline was working at Mount Sinai on 9/11 and began seeing patients with 9/11 illnesses that month. In her capacity as an epidemiology and prevention researcher, she was funded to observe but couldn't offer treatment. They call that "medical surveillance," which is every bit as creepy as it sounds. She tells the committee: "As medical professionals, we never believed the air was safe to breathe." And she gives the prognosis for our community: 11,000+ cancers treated; 55,000 of us certified with at least one 9/11 illness; new disease clusters and cancer links being discovered all the time.

Among the survivors are 20,000 kids who were attending schools below Houston Street on 9/11 and during the cleanup. These kids were innocent. Nothing they did or didn't do contributed to their exposure. No duty or oath required that they be there. As minors, they couldn't legally make the decision to return to contaminated schools, and the adults making that decision for them had been lied to. Lila Nordstrom, director of StuyHealth, a high school senior at Stuyvesant on 9/11 and the youngest person on the advisory committee to the WTC Health Program, speaks for the kids and the survivors. She is professional and prepared, the only one who stays within the five-minute time limit (which was just a guideline anyway). On her trips to DC she gradually dressed down because she often got confused for a staffer, being young and in business casual attire surrounded by FealGood hoodies and T-shirts. She bore, with grace and humor, the sexist indignity of being asked constantly if she was with us because her dad was a responder.

Lila tells how Christine Todd Whitman, then head of the EPA, sacrificed her classmates in the name of a return to normalcy following the attacks, based on the lie that the air was safe.

"I haven't had my twentieth reunion, and I know five former classmates with lymphoma. My friend Michelle is in remission from thyroid cancer . . . and classmates are starting to die . . . A couple of months ago, Kathy Choi passed away, aged thirty-three, from a 9/11-linked gastric cancer. Her VCF award has not been paid yet. When it's paid to her husband, it will be cut by fifty to seventy percent. And that's just my school . . ."

Lila herself has asthma, chronic acute allergies, GERD (which leads to esophageal cancer), and PTSD. All 9/11 linked. As a woman and self-educated public health advocate, she is uniquely qualified to speak to 9/11-related women's health issues.

"Women have special reason to be concerned because much of the data on post 9/11 health is taken from the first-responder community, which is an overwhelmingly male population, so there's less data to show the link between 9/11 and women's health problems."

The kids were just one overlooked group in the 9/11 story. My friend

Jevon Thomas, who died of 9/11 cancer in 2012, cleaned the Porta Potties at Ground Zero, work that wasn't going to get him on the cover of *Time* with the heroes of the FDNY, but work he was proud to do nonetheless. Our next panelist, the widow Anesta St. Rose Henry, tells of her husband Candidas's work cleaning the trucks that hauled away debris from the Pile. When Nadler tells the widow to reposition her mic, we can hear every stifled sob. She opens with a story about how much she missed Candidas while shopping for her son's recent prom, how much they would have laughed over his undersized jacket. She speaks to an important truth that can get lost in grand talk about duty and heroism and sacrifice: Every life lost deprives a family of little moments like these.

> *His job at Ground Zero was to wash the dust and debris from the trucks. He made sure everything was secure . . . and that no human remains would fall out of the trucks. While his job may not sound glorious, he was proud of his work and proud to say he worked at Ground Zero . . . He was a proud American.*
>
> *He cherished his pass from Ground Zero, a reminder of the important work he had been a part of.*

Candidas died a few weeks prior of a rare brain tumor that's not so rare among 9/11 responders. In her seat at the long table, Anesta clutches a large photo of Candidas in happier times, dressed all in white for a special occasion.

Their VCF claim had been cut by 70 percent. Now, the dream of using that money to send their son to college, the first person in their family to do so, is in jeopardy. Anesta tells the committee:

"If he had died two years earlier, everything would have been okay."

Thomas J. Mohnal was an FBI agent and expert in explosives. When the towers were hit, he was sent home to pack for New York. Stuck in traffic, he watched American Airlines 77 fly into the Pentagon. He alerted FBI headquarters and responded to the scene. In the months that followed, Mohnal and agents from nearly every FBI Evidence Response Team in the country sifted through a warehouse full of evidence from the attacks. They found fragments of the hijackers' passports and the infamous box cutters used in the hijacking.

(L-R) Special Agent Thomas J. Mohnal, FBI; Detective Luis Alvarez; Anesta St. Rose Henry (holding a photo of her late husband); Michael O'Connell, FDNY. (Photo/Faye Murman-Dorsey)

His colleague, Agent Dawnele Holbrook, a two-time survivor of the same cancer, sits in the back row quietly sobbing as her dear dying friend testifies. For years, 9/11 illness was a secret they shared, having been told by the Bureau to keep quiet.

I look over Stewart's shoulder and see he's still marking up his pages. I text him.

Look at those empty seats. Such disrespect.

FDNY Lt. Michael O'Connell recalls the Pile.

> *To this day, there is only one true memory etched into my brain, and one that still haunts me when I put my head on the pillow at night. As firefighters, we wear Scott packs that are equipped with PASS alarms. A PASS alarm is meant to go off and make a loud screeching sound in the likelihood that a firefighter is stuck and is motionless. For the first few minutes of our arrival, and the countless hours that passed, that is all we heard. Our brothers were trapped beneath that pile of concrete and steel and we could not get to them. It is a difficult memory, but one that keeps me going. It reminds me that those men and women who gave their lives that day were selfless, and I try my best to live my life to that standard.*
>
> *In the midst of the chaos and loss of life, I can tell you that there is another thought that I had. I would not want to be anywhere else in the world at that moment. We were there to help, and I was part of something that showed the world that we would not back down to anyone. We helped bring closure to families that just wanted something tangible, some part that remained, to bury. Now it is your turn, you were not there on the Pile, but what you do in this moment is just as important as what we all did at Ground Zero.*

Michael has sarcoidosis, a very rare autoimmune disease that is very common among 9/11 responders. Thanks to his full VCF payment, his family is taken care of. He doesn't have to be here today. But anyone who heard those alarms knows: They aren't as loud when you're doing your best to live up to the standard set by the men and women for whom that sound was a death knell.

Maybe someday we won't hear them anymore.

Lou Alvarez gets five minutes to do what he devoted his life to for the last time: protecting and serving. He holds the gallery in stunned silence while he stands up for VCF recipients and tells the committee what it's like to die of 9/11 cancer. Like Mike and Agent Mohnal, Lou

L: Lou's speech in his tattooed hand. R: On our feet for Lou.
(Photos/Faye Murman-Dorsey)

already received his VCF; that's what he means when he says, "I'm okay." He's not okay, but thanks to the VCF, his family will be.

"Less than twenty-four hours from now, I will be starting my sixty-ninth round of chemotherapy. Yeah, you heard that correct. I should not be here with you, but you made me come."

I'm bawling my eyes out. I can see Stewart breathing, trying to keep it together. Lou may have finally pushed Jon to set aside his prepared remarks.

"I have been to many places in this world"—Lou takes a long pause, his voice choking with emotion, maybe thinking of one place in particular he'll never see again—"and done many things. But I can tell you that I didn't want to be anywhere else but Ground Zero when I was there."

He closes with a few words that could be the epitaph for our community and our long struggle.

"You all said you would never forget. Well, I'm here to make sure that you don't."

In the standing ovation that follows, I lean over to Stewart for one last bit of coaching:

"Follow that, bitch."

Between rounds of applause, I wipe tears from my eyes. I look at Jon. I look at the empty chairs in front of him. The disrespect. Such disrespect . . . While Lou was speaking, something was happening on the floor, and I could see that Jon saw it. People were filing in, staff and members, to see the TV funny man Jon Stewart serve up some rhetoric. They were too busy for Lou, but they weren't going to miss Jon Stewart. That must have set him off. He hates that starfucking shit, and at a time like this? *Such disrespect.*

> *I want to thank Mr. Collins and Mr. Nadler for putting this together. But, as I sit here today, I can't help but think what an incredible metaphor this room is for the entire process that getting health care and benefits for 9/11 first responders has come to.*
>
> *Behind me: a filled room of 9/11 first responders.*
>
> *And in front of me: a nearly empty Congress.*
>
> *Sick and dying, they brought themselves down here to speak—to no one.*

We're all thinking it. The others are too polite to call it out. These aren't his prepared remarks, his eyes aren't on the page, he's staring down the committee. A few rows back, Bridget Gormley mutters to the person beside her, "Holy shit."

Jon tells of walking the halls with Ray, being dismissed with business cards and empty promises from staffers.

> *You know, I used to get . . . I would be so angry at the latest injustice that's done to these men and women and, you know, another business card thrown our way as a way of shooing us away like children trick-or-treating, rather than the heroes that they are and will always be.*
>
> *Ray would say, "Calm down, Johnny. Calm down. I got all the cards I need." And he would tap his pocket . . .*
>
> *[Stewart chokes up, blinking tears from his eyes. His hand trembles until he finds his pen. He bobs the pen in his trembling hand, the signature fidget of his* Daily Show *monologues.]*

. . . where he kept the prayer cards of 343 firefighters.

The official FDNY response time to 911 was five seconds. Five seconds! That's how long it took for FDNY, for NYPD, for Port Authority, for EMS to respond to an urgent need from the public.

Five seconds . . .

The breathing problems started almost immediately. And they were told they weren't sick—they were crazy. And then, as the illnesses got worse and things became more apparent, "Well, okay, you're sick but it's not from the Pile." And then, when the science became irrefutable, "Okay, it's the Pile—but this is a New York issue. I don't know if we have the money."

And I'm sorry if I sound angry and undiplomatic, but I'm angry—and you should be too; and they're all angry as well. And they have every justification to be that way. There is not a person here, there is not an empty chair on that stage that didn't tweet out, "Never forget" the heroes of 9/11. Never forget their bravery. Never forget what they did, what they gave to this country.

Well, here they are! And where are they?

And it would be one thing if their callous indifference and rank hypocrisy were benign. But it's not. Your indifference cost these men and women their most valuable commodity: TIME! It's the one thing they're running out of.

[He's shaking like one of those beds you put a quarter into. He taps his pen on the table.]

. . . And the idea that you can only give them five more years of the VCF 'cause you're not quite sure what's going to happen five years from now—well, I can tell you I'm pretty sure what's going to happen five years from now: More of these men and women are going to get sick and they are going to die.

And you can end it tomorrow. Why this bill isn't unanimous consent and a standalone issue is beyond my comprehension. And I have yet to hear a reasonable explanation for why. It'll get stuck in some transportation bill or some appropriations bill and get sent over to the Senate, where a certain someone from the Senate will use it as a political football to get themselves maybe another new import tax on petroleum—'cause that's what happened to us in 2015.

And we won't allow it to happen again.

Thank God for people like John Feal.

Thank God for people like Ray Pfeifer.

Thank God for all of these people who will not let it happen. They responded in five seconds. They did their jobs with courage, grace, tenacity, humility.

Eighteen years later—do yours!

Thank you.

For as long as I can remember, I've always been an Olympic buff. Doesn't matter what sport, I love watching excellence in action: the vicarious drop in my stomach as a gymnast vaults through air or a diver tucks into a backflip. Watching Jon speak takes me back to 1976. I'm ten years old on the floor of our living room, on my belly in front of the TV, watching Nadia Comăneci earn the first perfect 10.0 in history. This tiny human moving with precision and grace, flipping through the air, making the impossible look effortless.

Jon Stewart gets a 10.0 today. For nine or so minutes, the 9/11 responders were the ones vaulting through the air as a great mind articulated our pain and suffering with humanity and brilliance.

All we wanted was to be heard, even if that means speaking to no one. Almost immediately, it's clear that the whole world was listening. From the time I get up to applaud to the time I sit down again, I have 300 text messages. I will have 10,000 emails by the end of the day and 37,000 tomorrow. Stewart gets a text from his wife asking if he's okay. It occurs to him that his wife doesn't sit around watching C-SPAN. Friends have already forwarded the clip to her. She's never seen this side of him.

The hearing continues for nearly two more hours while footage of Jon's testimony makes the rounds online. The panelists keep pointing out the technicality that this is only a subcommittee meeting and that no disrespect was intended by the low attendance, but nobody at home will hear those corrections, and everyone will remember Jon wagging his famous pen at those empty seats. Jon will tell you that he knows it was a subcommittee. I'm telling you he didn't. Either way, as Stewart remembers, this was our whole lives. It was not where Lou should have spent one of his last days. But to these suits, it was like a zoning hearing. Jon compares it to those movie scenes where an actor sweats blood in audition while the casting director looks on disinterested and finally says, "We'll let you know."

Rep. Steve Cohen from Tennessee doesn't even hide it. He tells Stewart, "Well, you have to understand, we're very busy."

I want to scream. *Look, asshole, you don't think Lou has all sorts of things he'd rather be doing?* But I don't need to say anything. I can sit there and maintain "normal order" because today the greatest sit-down comedian of all time has put eighteen years of heartbreak and anger into words. Maybe tonight the smoke will let me breathe, maybe the PASS alarms won't chirp so loud.

When it's over, we sob in each other's arms.

After the hearing, we gather outside in the muggy June air. It went well, but there's no joy in it.

"This wasn't *Rudy*," Stewart will recall, a reference to the classic feel-good underdog football movie.

Matt McCauley walks Lou out to Rizzo's car. Lou asks him, "What do you think?"

Matt says, "I don't think we can do better than we did today."

Pretty soon, Matt's phone starts blowing up. His daughter, Emma, texts him: *Was that you behind Stewart??? Dad, my friends are telling me you're trending on Instagram.*

We're all very tired, and now we have to prepare for the vote.

I thank everyone for being there even though none of them had to be. Most of our crew goes home. I take a few guys to Albany where we get three bills passed, riding the wave of Stewart's viral return to the spotlight. I have to keep moving.

There's something I don't tell Stewart or any of the guys, something I've kept to myself until now: If that gamble to get a standalone bill passed before summer fails, I plan to take my own life.

My "Dear John" note will be a goodbye note. I know I won't be able to live with the shame of having let everyone down and having used Lou as a rhetorical pawn when he should have been holding his wife and his boys one more time. Even though the gamble pays off, I will have to live with what I asked of Lou. When I find myself consumed with survivor's guilt, I will remember his relentless determination and how I couldn't have stopped him from speaking if I wanted to. He didn't want to be anywhere else in the world. When asked to speak about PTSD I will tell audiences about the hearing and how sometimes you do your best work on your worst days.

Eighteen days after the hearing, Lou is gone.

The bill passes in late July. I will join Ray in Valhalla another day. The 9/11 Museum will get the pens Pelosi and Trump use to sign the bill into law. I have the pen from the Marriott that Stewart waved at the committee when he told them to do their jobs.

ACTION FOR ACTIVISTS: PUT YOUR SPEECH AWAY

As Jon Stewart's testimony demonstrates, you have to know when to put away your prepared remarks and speak from your heart. After you've simplified your rhetoric, spend some time working with your feelings. Find a way to express those feelings as part of your message.

Going back to your A, B, and C teams, you might delegate different parts of your message to different team members, in the way the 9/11 panel ranged from data-driven medical experts to an agonized widow.

A word of caution: This is not the same thing as having no plan. Don't just say whatever pops into your head.

I worked with Mike, Lou, and the other witnesses for hours to craft their statements. We gave Lila a little more leeway as the sole voice of the survivors and because she's so damn educated and smart. The widow St. Rose Henry didn't need crafted lines; she just needed to be heard. The point is, we thought through all of this. Jon's spontaneity was calculated and tactical. Nobody was winging it.

Testimony

MATT MCCAULEY

They called the 32nd precinct house "The Tomb of Gloom" in those days. Now there's a Starbucks across from the building. But when I graduated the Police Academy, in 1990, Harlem was a different world. I tell people: "I'm a Chinese food connoisseur, and if it isn't served from behind four inches of bulletproof glass, it doesn't taste as good."

Matt McCauley, aka "Unicorn," is a retired NYPD police officer, paramedic, and 9/11 responder who now works as a lawyer for the 9/11 community. He represented Lou Alvarez.

Even with overtime, I needed a second job. My B job was working as a paramedic. I'd leave one job, put the portable radio away, and pick up another portable radio. One day in 1993, I was working a day tour, and when I got off and started working four to twelve in the ambulance up in Yonkers, they sent us into the city where there had been a bombing at the World Trade Center.

I started going to law school nights. At that point, I was married, and my wife was doing another master's. We were a busy family. Law school led to work with the DA's office, which led to an internship downtown in the US Attorney's Office for the Southern District of New York in the organized crime and terrorism department. The guys in that office were incredible. They were wrapping up the trial from the WTC bombing and working on the Al-Qaeda attacks on our embassies in Kenya and Tanzania when I got there. It was an exciting time for me, as a thirty-one-year-old law clerk, loving every minute of this new career.

On the morning of September 11th, I was in the office, which has a view of the towers, when I heard a roar and saw the first plane hit. I just happened to be looking out the window. I picked up the phone and called the place in Westchester where I was working as a paramedic.

"Hey, you're not going to believe this . . ."

We said we would meet over by the overpass where we met in '93 when we responded to the bombing. I looked out the open window from my office and watched the emergency vehicles showing up. Then the second plane hit. We could feel the concussion from the impact. I told everybody to get the fuck out of the building, or words to that effect.

I worked on the ambulance down there, taking firemen to the hospital who had come off the Pile and were dangerously dehydrated. We were constantly flushing people's eyes out. I remember being in one of the temporary morgues which was in a Brooks Brothers across the street from the Trade Center. It was surreal because they cleared the store for these plywood examination tables, but the clothes were still hanging on the walls and in the window displays. On one of the tables, there was a fully intact body, burned to the point where I couldn't tell whether it was a man or a woman. In the warped logic of the recovery effort, I remember thinking: *That's nice, some family is going to get a whole body to bury.*

Fast forward, five years later, I was working at a firm downtown. One day, I was rushing up to the court, and I realized I needed to get a tie. I ran into Brooks Brothers. 9/11 was the last thing on my mind; I just needed a tie. As soon as I walked in, I just froze. The same displays

hanging on the walls, the same decor. This was the morgue. That was the day I realized those memories don't ever leave you. A flashback isn't always a bang or the roar of a jet engine. In my case, it was the sight of cardigans and polo shirts hanging on a sale rack.

Physically, I have the gift that keeps on giving, the same sinus conditions that everybody else has. I wake up every morning with a runny nose, feeling like I have a sock stuck in my throat. It is what it is, and I'm thankful that's it. I was exposed to the same dust and debris as people who died from their exposure. There's survivor's guilt that goes along with that, and there's a reluctance to put your hand up and tell your story when so many have it so much worse. But it's like I tell the people I enroll in this program: If you were there, "eligible." I don't use the word "deserve" because that's not what this bill is about.

For Lou Alvarez, that sense of fairness meant everything. He was adamant that his family should not get any more than they "deserve," but they shouldn't get anything less either. That was our starting point when I worked with him on his speech to Congress. Lou didn't believe he and his family were worth more than anybody else, nor was anybody else worth more than them. While we were writing, he was on his sixty-something round of chemo. We put that in the speech too.

When he was in hospice, the Yankees were on a tear. One night, we were watching the game and he got out his chewing tobacco. The doctor walked in just as he was tapping the tin, and they looked at each other for a moment. Here's this guy with stage 4 cancer packing a lip. Finally Lou goes, "What?"

The doc goes, "No no, you do whatever makes you happy, Lou," and goes about his rounds.

Lou turns to me. "You want a fatty, Matt?"

I quit a long time ago, but I threw a dip in with my friend in his hospital room that night.

It was really important to him to be buried in a military cemetery; that was his last request to me. And it was important to him that I knew why he wanted that last honor. He said it wasn't just in recognition of his time in the Marine Corps and his life of service to this country, though that certainly mattered a great deal to him. His deeper reason went back to fairness. As was always the case with Lou, it was never about him.

He told me, "I want my kids to see how we all are." He explained that in a regular cemetery, you can do whatever you want, you or the guy next to you can erect a mausoleum. "But I want to be buried where every headstone is the same. When my kids visit my grave, I want them to see that there's no greater honor than to be treated with the same respect and dignity as the person to your left and to your right."

That blew my mind. I was going to do whatever it took to make that happen for him. It wasn't as easy as we expected, or as it should have been, to get him buried there. We called Congress, we called the military. The wheels were in motion in the background, and all we could do was wait. Finally, Congressman Peter King's (R-NY) assistant called to say we got it. I felt weird celebrating, but I was delighted to accomplish what Lou had asked me for.

Lou was laid to rest at Long Island National Cemetery.

We talked on the phone about twelve hours before he died. We both said, "I love you."

Eleven

SEE IT THROUGH TO THE END

On our way back from Albany, we get pulled over. It's me, Matt McCauley, Rich Palmer, and Michael O'Connell in Matt's SUV. Matt's driving one hundred past a state trooper, who turns his lights on and pulls us over.

Matt says, "Don't worry, I got this."

He gets his badge out along with his license and registration.

The trooper approaches. Matt rolls down his window. Rich has "got this" too. He takes his badge out and says, "Excuse me, Trooper, sir, I'm a retired deputy warden . . ."

The trooper goes, "Yeah . . ."

O'Connell rolls down his window and shows his ID. "Sir, I'm a lieutenant with the FDNY, retired. We're coming back from Albany. We just got a bill passed for first responders."

The trooper looks at me and says, "And what's your story?"

"Sir, I got nothing, I'm a civilian. My name is John Feal from the FealGood Foundation."

"Oh my God. Mr. Feal, I'm in the health program. Thank you so much for everything you've done."

Needless to say, we get off with a warning. As we're driving away, nobody says anything, and I'm dying to rub it in.

Finally, I say, "Badges? We don't need no stinkin' badges."

Heading into the vote, I have to go see Crenshaw and apologize for the way my guys dragged him through the papers. I also have to win his vote. I do the thing I teach my guys to do in every meeting—I listen so that I can understand where he's coming from and meet him at his level. Hearing him out proves essential, because I learn that the congressman has been fed bad information and deliberately misled. His main issue with the bill is "all the fraud," to use his words. Luckily, I have documentation and sworn expert testimony that shows there has been zero fraud, and the few isolated attempts to exploit the program have been caught before any awards were given. This was an ugly slander against the 9/11 community, and one that might ring true for a Texan who may already have a dim view of a liberal East Coast metropolis.

The meeting goes well. Crenshaw is a good man whose love and devotion to his country is undeniable. Lt. Commander Crenshaw of SEAL Team 3 lost an eye in our nation's response to the attacks of September 11. He could give a master class to his colleagues on sacrifice and duty. I come to this meeting with no animosity toward the man, but I'm full of rage that he would be misled and manipulated by party operatives who oppose this bill. We shake hands, and he signs on as a co-sponsor. We stay in touch, and for about a year, he calls me every Friday to talk about life and politics. I give him a hard time, tell him he does a lot of complaining for a big, tough frogman.

Not everyone can be moved by common sense and decency. When all else fails, threatening their career will get their attention. Congressmen want to stay congressmen, and sometimes it pays to remind them of looming midterms.

Speaker Paul Ryan was in office until January 2019, just long enough to be a pain in the ass and a vocal #WorstResponder, to quote *The Daily Show*. I went to see him with Rafael Orozco, aka "The Preacher" or "Puerto Rican Jesus," a retired NYPD civil affairs officer and devout Christian with a touch for politics. Typically, when I'm with Raf, we do good cop/bad cop, where I'm the bad cop, and Raf is "the balm," to quote the book of Jeremiah, as he is so fond of doing, particularly with congressmen who have Bible verses on their walls. But with Ryan, Raf went out of character, as all the guys do eventually after they hear enough bullshit and watch me get results by going rogue. I was there, hat in hand, hearing Ryan out when Raf snapped and decided this was just nonsense.

He interrupted "This is total nonsense. You know what, all we have to do is have a group of people move into hotels in your district for thirty-one days, and then we can register to vote in your election. I already know how to run campaigns. I can guarantee the press will eat this up. We could run a freakin' refrigerator against you, man. And it won't matter if we win or lose, you're going to have to waste so much money and effort."

Raf was yelling. I had never heard him raise his voice.

When Ryan's people called back later, the first thing we asked them was: what do we tell all the people who stepped up to rent hotel rooms in the Speaker's district?

"No, no, no, tell them they won't have to do that."

Unbelievably, his staff had taken the threat very seriously and had been freaking out. We had shown up desperate for his support and now had the upper hand, as the ranking GOP member would do anything to avoid the scenario Raf had described.

Lou checks into hospice immediately after the hearing. Matt McCauley goes to see him and suggests one last way to help get the bill passed. "What do you think about giving Mitch McConnell your shield?"

He asks if Lou has a "dupe," cop-speak for an extra shield. Detectives use their dupes and put the originals away, so they don't lose them. That's important because Lou isn't giving his shield to anyone if it means not having one to give to his kids.

"Of course I have a dupe."

"Would you give it to Mitch?"

"That's a great fucking idea. He'll never be able to say 'no.'"

So, McCauley brings me the shield along with a note Lou wrote to the senator:

I want you to know that my time to leave this world is fast approaching.

My goal and legacy in this world was to see the VCF bill passed.

The senator agrees to a meeting under one condition: We do not bring Jon Stewart. No AR-15s this time, no Capitol Police chaperones. Our plan is to talk first, and if things go south, I will end it with a vengeance. We want to go outside and tell everybody that McConnell is a co-signer for the bill. If he won't get on board, we'll go out and tell people that. We let him know those are his options. Kenny speaks—he's a die-hard Trump supporter, but nobody is more loyal to our cause, and nobody runs a meeting like Kenny. A couple of the guys follow with brief remarks. Then McConnell goes to speak.

I say, "No. Mitch, it's my turn. There are a few things I need to get off my chest. I've been coming down here for years, and I'm tired. We are tired."

I keep going for about seven minutes. He tries to interrupt. I feel Lou's shield in my hand.

"Give me your word, Senator, that when we leave here, you're behind this."

He says nothing.

"Give me your word that you're going to support this and put it on the floor before your summer recess."

I reach out to shake his hand, and I press Lou's shield into his palm.

"This is from Lou Alvarez. He's gone now, and this is his shield. If it were up to me, I wouldn't give it to you. You're not worthy of it. But Lou wanted you to have it, not as a gift but as a reminder of your responsibility."

We watch as the blood drains from his face and he goes white. His eyes well up. Sensing the intensity of the moment, a stupid staffer gets up and approaches with the stupid blank-piece-of-paper trick, but the senator raises a hand to shoo her away.

"I've gotta go outside and talk to those cameras. What do you want me to tell them?"

"You have my word."

We go outside where there's like a hundred cameras in our faces. I tell them McConnell and I will never agree on politics, but we've come to an agreement on this bill, and he's kept his word, which is the best compliment I can give him. I vent, to the cameras, to the country.

"Look at these guys, they're not pretty . . . Yeah, I'm frustrated. I've been to 181 funerals. I'm about to go to 182."

On Fox with Jon Stewart, I tell them about Mitch's tears: "He may not have a soul in there, but he's made of water just like everybody else."

The papers will point out the tremendous significance of Lou's gesture, that a detective's shield is like a vital organ. It's a good analogy, because as Lou demonstrated in the way he spent his last days, he was someone who would have carved the bill from his flesh if he could have.

After our meeting with Mitch, the dominos start to fall. Liz Cheney's (R-WY) break with her party proves decisive—she calls the bill a "no-brainer." Soon Susan Collins (R-ME) is on board, and others soon follow.

Bill Clark, a photographer, will snap an iconic photo of McConnell walking down the marble hall to roll call ahead of the Senate vote. Jon Stewart stands off to the side, looking straight at the camera with a shit-eating grin, wearing an FDNY T-shirt.

Going into the vote, we have overwhelming bipartisan support: 333 sponsors in the House and 76 in the Senate. Those numbers really mean something when you look back on the work it took to get them on our side. On July 12, 2019, thirteen days after Lou left us, Congress voted to pass the renamed "Never Forget the Heroes: James Zadroga, Ray Pfeifer, and Luis Alvarez Permanent Authorization of the September 11th Victim Compensation Fund Act." I made some bets we'd be over four hundred. Peter King paid me a dollar; Anthony Weiner paid me a dollar. I had to explain to Nancy Pelosi how over/under works—she still owes me a dollar.

The bill passes by 410 to 12. I watch it from a TV in Schumer's office, right down the hall from the chamber where the vote is taking place. The members come in and out. Some give me dirty looks, I stare them down, a blank look on my face: *They're the ones who should be nervous.* I have no reaction when it passes. I can count. I knew it was going to pass. The group comes down the hall, Jon and the guys.

We hug. I fucking lose it. All these years. All this work. The funerals, the surgeries, the friends who aren't here anymore, the people who will never be the same again. It feels like I can finally exhale. Somebody snaps a great picture of me and Jon crying and hugging and smiling. The hearing back in June had felt like such a triumph for everybody, but I was quick to point out at the time that it wasn't over, we couldn't ease up. Now, it feels like I can finally let my guard down.

On July 23 the bill passes in the Senate by a vote of 97 to 2. The two are Rand Paul (R-KY) and Mike Lee (R-UT). It would have gone straight to the president from the House by unanimous consent if it weren't for these two profiles in cowardice. Their comments in favor of blocking the vote are too asinine to repeat. Mike Lee rehashes fantasies of fraud. Rand Paul wants an amendment to offset the cost. Both drone on about debt, an issue that hadn't stopped them from approving Trump's tax cuts, which added hundreds of billions to the deficit.

On NBC, Stewart calls this what it is: "Pardon me if I'm not impressed in any way by Rand Paul's fiscal responsibility virtue signaling."

Special master of the fund, Rupa Bhattacharyya, who testified on the panel with Stewart, speaks to the thorough background checks and verification standards already in place, which include FBI background checks for all recipients (a concession to Republicans from an earlier version of the bill) and verification from third parties to prove presence and eligibility. She says, "The VCF under the Zadroga Act has not documented any instance of fraud in a paid claim."

Having to defend the program and justify the existence of the fund, even after the House passes its permanent reauthorization and funding, is frustrating. Stewart sets an example with his humorous dismissal of these clowns, telling reporters that he "hopes Paul finds his libertarian paradise."

All I can manage is what I tell *Fox & Friends*: "They [Lee and Paul] have no humanity."

I call them bottom-feeders and assholes on the air. I apologize for my language to Alisyn Camerota and John Berman.

If you watch me and Jon on *Fox & Friends*, we both look so tired.

A little while later, the phone rings. The White House is calling. The operator connects Rudy Giuliani's son, who's working for the president. I hand the phone to Rich Palmer and loudly say, "Here, Rich, you can talk to this clown."

They were giving away 250 tickets to the Rose Garden signing and asked us how many we wanted. We took 100. The rest went to VCF attorneys and law firms, and unions, some who were with us through it all, some who just made a buck off the work of guys who walked the halls of Congress on oxygen.

Some people can put their anger to one side and just enjoy a day like today for what it is and get back into the fray tomorrow. I'm not one of those people. It's hot in the Rose Garden. We've been standing around waiting for the president. This day has come nearly two decades too late for so many of us. I don't know how to turn it off, so I don't. We got what we wanted, and I'm still so angry. It took so long. So many good people died or went broke or lost their minds. I'm in no mood for the fanfare.

Mike Pence comes over. Somebody says, "Let's get a picture of you with the vice president."

I say, "I'm good."

The VP, who calls his wife "mother," grins through the awkward silence that follows. He shakes my hand. "Congratulations, you did a really good job."

I don't let go. "You were a senator in 2015. You voted against the bill in 2015. What changed between now and 2015?"

He gets this smug look on his face like he's about to blow me away with the profoundness of what he's going to say. "Well, for one thing, the urgency."

"Mike, do I look dumb? It wasn't urgent in 2015? People weren't dying in 2015 or 2010? Wasn't it urgent for Ray Pfeifer?"

He smiles and nods and walks away to go smile at someone else.

Finally, President Trump comes out.

From where I'm standing, I can see the massive letters on the teleprompter. He speaks about the courage of the responders and ad-libs these extravagant, self-seeking, untruthful asides: "I was down there (at Ground Zero) and I saw what you went through, firsthand, and it was big league."

He repeats a pet lie of his, that he sent 250 of his employees to help out on the Pile. To my knowledge, nobody in the Trump organization is in the health program. He didn't go to hundreds of 9/11 funerals—there's no record of him going to a single one. He did not see Muslim Americans celebrating the attack from his window in Trump Tower as he would claim on the campaign trail. He did, however, brag on live TV on the day of the attack about the height of one of his buildings, saying "Forty Wall Street actually was the second tallest building in downtown Manhattan [which wasn't true to begin with] . . . now it's the tallest." We've had nearly twenty years of politicians and public figures using that horrible day as their little flag to wave, but nobody knows how to make it all about himself like that guy.

He rambles for a while. I keep thinking, *hurry up.*

When he's finished, he invites responders up to the signing of the bill. Everybody crowds around his desk. I walk up there slowly, and people make room for me. He signs. I'm standing next to Joe Zadroga, James Zadroga's father. There are guys with cancer on the other side of me. He reaches out and shakes my hand. He tries to squeeze; I squeeze back. He's got a handshake like mashed potatoes. He hands me the pen and says, "Nobody deserves this pen more than you."

All the faces and names flash through my mind, guys I can think of who deserve it more than me. I think it; I don't say it.

I say, "Thank you, sir, that's an honor."

He's not finished: "You, you are going to be famous."

"Sir, I don't want to be famous."

"No, you and your friend are always on TV."

"My friend?" He won't say Jon Stewart's name.

"You know the guy. But, listen, you're going to be famous. I just have a feeling about you."

It's a weird encounter. It's weird that it's over. I'm tired. I'm so tired—207 funerals at this point and counting.

The day we got the bill passed and knew we were going to the White House, I gathered everybody in the parking lot. We took a group picture, then I got everyone around me in a huddle.

"I'm going to be serious for a minute. What you did is historic. What you did, nobody can take away from you. This was your moment.

"You guys were all farmers. You were forced to put down your rakes, and I asked you to pick up your swords. But today, I want you to put down your swords. Go home. Pick up your rake again, plant something, and watch it grow with your family in the time you have left."

ACTION FOR ACTIVISTS: PREPARE TO WIN

What does winning look like? What will you do after you achieve what you set out to accomplish? This is a vulnerable moment for any movement, and it's a time to be careful and stay focused. You need to be ready to win and ready to defend what you've gained. You don't have to go back very far in the history of American democracy to find examples of times when we prematurely declared that we had conquered some social problem once and for all, or finally put some ugly outdated attitude like racism behind us, only to have it come back with a vengeance. Hard-won rights that we now take for granted can be taken away with a show of hands from Supreme Court justices who are appointed along partisan lines. These are features, not bugs, of American democracy. And there is no shortage of people eager to exploit them. So, anybody in the business of activism has to be ready for a rematch. Your opponents will be doing push-ups while you toast to your accomplishment.

But that's not to say you shouldn't celebrate your wins. Take the time to recognize your accomplishments and the work that got you there. Express gratitude to your team. Be the person you didn't let yourself be in meetings and press conferences; take some time to breathe. Celebrate your small wins too. Even if you have a long way to go, the morale boost from that celebration could carry you through the next slog and on to the next victory.

Most activists spend more time thinking about how to handle setbacks than how to handle success. Winning can be just as draining as defeat. There is always a comedown, and normal life can feel dull and meaningless compared to the battle you've just been in. As any veteran will tell you, coming home is the hardest part. Give yourself time to adjust, and stay connected to people who get what you're going through. The good news/bad news is there will always be another fight, more wrongs to right. So if you, like me, don't know how to "pick up your rake," there is plenty of work to be done.

Testimony

DANIELLE ROBINSON

I wasn't sure how I felt about a long-distance relationship, and I really wasn't sure about a long-distance relationship between Ohio and Iraq. But Heath and I decided to give it a shot.

Danielle Robinson is the widow of Sgt. First Class Heath Robinson, Ohio National Guard, for whom the Heath Robinson PACT Act (aka the Burn Pits bill) is named.

I was a student at Ohio State at the time, and Heath was a soldier in the Ohio National Guard who I had met between his deployments to Kosovo and Iraq. He asked me out right before he deployed. I sent him care packages and didn't get my hopes up too much. He came home for two weeks at one point, it happened to be over Valentine's Day. There was a huge blizzard that caused Ohio State to cancel classes for the first time in like twenty years. So, we had a little stay-at-home date. I couldn't wait for him to get home for good, and when he did, we made up for lost time and had a really good year. Then I got into a program for physical therapy, and it was back to long-distance while I went to Youngstown State. Heath went back to part-time National Guard duty, "one weekend a month, two weeks a year," like they say in the recruiting ads. He was running a locksmithing business and attending the Ohio Fire Marshal Academy to become an EMT and firefighter. Around the same time, he found a full-time job with the army and ended up going with that instead.

I graduated my program and started working as a physical therapist; Heath proposed, we got married, and had our daughter. Life was so good. We were enjoying being young parents, watching Ohio State football, and staying close with his National Guard buddies and their families. He trained for NCO of the Year and won it. It was a grueling process: physical tests, specialized shooting drills, navigation with a compass, and a two-hour written test. He took it so seriously, training all the time and quizzing himself constantly. He ended up going to regionals but placing second due to a meniscus injury that hurt his running time. He wanted to try a third time for nationals.

He was getting ready to run a half marathon and noticed he was starting to get short of breath on the last miles. This was in August 2016. He had two weeks of Guard training down in Georgia, and he started to have nosebleeds when he was down there, which he blamed on the climate. But the nosebleeds kept coming when he was home. I insisted he go to the doctor; they did a workup on him and his blood cell count came back normal. At the same time, he was starting to feel fatigued, and his one-rep maxes were lower in the gym. The doctors told him it was probably just that he was getting older. It got to where he was sleeping all hours when he wasn't at work. This wasn't a midlife slowdown. They ran more tests and referred him to an autoimmune disease specialist at Ohio State who diagnosed him with a rare condition that causes the body to attack the epithelial linings in your body, like inside your nose and mouth. It's normally something they see in patients in their seventies. He would have to deal with it for life, but it would be manageable with steroids. Then he lost his voice. They did a CT scan, and that's when they saw his lymph nodes were all huge. It was time to see an oncologist.

Anyone who's been given a cancer diagnosis knows how hard it is to focus on what the doctor is saying and take it all in. You go into tunnel vision. The first thing he said really stands out because of what a shock it was to us at the time and how obvious it seemed to the doctor.

He said, "What have you been exposed to?"

We were incredibly lucky that the doctor was from the Middle East and had spent a lot of time over there. He made the connection right away. He told us the way Heath's cancer is presenting could only be due to toxic exposure. I could see Heath racking his brain. We both said we didn't know, and we asked if we should test our home. I thought radon maybe; I worried about our little girl. And then the doctor said:

"I want you guys to prepare yourselves because, if we don't get this under control, you have four to six weeks to live."

At that, the doctor started tearing up. He had read Heath's whole file and knew we had a three-year-old daughter at home. After giving us a few minutes to process, he pulled out the bell curve of survival that showed Heath having a max of five years if he responds to immunotherapy and/or chemo; eighteen months was more likely. Heath said he was up for anything they could throw at him. He wanted to tackle this head-on, just like everything else in his life. That was on a Friday. At six o'clock on Monday morning, we were starting his chemo, with the most aggressive kind they could give him.

Over the weekend, before his treatment started, a military spouse sent me an article about burn pits. I read it and read it again.

I went downstairs and asked him: "Heath, were you around a burn pit at all on your deployments?"

"Yeah. We all were."

This was my first time hearing about burn pits. He never mentioned them in his letters and calls. I had accepted that he could be killed in action, or even in training. He was a soldier; that's part of the job. I accepted that his service meant missing our daughter's birth and my graduation and weddings and funerals for loved ones. These are sacrifices soldiers and their spouses make as part of their service. And men like Heath would sacrifice more if they could. I accepted that being his wife and sharing my life with him meant duty and service would come first. Always. But I also believed that once he came home, he was safe. His war was over. He stepped down off that transport plane, walked across the tarmac and into my arms, and we got back to living our lives together.

Back at the clinic, Heath told the doctor that he had guard duty for three months about twenty yards from a burn pit. That proximity and duration meant his exposure was extremely high. The doctor told us that made sense. He told us about the lethal combination of toxins and how it was exactly like the dust exposure from 9/11 that was killing first responders. He said veterans would be getting sick over the next ten, fifteen, twenty years. The signature of these cancers was that there was no primary tumor, which is normally where doctors focus their treatment. Heath's cancer was everywhere: all the through the lining of his lungs and the pericardium sac of his heart. It was in his esophagus. But it hadn't started in any one place that was clear to the doctors. This was exactly what they were starting to see in cancer patients with burn pit exposure.

While Heath was fighting for his life and we were dealing with our personal, family tragedy, big things were happening nationwide in research and legislation around burn pits. A woman in Texas, Rosie Torres, whose husband was sick from burn pit exposure, was organizing a movement from their garage: Burn Pits 360. Doctors and scientists were doing research. In 2015, a year before Heath got sick, Vice President Joe Biden's son, Beau Biden, died of brain cancer linked to burn pit exposure. Beau had been stationed at Camp Victory, part of the Liberty/Victory complex where Heath was stationed, their deployments a year apart.

Heath was luckier than some, because at least the VA acknowledged that his illness was 100 percent service related, but we still had issues.

The VA didn't provide us with caregiver benefits, they declined medications, and delayed imaging. The acknowledgment of the burn pit connection was already there in Heath's case, and they were still fighting us.

We lost Heath in May 2020. Right up to the end, he was an example to everyone around him and a real anchor to our family, our friend group, and our community. He was never too sick to make us laugh, even at the very end when his quality of life was so poor and his oxygen levels were borderline for maintaining consciousness, his focus was always on the people he loved. He coached our daughter's soccer while he was undergoing treatment, he helped a friend build a deck, and he painted a gym at the armory for his guys. The pain he went through to extend his life, all so he could have a little more time with her and with me. They had to puncture his lungs for a special type of radiation, and they had to do it while he was awake. He just fought through the pain. As Brielle grows up, that drive, that will to keep going with a smile on your face no matter what, that is what I want her to remember about her father.

In September of 2020, I got in touch with John and Jon [Feal and Stewart]. At this time, the veterans were getting the same pushback and denial the 9/11 responders had experienced. John and Jon were helping us organize and fight for burn pit legislation using their blueprint for the 9/11 bill. They told us it was going to be a long fight, and we would have to be committed.

"The train's leaving the station. We're getting this bill passed," John said, speaking to a group of veterans and their families. "You're either onboard, or you get off the train now."

I was on board.

They asked me to tell Heath's story outside the Capitol. I kept coming to DC. My daughter came with me when she wasn't in school. I was working full-time, raising a daughter, and grieving. When I was home, I got on virtual meetings with the burn pit groups. Things would go quiet between trips or while Congress was on a recess, then one day my phone would blow up with calls from John. One day, I was treating patients, so

I wasn't picking up. John called my mom who called the front desk at my work. They told me my mom was on the line; it's not an emergency but I needed to answer right away. I got back to John.

"You need to call Jon Stewart right now."

"I don't have Jon Stewart's number, John."

"Alright. If I give it to you, you need to swear not to give it to anybody."

He gave me the number. I called Jon Stewart.

"Danielle, good to hear from you. What are you doing tomorrow?"

"Ummm . . . Treating patients."

"Well, what if I told you the First Lady wants you to come up to be her guest at the State of the Union?"

I was speechless, I immediately thought he was pranking me. It was close to April Fool's Day. I had no heads-up, nothing.

"Are you still there? So, listen, what time are you getting off work? I'll call you then and we'll go through a bunch of stuff and get you cleared through White House security. We're going to fly you out and put you up in a hotel."

"Okay. Sounds good, Jon. I'll call you when I'm off work."

That was a whirlwind, going to the State of the Union, siting in the First Lady's box. After that came the signing and naming of the bill. That was another memorable call from John. My daughter and I were out at sea on a Disney Cruise we had planned to go on as a family while Heath was still with us. Wherever we were on the ocean there happened to be cell coverage, but it was spotty. I couldn't hear John very well, but he said something about a meeting next week.

"Senator Schumer wants you there . . . Just be there, and bring your daughter. The senator wants both of you there."

So, we finished up our cruise and headed to Washington where we went to a press conference with Jon Stewart and Senator Schumer. And that's where they announced the bill would be named the "Sergeant First Class Heath Robinson Honoring Our Promise to Address

Comprehensive Toxics (PACT) Act." I was totally blindsided and felt so many emotions all at once. It was an honor, but I immediately thought of what Heath would say, that there are all these other veterans who might be more deserving. I thought of one guy in particular who fought hard for the bill, walking the halls of Congress with a double lung transplant before his illness took him. And the more I thought about it, I started to feel this overwhelming sense of responsibility to help make this bill as good as it could possibly be. I was going to give this bill 110 percent, because that's what Heath did with everything. There was a lot of work to be done; we had to fight for this bill in the House and the Senate. It was the kind of all-in suffer-fest of grit and endurance in the name of a good cause Heath would have absolutely loved.

Twelve

PICK UP YOUR RAKE, PUT DOWN YOUR SWORD

When I was in the hospital, the first time, when the docs were trying to save my foot, there was a nurse who was always singing "The Wheels on the Bus" to a kid somewhere on the ward when she did her rounds. She had the most incredible singing voice, even singing this silly kids' song.

One day, when she was checking on me, I said to her, "No 'Wheels on the Bus' today? I missed hearing your beautiful voice."

She said, "That little boy passed away last night."

Fuck.

Now whenever someone asks me my favorite song, I always say, "The Wheels on the Bus." At one point someone on Twitter asks, and it becomes a thing among my fans and trolls alike. When someone wants to tweet at me and I don't reply, they come back with, *@TheJohnFeal9117's favorite song is "Wheels on the Bus."* One day, I tell the story behind that, and it blows up.

There are more bad times in life than good, if you ask me. And if you think otherwise, wait. Through all this death and grief and loss, I haven't thought much about the afterlife or where exactly my friends have gone. If you haven't noticed by now, I like war-fighting analogies, and my concept of an afterlife is borrowed from the Vikings who believed in Valhalla, a heaven reserved for warriors who died in battle. If there is such a place, Ray is there, and Lou, and those responders under the Pile we couldn't get to. I have no choice but to seek out new battles so I can join them there one day. Until then, when I'm having a bad day, I think about what they would trade to have just one more bad day, and I stop feeling sorry for myself.

Back in 2007, not long after I started the foundation, I got an email offering me an opportunity to be helpful in a way I never imagined. The sender was giving me the chance to give a stranger the gift of life. Paul Grossfeld, from New Jersey, thanked me for the work I was doing and asked if he could put his story on my website: He was looking for a kidney. He told me he wanted to see his son, who was in eighth grade, grow up and graduate and get married. He wanted the FealGood Foundation to get the word out.

I called him up. I told him I can't put his story on the website because that dilutes what the website is for.

"But I'll tell you what, you can have my kidney."

He said something like, "Don't fuck with me."

"No, I'm serious, you can have my kidney."

"Why would you do that."

"Why wouldn't I?"

There was a long pause before he said, "If you're serious, you can meet me in person and we'll talk next steps."

Two weeks later, I met him at Columbia Presbyterian. Now, I'm never late for anything. If I'm half an hour early, I consider that late. But there was bad traffic getting through the Bronx. The whole time, he was texting and calling, thinking I stood him up. Finally, I got there, and they tested both of us. I was compatible but not a perfect match, and he wasn't ready for a kidney. Two or three weeks after that, Columbia Presbyterian called me to say that if I give my kidney to somebody else, they will make sure Paul gets a better one. I was delighted. I got to keep my word to Paul and help two people instead of just one. I told them that, and they said they liked my spirit. From there, it was a long process, complete with a psych test—which by some miracle I passed.

Did anybody offer you money?

No.

Have you been threatened?

No.

Do you want to kill yourself?

Not lately. I just want to help people.

In the middle of this drawn-out process, the hospital brought up the idea of a six-person swap, where we crisscross donors and recipients to help more people. I liked the sounds of that. It had been done at Johns Hopkins, and they were eager to try it. The three-way swap would be newsworthy and hopefully inspire others to become kidney donors.

On August 30, 2007, we did the surgery. About a month later, we all met for the first time. My kidney went to a woman in Connecticut.

Three strangers get the gift of life from pieces they carve out of me and five other donors. And what do I get in return? I get to remain human.

Most of my adult life was shaped by an act of destruction perpetrated by fanatics who thought mass murder was their ticket to paradise. I spent two decades fighting elected officials who cared more about money, power, and their own careers than human life. By giving life, by trying to help others when I can, I chose humanity. I remain human.

At the end of the day, 9/11 will not define me. I won't let it. My mother's love is what defines me. Everything I've done was an attempt to follow her big-hearted example. She never would have cared about my salary, my title, or any awards or publicity around my work. All she would want to know is who have I helped?

At a press conference following the hearing in 2019, Stewart turns to me from the podium and says, "I will follow you anywhere." It isn't long before I take him up on that offer. One day the phone rings, a woman named Rosie Torres is calling from Texas, where she has been working from a home office in her garage, tracking and documenting illness among veterans exposed to burn pits during their deployments. She learned about the World Trade Center Health Program when googling some of the chemicals her husband, LeRoy, had been exposed to while deployed to Camp Anaconda at Balad Airbase in Iraq. A quick search of the toxins found in air sampling of US bases brought up the same chemicals from samples of the dust and the smoke plume at Ground Zero. Further googling brought up pictures of me and Phil Rizzo talking to senators, Congresswoman Maloney wearing a bunker coat in committee, Stewart's testimony in 2019, the triumphant group shot after we finally got our bill passed. She said to herself, "Those are the guys we need on our side."

Up until this point, Rosie had been doing what I had done in the early days, stacking documents and reports, answering the phone all hours, and building a network of sick and dying people who were being ignored. Her husband had called her from downrange complaining of fatigue, headaches, and shortness of breath. The army threatened to accuse him of malingering, a very serious charge. Thousands of our troops were going through the same thing. They were getting sick and being told they were faking it. Rosie started collecting their stories and meeting with experts in toxic exposure to build a case she could take to Washington. She founded Burn Pits 360, a grassroots action group. As soon as she found out about our work on the 9/11 bill, she called a friend at Fox who had covered the burn pits. She gave Rosie my number.

Then she called me and gave me a summary of her decade of work.

"We've already done all of the work, we just need you to help us finish this."

I tell her I'll call Jon Stewart and get back to her.

The United States Army field manual outlines five ways to dispose of nontoxic solid waste: incineration, burial, landfilling, tactical burial, and burn pits. The manual states, "Within the U.S. all solid waste generated during field exercises must be backhauled to garrison or picked up by contractors." In Iraq and Afghanistan, the DOD opted for burn pits to dispose of solid waste both toxic and nontoxic.

So, what was in the burn pits? The answer is the same as the 9/11 dust: *everything*. Everything an army base consumes and discards—human feces; food waste; Styrofoam; paint; petroleum and lubricating products; munitions and unexploded ordinance; rubber; aluminum cans; plastic in many forms; uniforms and clothing, which are often made of Gore-Tex, which contains PFAS or "forever chemicals"; and medical waste. They used jet fuel to ignite these toxic mixtures, releasing the same carcinogens and alkaline compounds as at Ground Zero and forging new compounds through combustion. Some of the burn pits, on remote outposts, were small like backyard firepits. The larger Forward Operating Bases (FOBs) and air bases had enormous burn pits. The one on Joint Base Balad, where Rosie's husband was exposed, covered ten acres, or eight football fields. These super burn pits operated like town dumps, with bulldozers pushing waste into the flames, drivers choking on the smoke. They burned 24/7.

Some of the worst exposure was among service members whose jobs kept them behind the wire and relatively safe from combat. The engineers who built and maintained the large burn pits spent their whole deployments being continuously exposed. And as with post-9/11 healthcare, there were civilians in harm's way who would ultimately have a harder time proving their presence and eligibility for care than those in uniform. These included civilian contractors, employees of the CIA, DIA (Defense Intelligence Agency), State Department, and other government agencies, civilian firefighters who kept the fires from burning out of control, and of course contractors working for Pizza Hut, Subway, Popeye's, Cinnabon, and other franchises that operated on American FOBs in a surreal effort to bring a slice of America and the comforts of home to foreign war zones.

And the locals suffered, too, of course. Between poor air quality and all that sand blowing around, Iraq already has high rates of childhood asthma and other respiratory illnesses. Now add toxic burn pits to the mix. There would be no VA benefits for the locals, no way to sue the American government or have their day in court.

The illnesses linked to burn pit exposure will all sound familiar: brain cancer, kidney cancer, melanoma, all the respiratory cancers, asthma, COPD, chronic rhinitis and sinusitis, sarcoidosis, pulmonary fibrosis, and many others. Burn pit cancer is like an insurgency in the body: everywhere and nowhere. A hallmark of these cancers is that there's often no primary tumor, making them much harder to catch in time and treat.

As with 9/11 cancer, the powers that be are more interested in protecting themselves and the government from liability than dealing with the consequences of a policy that anyone with the most basic understanding of air pollution could tell you was bound to end in disaster.

I call Rosie back. "Listen, I can help you, but you're going to have to do this my way or not at all."

"What's your way?"

"Okay, first thing. I need you to promise that you're not going to take 'no' for an answer."

"You got it."

"Next thing, and I'm going to tell all your people this: Buy a treadmill. We're not going to DC once, not twice. We're going again and again until they do the right thing."

"Let's go."

We go to DC. Rosie brings her guys. Just like my guys, the best ones are falling apart. They're on oxygen. One dude is throwing up blood and has been told by the army that he's faking it. Just like the 9/11 responders, the elected officials pushing back the hardest are the ones who tweet the loudest about supporting our troops. Those flag-waving fucks.

I have no doubt these people are going to get their bill, with a little help. Their worst enemy, when I start working with them, is themselves. The various VSOs (Veteran Service Organizations) are negotiating against each other and against themselves on this issue. They're setting themselves up for a compromise that isn't going to help the people who need it most. The VSOs were creating disorder in the movement by approaching the problem in silos: the VHA (Veterans Health Administration) had been focusing on health while the VBA (Veterans Benefits Administration) was focusing on benefits, without a common purpose or stated goal. We get them working on the same page and make priorities clear. Healthcare has to come first, because people are sick and dying, and they can't wait. But just as important, especially for those who aren't sick yet, is presumptive causation. We drill our sound bites, just like the 9/11 responders: *We no longer have to prove the burn pits made us sick; you have to prove the burn pits* didn't *make us sick.*

These service members and their families take a unique, military-inspired approach to making their presence known to Congress. On the night of July 28, 2022, Burn Pits 360 teams up with the Grunt Style Foundation to host an overnight "fire watch" on the steps of the Capitol, "camping out" in civilian terms.

Earlier that day, twenty-five Republicans flip their votes, effectively killing the bill over a budgeting technicality in the revised language of the legislation—and GOP retaliation for an unrelated bill. They now have until the August recess to get it passed.

I tell Rosie, "We need to scorch the earth."

She organizes the fire watch.

One of the flip-floppers, who Stewart will do a hilarious impersonation of in a press conference, is none other than Mitch McConnell, who looks a war hero from his home state of Kentucky in the eye and says, "We'll get it done," before flipping his vote.

Sometimes politicians find their conscience on their way out the door and act righteously when free of the pressure to seek reelection. Others "step in a pot of gold," to use Stewart's idiom. That seems to have been the case with Senator Pat Toomey (R–PA), the architect of the flip.

We're all livid.

Senator Gillibrand tells the press, "There's no excuse, it's total BS."

I go on Andrea Mitchell's show and say "Toomey, I hope your wife divorces you and your dog bites you."

Mitchell stares at the camera, stunned, and then cuts to a commercial break.

Jon Stewart speaks to the media. I know this is going to be explosive. We've just come from a meeting where he went rogue, full-on bad cop for a change, laying into Senator Shelby from Alabama and his "brain trust," so angry that I didn't have a chance to speak up or cut him off. He uses words that make me blush—and a little jealous. I defuse it, and before the meeting's over, we get them on board and shake hands.

In the hall, I say to Stewart, "What was that?" This is not how we operate. He's supposed to be in command of rhetoric, a man of letters. He doesn't need to swear or lose his temper. If he were just one of the guys, I would send him home. Now, for the first time in all my years working with him, I'm actually nervous about what he's going to say to the cameras.

He takes to the podium:

> *America's heroes, who fought our wars outside, sweating their asses off with oxygen, battling all kinds of ailments while these motherfuckers sit in the air-conditioning walled off from any of it. They don't have to hear it. They don't have to see it. They don't have to understand that these are*

human beings . . . I . . . I . . . I don't even know, honestly, I don't even know what to say. I've been coming down here ten, fifteen years. I'm used to the hypocrisy . . . I'm used to the cowardice. I've been here a long time.

The Senate is where accountability goes to die.

These people don't care.

He goes on to point out the most frustrating thing: They already passed the bill before they took it away.

. . . 84 to 14, you don't even see those scores in the Senate anymore . . .

Every one of these individuals that has been fighting for years standing on the shoulders of Vietnam veterans who have been fighting for years, standing on the shoulders of Persian Gulf War veterans fighting for years, Desert Storm veterans to just get the healthcare and benefits that they earned from their service. And I don't care if they were fighting for our freedom. I don't care if they were fighting for the flag. I don't care if they were fighting 'cause they wanted to get out of a drug treatment center, or it was jail or the army. I don't give a shit. They lived up to their oath and yesterday they [the Senate] spat on it. So they can't leave until this gets done because these people will not give up. They will not give in and they will not relent. This is an embarrassment to the Senate, to the country, to the founders and all that they profess to hold dear. And if this is America first, then America is fucked.

The veterans keep watch while Jon and I go to meet with Speaker Pelosi. She and I have stayed in touch through the years. She sent me flowers when I had hip surgery. She gets us a meeting with Congressmen Mark Takano and Raul Ruiz. If the Speaker gives you ten, fifteen minutes, that's a big deal. She gives us an hour. Between the heat and the pressure to get this done for those men and women who aren't leaving until we do, I am sweating and emotional. For forty-five minutes of that hour-long meeting, Speaker Pelosi holds my hand and doesn't let go.

Her presence soothes me. She wears this perfume that's indescribably lovely. The meeting goes well. Stewart and I are more relaxed than we were going in.

When we're out in the hall and it's just the two of us, Stewart leans over and says to me, "So... What's the story with you two?"

I turn red, and as soon as I recover from being doubled over laughing, I kick him in the shin with my work boots. It's like he crossed a line. He might as well be talking about my mother. But oh my God, is that man funny.

On August 2, 2022, the bill passes the Senate by 86 to 11. On August 10, the PACT Act is signed into law by President Joe Biden, whose son Beau died of brain cancer linked to burn pit exposure. I had a meeting with Schumer beforehand and told him the bill needed a name, because, as I told him, as Ben Chevat once told me, "When you give a bill a name, you give it a pulse." The Sergeant First Class Heath Robinson Honoring Our Promise to Address Comprehensive Toxics Act of 2022 covers healthcare and environmental health screenings for over three million veterans. The bill took just a year and a half, using a recipe that took us twenty years to perfect.

When the veterans finally stand down, having got their bill, I gather them around and give them the same rake speech I gave my guys in 2019. This time I add one important caveat from personal experience: "Some of you will go home and find that you can't pick up your rake. This work gave you purpose and meaning again, and you don't want to give that up. The bill will need you to defend it."

I have the words "hired gun" tattooed on my neck. I will use our recipe to help anyone with a worthy cause who's willing to pay my per diem: one bottle of water.

Stewart once said to me, "I hope one day, you take a step back and appreciate what you've done."

"Someday," I said, "but not now."

He knows I'm not ready to pick up my rake, and he keeps asking, "When are we going back?" All I can say is, given the way things are going in government, probably sooner than either of us would like.

I go where I'm needed, and sometimes that means going to the 9/11 Memorial Museum, where the Twin Towers once stood, for events, memorials, and forums. We all have a different relationship with the place. Some will never darken the door. Lila will go there for events in the Foundation Hall but won't go into the museum. That hall, where the Last Column of steel stands thirty-six feet high, faces "the slurry wall," a retaining wall from the foundation of the World Trade Center. Visitors who were on the Pile swear that they can feel the damp from the Hudson.

Ivonne Sanchez says the museum, particularly the room with photos of everyone who lost their lives, makes her feel a heavy guilt that manifests physically in a headache: "It's like they're all saying 'Why didn't you find me?' That was my job and I failed. I know I'm not the only one who feels that way. I always have that guilt, but the museum is where I feel like I can say it out loud, 'I'm sorry I didn't find you.'"

In a corner of the Foundation Hall, there's a small exhibit on post-9/11 illness and advocacy. They have photos from our trips to DC, business cards from representatives, and the mass cards we would hand out in return, including Ray's. They have my jacket and the pens Pelosi and Trump used to sign the bill. They have dozens of empty prescription bottles prescribed to Westchester probation officer and volunteer EMT Keoni May. There's a protest sign with prescription bottles from the twenty-three different medications Freddie Noboa was taking attached to it with zip ties, along with various inhalers and breathing devices. Written across the top of the sign: *THERE ARE NO WORDS THAT EXPRESS OUR SUFFERING.*

Ray's wheelchair sits empty at one end of the exhibit.

Above ground, facing the entrance to the museum and the memorial pools, there is a walking path among the white oak trees, flanked by six stone monoliths, where the main ramp to the Pile once stood. This is the 9/11 Memorial Glade, built to honor the responders and survivors. The fissures in the big rocks are filled with World Trade Center steel, smelted to fit by a foundry in Missouri. The committee to establish a monument to the responders and survivors was established in 2014 and I was on it. The Glade was designed by Michael Arad and Peter Walker, with support from Jon Stewart, and representatives from the survivors and responders. It was dedicated on May 30, 2019, the seventeenth anniversary of the removal of the last piece of steel and the end of the recovery effort.

At one end of the path, an inscription reads:

This Memorial Glade is dedicated
To those whose actions in our time of need
Led to their injury, sickness, and death
Responders and recovery workers
Survivors and community members
Suffering long after September 11, 2001
From exposure to hazards and toxins
That hung heavy in the air
Here and beyond this site known as Ground Zero
And at the Pentagon
And near Shanksville, Pennsylvania
In the aftermath of the terrorist attacks.
Here we honor the tens of thousands
From across America and around the world
Who came to help and to heal
Whose selflessness and resolve
Perseverance and courage
Renewed the spirit of a grieving city
Gave hope to the nation
And inspired the world.

Every year, on the Friday after 9/11, the night before the reading of the names, I go to the park we built in Nesconset and sit with them for a while. I ask them to forgive me for how long it took. We got the best bill we could, but I can't face those names in stone without feeling like it was too little too late.

In the time it took me to write this book, around four hundred responders have died of 9/11 related illnesses. One hundred five died between the reading of the names in September 2024, and New Year's 2025. Over seven thousand members of the World Trade Center Health Program have died. The exact number of deaths from 9/11 illness may never be known, but by the most conservative estimates, they already outnumbered the death toll on the day of the attack before the twentieth anniversary.

Over 37,000 responders and survivors are living with cancer, with all the suffering and hardship that entails: from the cost of co-pays to the awkwardness of making love to your spouse on oxygen. The average age of a 9/11 responder was thirty-eight in 2001, so most of us arc in our early sixties. The VCF is quickly becoming a program to settle wrongful deaths. Someday there will be no names left to read.

There's a joke in the 9/11 community: We say "happy 9/11" when the anniversary rolls around, because you would think it's a day for festivities, judging by the TV specials and ceremonies. My Septembers are always booked solid with TV appearances, interviews, and events. But when we hit twenty years, it's "happy 9/11" on steroids. I do my part, say what needs to be said on behalf of my fellow responders and survivors, I go home and take a lot of long showers.

On the twenty-first anniversary, Pearl Jam plays Madison Square Garden in honor of the first responders who died on 9/11 and to support "healthcare for heroes." They invite us along: me, O'Connell, and some of the guys.

In a conversation with O'Connell before the show, their front man, Eddie Vedder, says something beautiful: "9/11 was horrific, traumatic, despicable . . . but in some ways, 9/12 was awesome. 9/12 people came together as one. We were supported by the rest of the planet. And most importantly in our country, we supported each other. There was a time when we supported each other. That's the part that we cannot forget. We can stay together. We don't have to wait for another terrorist attack and suffer this thing of being divided."

In the middle of their set, Vedder stops, points up into the crowd in my direction and goes:

"John Feal, you're baddest motherfucker on this planet."

People in the audience come up to me and ask, "Who are you?"

All I can think is Ray would have loved this, the music, the shout-out, my embarrassment, and the concertgoers bringing me back down to earth. I close my eyes and enjoy the show for both of us.

In 2002, a few days after I get home from the hospital, I hear a knock at the door at my mother's house. I'm in my room watching *SportsCenter* or something. I shout:

"Yo! Who is it?"

Nobody answers. They knock again.

Finally, I get up. It probably takes me five or six minutes to get on my feet and hobble to the door. Just checking the mail is an Olympic event at this stage of my recovery. I hear a car drive off. I look out the window, and there's nobody there. I open the door and see a Rottweiler puppy in a basket with an unsigned note: *Hope this makes you feel better.*

That was Cain; he grew to be 140 pounds, a gentle giant who was always at my side while I got my strength back. He left this world in 2009. I had to do the first bill without him. It was cancer. Fucking cancer. When I went to bring him to be put to sleep, I got to the vet's office and turned around and went home.

We lay on the kitchen floor for three hours, and eventually, I said, "Sorry, buddy, we gotta go back."

The vet came and explained everything, then said, "Take all the time you want."

He came back maybe a half hour later, and I looked at him and said:

"You said I can have all the time I want. Leave me the fuck alone with my fucking dog. We're not ready."

When it was all over and I left, I apologized. I came back the next day with Dunkin' Donuts for the whole office. After a tough couple of months, this girl Debbie, who runs a dog shelter on Long Island, called me to say she found a gorgeous female Rottweiler tied to a broken-down truck with an extension cord.

That was "Seven," named for WTC 7, where I got hurt. Always got her way. Moody. But I spoiled her. We used to go on long drives together. All my dogs love that. Seven moved on in 2019, after the bill. The vet made a house call when it was her time. I didn't make a scene or cry, but I stayed in bed for a couple of days.

A few months later, Debbie calls again. There's a dog at a shelter in South Carolina, a pit/terrier mix. It's Thursday night. They're going to put her down on Saturday morning.

"What's wrong with her?"

"Nothing," says Debbie, "it's just a kill shelter. Someone abandoned her, they found her drinking from a puddle in the street. She must be a sweetheart because she walked right over to the dogcatchers and tried to make friends."

I call the shelter in South Carolina Thursday night but get no answer. I call again Friday morning and stop the execution. I fly her up to New York, and Debbie brings her to my house on Tuesday. First thing she does is run inside and take a massive dump on my white living room rug.

I name her LouRay, after two of the best guys I ever knew.

If I give you a nickname, it's because I'm afraid of how much it will hurt when you're gone. It's my way of saying I love you. In 2024, I meet the young woman I'll dub "Samsonite" because she has as much baggage as me. She's a scientist, with an alphabet soup of degrees. She makes medical devices for women's health, finding ways to drive down the cost of ultrasounds for underserved communities. In her spare time, she rescues pigeons and cares for geriatric turtles. All of which is impressive but it's not why I'm crazy about her. She thinks what I've done is pretty cool, but that's not why she's crazy about me, and she didn't know a thing about my story or the bills before we met.

With her, I don't have to be John Feal, I can be just John. One day, we're out walking in Manhattan. She's feeding the pigeons, and a cranky old lady tells her not to. So, I run to the nearest bodega and buy more bread. Love is scary for both of us, but we were lucky to meet at a time when we had each come to the realization that the only thing scarier than allowing yourself to be totally vulnerable with someone is the emptiness of a lonely life where you're too scared to let anyone in. We're beginners learning how to love and be loved. She sets down her baggage while I clear a place for us in the rubble. She met me on my way home, a journey of twenty-four years and counting. I used to think home was a place or a state of mind or maybe a person. It's been so long, I don't know if home will be a place I recognize when I get there or if I'll ever arrive. But I won't be alone.

ACTION FOR ACTIVISTS: PICK UP YOUR RAKE (IF YOU CAN)

It will be tempting to broaden your purpose and take on new causes. Social media pressures everyone to care about everything. But you need to stay focused. Scope creep kills causes. The lesson for contemporary activists from Feal and Stewart is to take focused action and expand your scope only after you are successful. That said, connecting with and learning from other causes will keep your messaging fresh and build your network.

Like I said in the last chapter, it's easier to stand up for people than for abstract ideas. Ground what you're doing in love and friendship. Don't wait to say what's in your heart. You will need the people you love when it's all over and you've won and it's time to pick up your rake.

I'm a bad example of picking up your rake, and I can't give you much advice on how to do that, because I haven't really done it myself. Maybe I never will. As emotionally and physically draining as it was to fight non-stop for two decades to pass nineteen pieces of legislation, it's nowhere near as awkward and uncomfortable as the fight being over. In the years since we got our bills passed, I've learned what it must be like to be a victorious general. One day you're a warlord, and the next you're a paper pusher whose job is to suck up to politicians. Ask anyone I've worked with in the last two years, and they'll tell you the transition to "peace time" hasn't been easy. So, if you're like me, and you find you can't pick up your rake, then my advice is to find ways to help others pick up their swords. Stewart once said to me: "This country is nothing but need." There's no shortage of worthy causes and battles worth fighting. It could be that the lesson from my story is you don't want to do what I did, you don't want to carry a whole movement on your shoulders. But maybe you want to do what Rizzo and O'Connell and some of the guys did. Maybe you want to document the work, like Bridget. Whatever your approach, there's plenty of work to be done, and the time to start is always now.

EPILOGUE

L: Walking the halls again, 2025. (L-R) Michael O'Connell, Tim Casey, John Feal, Tom Willson. R: Alone in the Capitol rotunda. (Photos/Bridget Gormley)

We turned in a draft of this book in spring 2025, on the eve of a government shutdown. Things are too chaotic and moving too quickly for this book to include an up-to-date and comprehensive accounting of every setback and every threat to the bill that has come up since the legislation was signed into law and permanently funded, but it's worth including an update on where we are as of this writing.

Things are, in the words of *Pulp Fiction*, "pretty fucking far from okay."

In 2015 there were 75,000 people in the program; there are now over 145,000 in the program, with an additional 10,000 signing up each year. One-third of those 145,000 have a certified 9/11-related cancer, roughly 49,000 people. But with this increased demand on the program as more people got sick coupled with medical inflation, we were heading toward a deficit by 2027 unless we got additional funding, or inclusion in the omnibus, to get us through the first decade of permanent authorization. So, we were authorized 'til 2090, but funding-wise weren't going to make it to 2027. And that was challenging before DOGE and the Tesla guy's purge of government programs.

In the first DOGE slashing spree, they tried to cut the WTC Health Program by 20 percent and then backtracked. I don't think that will happen again before this book is out. But the PACT Act is going to suffer mass cuts and layoffs at the VA. Many who work on that program are among the 80,000 VA employees laid off by DOGE. It remains to be seen how cuts to the NIH, NIOSH, and other sources of medical research and funding will impact these programs. It won't be good.

The scientists and doctors who work for these programs are talented and sought after, and they're not going to sit around in jobs that might not exist soon, and their loss would be disastrous for all of us. For that reason alone, we can't afford shortfalls and deadlines running out.

We were dealt a body blow, via email, at 5 AM on April 2, 2025, with the firing of Dr. John Howard, director of NIOSH. Here is part of the statement I sent out in response to his termination:

> *The World Trade Center Health Program works because of its leadership from Dr. Howard and those that have worked tirelessly in NIOSH on*

issues directly for the 9/11 community. From signing certifications for coverage to entering into contracts to cover new illnesses, these people directly provide care across the country for those in need. Since it was developed in its current form in 2011, we have challenged any member of Congress or sitting president to come forward with examples of fraud, waste, abuse, and they have never done so. That is why we have received funding every single time we needed it, despite having to fight for it. You have spit in the faces of the 9/11 community for the last time.

I will not let this administration undo what thousands of people have given their lives for. You will not destroy a program and those it serves with your nonsensical rhetoric and reckless actions. While you have clearly shown those who wish to destroy this country that you have forgotten about the sacrifices the 9/11 community has made since September 11, 2001, I will show those same people that there are people with spines who will stand up for each other in need and in an instant. I will very publicly come to your doorsteps and make sure that everyone in this world sees that we will not bow to anyone who attacks the 9/11 community, whether foreign or domestic. Those of you who are responsible for these actions disgust us all and will be forgotten about, and we will put this program back where it was and continue to move forward.

I've been back to DC in a "break glass in case of emergency" capacity, and I will go again when I'm needed. I've done eleven trips and attended 280 meetings, in person and on Zoom. We're confident we will be attached to a larger vehicle by January 2026. Stewart and I have spoken to veteran service organizations about the future of the PACT Act and the VA, we've spoken to a congressional committee on the subject, and we're ready to help defend that legislation any way we can. Walking the halls in 2025, it's a different game. Where we once had a political party opposing us, now we're up against a cult. Where we once had dialogue, it's now nothing but rhetoric. There's no conversation. Our "bible" is almost useless because we're not going there to educate and persuade, we're having to challenge their humanity and urge them to look past their spray-tanned demigod. But I won't stop. Democrats, for their part, need to learn how to street fight. I've been giving lessons.

Press conference, 2025.
(Photo/Bridget Gormley)

I plan on being a dick. I'm not going there to try and make friends with anybody. If you're a Republican or a Democrat and you don't get it, then you're going to wish you never met me. It's that simple. A lot of my guys are Trump guys, it's no surprise that he did well among the first responders, and trades, and the good people who make our society function and are sick of being ignored. I tell them the same thing I tell the Democrats on my team: Put aside your politics. We're here to defend human life, not to settle partisan scores. Recently, on social media, I've had assholes from the left comment that these guys (9/11 responders) voted for Trump and are now getting what they deserve under his program cuts. I point out that I didn't vote for Trump, and I defend my guys who did against that kind of divisive trolling.

Back in 2019, I told my guys to go home, plant something, and watch it grow with their loved ones. Now, they all have ten-foot trees, and for those who want to pick up their swords again and defend this bill, the gardening is going to have to be put on hold. This is what I meant about "buying a treadmill." When I told the burn pit families that their legislation would need a few good people to defend it and hold the line, these are the trying times when that is needed.

At the end of the day, we're talking about a lifeline for 150,000 people, and three million-plus in the case of the PACT Act. My guys aren't the kind of people to keep tending to their gardens when human life is on the line, and a lot of them, like me, were bored watching trees grow. They were sharpening their swords, polishing their armor, and waiting for the call.

LET'S GET YOUR BILL PASSED: A FEW MORE TIPS FOR ACTIVISTS

I hope you didn't use reading this book as an excuse to put off starting your activism. You can read on the bus to DC or listen to the audiobook in the car. If you take one thing away from this story, it's to start before you're ready. You'll figure out the rest as you go.

There are some books out there on how to get things done in our nation's Capitol, by people much smarter and more qualified than me. I would recommend *The Beltway Bible: A Totally Serious A–Z Guide to Our No-Good, Corrupt, Incompetent, Terrible, Depressing, Sometimes Hilarious Government* by Eliot Nelson. And Lila Nordstrom's *Some Kids Left Behind: A Survivor's Fight for Health Care in the Wake of 9/11* contains practical tips for activists of all ages.

You're going to learn a lot about yourself through your work as an activist. Some of what came naturally to me might be a struggle for you, and I'm sure there are things that come easy to you that I'd never get my arms around. I'll leave you with a few more pieces of random advice I picked up along the way that might help you in your work and save you from having to learn things the hard way.

If I can do it, you can do it, and probably do it better.

Godspeed!

BE YOURSELF

The lesson from my story is not to copy my style, it's to find your own and be true to it. I'm an in-your-face, knuckle-dragging kind of guy. That's not an act, it's who I am. And I couldn't be any other way if I wanted to. That's how I carried myself in the Capitol. I didn't pretend to be someone else, and you shouldn't either. Now, that's not to say that you shouldn't smooth over some of your rough edges or fill gaps in your knowledge. The lessons I have to offer activists come from that process of self-education. But I stayed true to myself along the way. When I say "be yourself," I mean be the best, most effective version of yourself, whatever that looks like.

Jon Stewart is an intellectual, a satirist, and a master of rhetoric. He leaned into those strengths in his remarks to the subcommittee. He didn't need to get tough with anyone, because his power is in his command of the English language and in his household name status from decades in the public eye.

START WITH WHAT YOU KNOW

Being true to yourself applies to how you think about activism as well as how you do it. I use a lot of military and wrestling analogies (if you've gotten this far in the book, I'm guessing you're not sick of them). That's what I work with because that's what I know. But if you're not a soldier or a marine, you probably don't think of a group of four as a "fire team." Find an analogy that works for you and resonates with your audience.

IT'S FREE TO BECOME AN ACTIVIST

It's a rookie mistake to assume you need funding or a foundation to start a movement. Raising money is a distraction, and you don't need it to get started. All you need is a worthy cause and your time. Writing blog posts and using social media is FREE. Press coverage is FREE. Networking and organizing is FREE. Calling your reps is FREE. You may end up traveling to DC like we did, and that comes with transportation and lodging costs, but don't start there. If there's a class action side to your cause, you can get a lot of your expenses covered by the law firms you work with. But try to start with no expenses.

REMEMBER WHO THEY WORK FOR

Lila likes to remind activists that legislators' offices are open to the public at every level of government. "Just because they're probably wearing suits doesn't mean they are your boss. They work for their district. If you're from their district, they work for you." (*Some Kids Left Behind*)

I would take it a step further and say that our elected officials are sworn to serve and protect their constituents, and if they're not doing that, then they don't belong in office.

Who are your representatives at the local, state, and congressional level? If your cause involves multiple districts, have everyone ask these questions. Make a list with emails, phone numbers, and social media. You'll use this info later when you make your "book."

MASTER THE SOUND BITE

I become a walking sound bite when you put a camera in front of me. I had all our talking points and figures down in TV-friendly statements:

We're here today because there are hundreds of thousands of people who are sick and dying from the aftermath of 9/11.

We no longer have to prove that we got sick from 9/11. They have to prove that we DIDN'T get sick from 9/11.

We ate at Ground Zero, we slept there, we cried there. The absorption through the nose, mouth, and skin made us sick.

I would throw a "shit" or a "fuck" in there, too, for effect. The main point was to make it simple for myself so that I could communicate it simply for others.

Instead of info dumping or throwing around scientific terms I could barely pronounce, I wove the science into these sound bites, communicating critical facts like the role of skin exposure. People have short attention spans these days. You have to keep it brief and make it memorable.

COMPILE YOUR BIBLE

We had two "books" that were invaluable in DC. One was our bible of stats and facts explaining 9/11-related illnesses and their nationwide prevalence. That book alone won us a few votes. Believe it or not, there are still some politicians in these insane times who can be persuaded by facts and reason.

The second book, Bridget called "the Burn Book." It was a collection of printed tweets and press clips documenting every congressional #NeverForget and every statement on the anniversary of 9/11. This was hard evidence of the hypocrisy and doublespeak we were there to call out.

We also put together intel and opposition research that would put the NSA, CIA, and KGB to shame. We knew every member's schedule, their hobbies, whether they were fire buffs or had served as volunteer firefighters. And if they had some sleazy ulterior motive for opposing the bill, like Mitch and his oil deal, we had all the dirt on that too.

A word of caution: DO NOT let the homework become procrastination or get in the way of the doing. Get to work and learn on the go. We learned some of these lessons the hard way after ten years of going to DC. We didn't wait 'til we knew everything before getting to work.

Get started on your book. Gather the facts and news clips that support your cause and the intel or opponent research you need to understand who you're up against.

"YOU CAN'T CARE WHO YOU PISS OFF"

That's one lesson from my work, according to Jess Fassler, Sen. Gillibrand's chief of staff. Beware of trying to be uncontroversial and inoffensive.

HOW TO WIN THE MEETING

The winning formula is this: Open the meeting, talk a little, then shut the fuck up. Get them to do the talking. If we had gone to the House and made our pitch while they listened politely, members who were against it could have cited the need to curb spending and shown us the door. By getting them talking, we forced their move. They made weak arguments about fraud that we could easily shut down, and they were left without a leg to stand on. When your adversary ducks you in the hall or gets out a blank piece of paper and pretends to be reading, like Mitch McConnell did, you've won. Once you find a crack in their armor, you just split them wide open like a lobster.

MEN MAKE A MOB, WOMEN MAKE A MOVEMENT

My mother was the first person who taught me that toughness has nothing to do with being physically intimidating and male. Women give your group a legitimacy and subtlety that a group of young men lacks. In *Freedom,* Sebastian Junger writes about how the involvement of women in early labor movements and the Irish War of Independence made it much harder for the powers that be to quash their activities with violence. When we walked the halls of Congress, having Bridget and Lila and responder widows with us made us harder to dismiss, and we looked less like a security threat.

Pay attention to the listen-to-talk ratio between the sexes. Are the men and women in your group given equal airtime? If you're a mostly male group like we were, what are you doing to make women feel included and heard?

BE KIND TO YOURSELF AND OTHERS, BUT KNOW WHEN TO BE RUTHLESS

Nobody wants to work with an asshole, but you won't get anywhere being a pushover either. It's all about balance. Defaulting to kindness will help you save energy for when ruthlessness is called for.

And when the time comes to be ruthless, scorch the earth and don't worry about trying to be everybody's friend after. Fuck your reputation! You can't be effective if you check your swing in the name of safeguarding future career prospects. Your reputation, the one worth having, will be secured by what you and your team accomplish. I don't have to give a flying fuck about what some suit thinks about my use of four-letter words. I can rest easy knowing families will be taken care of because I put them ahead of my own reputation.

"TAKE A SHOWER," SELF-CARE IS CRITICAL

I play golf to clear my mind. It's the one time I don't want to talk about 9/11 or people getting sick. It's my time to decompress. After a tough conversation or a therapy session, I'll take a shower to reset. A lot of showers went into writing this book.

You're no good to anyone if you become an exhaustion casualty, or burn out, so take self-care seriously as part of your work.

As a leader, you're going to spend a lot of time alone, even when your team grows. It helps to have a support network of family and friends outside of the group. You need to be able to vent to someone who can listen with compassion.

THERE WILL BE CASUALTIES

Literally and figuratively. You are going to lose people along the way, and you have to be prepared for those losses. The only way for nobody to get hurt is to stay home (and that's not even true, because home is where most accidents happen). The only way to never get your heart broken is to never fall in love. You can protect yourself from grief by never making a friend, but what kind of life is that?

Make time to mourn, to say goodbye, to feel your feelings. Then take a long shower, dry off, and do something worthy of their memory.

AUTHOR'S NOTE: JOIN THE WTC HEALTH PROGRAM

If you worked, lived, or went to school in Lower Manhattan between September 11, 2001, and May 2002, or at any of the three attack sites, and have a 9/11-related illness, you are eligible for the World Trade Center Health Program and the September 11th Victim Compensation Fund and should be in the program.

Even if you're not sick, get in the program.

You do not need to be a first responder. By enrolling, you won't be taking anything from anyone else. Thanks to the hard work and sacrifice of the VCF recipients you've read about in this book, the program has enough funding for everyone and it always will. If you know someone who was there, tell them about these programs and help us spread the word. You could be saving a life. It's that simple.

Like many 9/11 responders, I am haunted by all the people I couldn't help. Telling my story is a way of putting that guilt to rest; it's my attempt to finally come home from the Pile. My journey is not complete until I've put as many people in the program as possible. By signing up, you'll be helping yourself, helping your family, and helping your fellow responders and survivors and their loved ones.

Find out more at www.vcf.gov. If you have questions about how to enroll or are ready to start the process, contact the law offices of Barasch & McGarry at 1-800-523-4671 or www.911victims.com.

If you are a responder or a survivor, or just a person who has been through something traumatic and needs to talk to somebody before it's too late, call the National Suicide Hotline at 988 anytime.

God bless you all,
John Feal

CO-AUTHOR'S NOTE

"I'll go with you then,
Since you must play this game of ghosts . . . "
—Siegfried Sassoon, "To One Who Was with Me in the War"

A machete is a rake and a sword. A gas-powered weed whacker is faster and more efficient but nowhere as satisfying to work with. That *thwack thwack thwack* through the brush, the care you have to take with each swing . . . It's like a form of meditation, and it's the perfect activity to pass the time when you're waiting on big news and need to get your mind off the waiting. Unlike a power tool, a machete lets you hear the phone ring when the waiting is over.

Lucinda Halpern is going to call any minute to let us know whether her agency will represent this project. Her team is meeting at the start of their workday in New York while I clear brush in Ireland. John has probably been up for hours already, done a workout, and downed six of his daily dozen eggs.

I'm slashing the path to the beach from the cottage where my wife, Dominique, and I live with our cat, Serge, and our many books on Ireland's Wild Atlantic Way. The path had become overgrown as daylight hours got longer, and I was too busy getting John's book proposal ready to clear it. My parents will be visiting from Cape Cod, Massachusetts, next week, and I want the path to look nice and be walkable for their visit. My meaning-seeking storyteller's mind has me thinking about summers here growing up. The seasons and passing of time are so pronounced in a place with so much rain, sun late into the night in summer, darkness and gales all winter. Taking over the cottage means jobs like brush clearing that had once been my father's are mine now.

He's ninety-eight, I'm thirty-five, he had me late in life. Like John, I'm the son of a Korean War veteran. Dad was climbing ladders, mowing the lawn, and fixing potholes in the gravel driveway into his early nineties. Now I do those things. I've delegated the killing of rats and mice to Serge, the black cat.

I look out at the calm bay and wonder: How many more stories by the fireplace, how many full Irish breakfasts and morning papers? At the end of the path in the cove where he would swim at dawn or leap off the nearby cliff at high tide, little waves rearrange the sand. I think about something Dad said about life, paraphrasing Keats: *Put your hand in the water, pull it out, what's left? Does your hand make an impression?*

I swing at a long, thorny vine.

I want Mom to have an easy path to the beach. She still walks miles every day with Parkinson's. I check the fence post and rope railing in the place where the path gets steep. We used to have a wire fence around the yard, when my brother and I were kids, to keep us in and our donkeys out. Parents getting older means railings and grab bars and reflective tape on stone steps. Mom will be in "wait mode" today too. My career is her favorite spectator sport. She loves the stories I've told her about this project, and she follows John on social media and watches his news appearances. She has a doctor's appointment today that should be over by the time I hear from Lucinda.

Taking a water break where the path bends and overlooks the bay and the Atlantic beyond, I imagine the courage it must have taken my mother's family to set out over the waves, *trasna na dtonnta*, in a wooden ship when the alternative was starvation. I think about Mike O'Connell and Bridget Gormley and how Ireland will always be a part of the 9/11 story because so many responders came from this island originally. There is a park of survivor trees planted in Kinsale, Co. Cork, not far from us, by a local woman who had been a nurse in New York on 9/11. There are dozens of famine ruins in the hills above our cottage, the abandoned one-room stone homes of families who emigrated. I wonder if our neighboring ruins sent any responders down the generations. John, whose mother is a Doherty, reminds me of those folk songs that warned Irish men about what can happen when you leave and get mixed up in foreign wars.

My roots will be useful in the interviews I do for this book. Cops and firemen and feds don't always like nosy journalists and writers, but they all love Ireland, or at least Irish whiskey. O'Hara's, the Irish pub kitty-corner to the World Trade Center, is my first stop on my research trip to New York. I sip a seltzer water while Bridget shows me "the Book" they keep behind the bar, full of press clippings from 9/11 and the days after.

I was eleven years old on 9/11. When we started working on this book, I was thirty-five, the same age John was when he got hurt. He and I hit it off immediately and have forged a friendship that transcends our working partnership as co-authors and defies the surface-level differences between a kid who grew up between two beach houses on either side of the Atlantic and a "professional pain in the ass" with scar tissue on his knuckles. We met through my friend Bridget (who also introduced me to Dominique). One thing about John's story that resonated with me is the way he was always willing to pay the price to be a teller of truths, even if that price was loneliness. It's not any easy way to be, but—as I'm sure John would agree—it beats going along to get along.

In my experience as a ghostwriter, I'm fascinated by the way an author will size me up and decide whether I'm the right person to trust with their life story. The green flags John saw in me were interesting: We both have one kidney—though mine was congenital, not altruistic. We drink our coffee black and start our days before dawn. When he mentioned his hernia repair surgery and I told him I was recovering from the same on both sides he asked:

"Did you take pain killers after?"

"No." I said. Not trying to sound tough, just stating facts.

"Good."

More importantly for the subject at hand, I had grown up with a secondhand familiarity with PTSD, from "the good and bad of having a marine combat veteran for a father," as Karl Marlantes put it when he dedicated *Matterhorn* to his children. *The bad* is an inability to relax, an intolerance of boredom, and extreme restlessness (sound like anyone in this book?). I learned to wield a machete helping Dad with his gardening, limited slightly by the effects of a gunshot wound to his left arm. His approach to yard work was compulsive and intense, never relaxing. I remember when I was in high school back in the States, trying to wake up before him on a snow day because he would be out shoveling the drive at first light, against doctor's orders. And *the good* was his obsession with the sea, which he shared with me from a young age. His idea of relaxation was long, offshore day trips in small boats, like mainland Massachusetts to Nantucket in an open skiff. I was his navigator.

Growing up in the shadow of my father's war prepared me to write this book. Everything I knew going into this project about how to talk to John and how to help him "go there" with his story I learned from an old man who sleeps with a night-light because of things he saw and did on the other side of the world when he was younger than I am now.

On one of our first calls, before I'm really at ease, still jotting notes nervously in my reporter's notebook, trying to look diligent, John sits in silence. He has just come from yet another funeral, Al Williams, one of his guys. Finally, he speaks. He's crying. "Cancer is the fucking devil. Write that down."

Early on in the project, a scheduling snag will cause a blowout that has John ready to walk and our representation feeling the same. I get on a call to try to save the project and point out that none of us know what it's like to lose friends to admin errors and delays. What's a minor scheduling conflict to an agency takes John back to a bad place.

But we're not there yet. I'm still waiting on the call. My ringing phone catches me mid machete swing. I bury the machete blade in the grass and answer.

We got it. Lucinda wants to sign John and represent the book and shop the proposal to publishers.

I call John.

"Okay," he says, not one to get excited before he's thought through next moves and ways this could go sideways.

I mask my own excitement, a dream I've had since I was an English major scribbling bad short stories in leather-bound notebooks.

The phone starts beeping with a call on the other line—Mom; I tell John I'll call him right back.

I blurt out the good news before Mom can get a word in. She's delighted. I don't even think to ask about the doctor's appointment. We've learned from her Parkinson's not to sweat those appointments in advance. And this one wasn't with her neurologist. She had a persistent cough she wanted to get checked before coming to Ireland. She thought it might be an infection she might need antibiotics for.

"How'd it go with the doc?" I ask.

"It's not good news."

What she says next, I don't remember verbatim, because it's like getting punched.

It's lung cancer, stage 4, spread outside the pleura of the lung and a few other places they're going to look at. I cling to the clinical jargon I only partially understand from my research on John's book because it gives me some illusion of control. It's the worst news five minutes after the best news.

Dominique is in the air on her way to see her family in Switzerland. Her Irish SIM card won't work when she lands. So strange how your mind goes to logistics like that.

I call John back and say those four words for the first time, "My mom has cancer."

I think about the question I knew to ask him based on my mom's Parkinson's diagnosis, when we worked on the chapter about his mom: *Did you think "I wish it was me and not her, if I could have it for her I would"?* He said of course that's how he felt.

As we're talking, I hang the machete in the shed. It's dangerous to swing a blade in an emotional state, and I don't feel like gardening or dwelling in nostalgia for summers past. I pace and look out at the calm water and talk to John about something he knows too much about at this point. This note you're reading originates in this phone call.

He says, "This needs to go in the book, do your wordsmithing. People need to know that you had this going on while you were writing down our stories."

It takes about a year to write a book, and the clock starts when you get your deal. I measure that year in scans, staging, and blood work. My workdays are all about cancer, hearing the stories that become this book. I don't often mention my mom in interviews, but I'm with the right people when I do. It's "a club I never wanted to be a part of" as Bridget put it. When I call her, right after I get off the phone with John, she makes us both laugh by saying, "Yeah, well, welcome to the club." Her late father's words will become a mantra my mother and I will repeat often: "There are kids who have what I have."

With lung cancer, there's this compulsion to point out that she wasn't a smoker. And it turns out, that's actually important because it means she's eligible for different treatment options. The genetic marker of her tumor is a match for a targeted treatment that means no chemo for now—which would be devastating with Parkinson's.

Her cancer wasn't from smoking, like most lung cancers, and it wasn't from deception and cover-up like the 9/11 cancers. "Just cancer" like John says about his own mother's illness. On the other side of the same unfair coin of healthcare in America, she has access to the best treatment at Dana-Farber in Boston through TRICARE For Life, my dad's insurance through the military as a medically retired marine. A buddy of mine, Joshua Maloney, an Iraq vet who helped me with the burn pit chapter, explained that hospitals love to take TRICARE because most of their policyholders are fit, young people, pre-screened for countless conditions. Put another way, my dad had to get shot for his wife's healthcare to be looked after no matter what.

After I tell John the details and what we know from her first scan, he says, "I know cancer, from my mother, my sister, the 9/11 responders. Your mother's going to live a long time. You can worry about what the future holds, or you can enjoy the good days you have with her. I suggest you do the latter."

And so far, that's what we've been doing. The primary tumor has shrunk considerably, and cancer has retreated from the places it had spread. If someday this targeted treatment stops working, there are other options that have been approved since she was diagnosed, and who knows what's right around the corner? Mom has read a draft of this book and read it aloud to my father. They will visit Ireland later in the summer between scans.

Writing down the stories of the 9/11 responders and survivors, I tried to be careful never to reduce anyone to a diagnosis. I tended to start with their jobs because that's how they ended up at the Pile and because the variety of work that needed to be done down there is truly fascinating. I want to extend my mom the same editorial courtesy . . .

In my parents' house on Cape Cod, there's a framed recruiting poster from the First World War of a woman in a sailor's uniform with the headline:

Geee, I wish I were a man, I'd join the NAVY!

The poster was a gift to my mother from Joe Moakley, a congressman from South Boston. It's a tribute to her work as an aide to Speaker "Tip" O'Neill, where she was what John Feal would call "a relentless activist" for women's issues, working on Title IX and the Equal Rights Amendment. She's a constant source of good questions to ask John and a resource for understanding the Hill. She gives us the O'Neill quote, "All politics is local" and the Capitol adage "Assumption is the mother of fuckup," two phrases that hold true in John's experience in DC. Through three and a half decades of unwavering belief in me, she has helped make this book possible in ways readers will never know.

After John and I get off the phone, I follow the half-cleared path down to the beach and sit for a while. Seabirds dive for their supper. A splash and the waves have already forgotten.

Charlie Daly,
West Cork, Ireland
2025
Charles Daly's father, Chuck, died in January 2026, while this book was being copyedited. His mother's cancer is responding to treatment, her Parkinson's is stable, and she recently welcomed two grandkids into her life.

JON STEWART'S SPEECH (THAT HE THREW AWAY)

Congress requires witnesses to submit their prepared remarks to be entered into the public record. This is the original speech Stewart prepared for the hearing. If you compare this to what he actually said, you can see that my plan to "take his speech away" worked.

Testimony of Jon Stewart
House Judiciary Committee
June 11, 2019

Chairman Nadler, Ranking Member Collins, and Members of the Committee, thank you for letting me join these 9/11 responders and survivors, these heroes, today on this panel. And thank you for this hearing today on the September 11th Victim Compensation Fund, and the legislation Never Forget the Heroes: Permanent Authorization of the September 11th Victim Compensation Fund that would fully fund the program and extend its authorization. You have just heard in agonizing detail why you need to act on this legislation. Many talk about 9/11 and how the country responded to it, but frankly the response on the impact of the toxins at Ground Zero, as these men and women have outlined, has not been as good as it should have been—to say the least.

First, the issues these heroes face is squarely the fault of terrorists. But in the rush to get Wall Street open again and move people back in, mistakes were made. People—local residents, students and commuters into the area (as well as responders)—were told that the air was safe. But it was not. Children were brought back to school next to a toxic pit, and then it was denied—for years—that there was a health problem. Those who responded and worked in the pit—and had the most exposure—were of course the first to feel the effects. But soon residents became ill, too—with persistent coughs or rare cancers. So, for many years since 9/11, these responders and residents had to walk the halls of Congress, looking to see if "Remember 9/11" is more than a cheap Twitter slogan senators and representatives use to nod in the direction of empathy without having to do anything. They had to work to get Congress to provide healthcare for these injuries from toxins; they had to work to get compensation for the injuries so that their families would not suffer. First responders, firefighters, police, construction workers, Red Cross volunteers, transit workers, FBI agents, and schoolteachers have had to go door to door down your gold- and marble-lined hallways, because seventeen years after the attacks on 9/11, they and their families are still dealing with the impact of the toxins at Ground Zero. They are in every state and 433 out of 435 congressional districts. The fact that they have had continue to do this is beyond my comprehension. But I have to say that my impression of Washington might be changing. Some things are getting done.

Just a few weeks ago I said that the Trump Justice Department was doing a good job running the program; I would never have thought that I would say it, but I did because it is true. The fact that this hearing is happening in this committee today is heartening. I understand there has been some recent unpleasantness. This legislation has over three hundred bipartisan sponsors. Three hundred members of the House agreeing to take action is pretty good.

I want to thank Ranking Member Collins for his support today; he and Mr. Nadler have set an example that the parties can come together. All of the support gives me some hope. There seems to be a general understanding and agreement that compensating the 9/11 heroes through this bill needs to happen. I thank all of you—Republicans and Democrats—for that.

These people can't wait—the cuts to them or their survivors are happening now. I know that this is going to cost a lot, but you need figure out how to pay for it. It is not their job to tell you how to pay for it—they did their job. I ask you to move this bill and get it to the floor.

Two weeks ago, I was at Ground Zero for the dedication of the National September 11th Memorial, for the dedication of a new Memorial Glade, with ragged stone monoliths that honor those who have become ill and those that have died from 9/11-related illnesses. The space will never bring closure to those who have lost so much and continue to suffer so deeply, but it recognizes the great courage and strength they gave so willingly and the price they continue to pay.

But they need this bill. Please help them.

SOURCES AND FURTHER READING

Barrett, Wayne, and Dan Collins. *Grand Illusion: The Untold Story of Rudy Giuliani and 9/11*. HarperCollins, 2006.

Brown, Michael Everett. *What Brothers Do: A Personal Story of Love, Loss, and Loyalty in the Aftermath of 9/11*. Archway Publishing, 2015.

Daly, Michael. *The Book of Mychal: The Surprising Life and Heroic Death of Father Mychal Judge*. St. Martin's Press, 2008.

Feinberg, Kenneth R. *What Is Life Worth?: The Unprecedented Effort to Compensate the Victims of 9/11*. PublicAffairs, 2005.

Graff, Garrett M. *The Only Plane in the Sky: An Oral History of 9/11*. Avid Reader Press, 2019.

Gonzalez, Laurence. *Deep Survival: Who Lives, Who Dies, and Why*. W.W. Norton & Company, 2003.

Jacobson, Sid, and Ernie Colón. *The 9/11 Report: A Graphic Adaptation*. Hill and Wang, 2006.

Junger, Sebastian. *Freedom*. Simon & Schuster, 2021.

Langewiesche, William. *American Ground: Unbuilding the World Trade Center*. North Point Press, 2002.

Lioy, Paul J. *Dust: The Inside Story of Its Role in the September 11th Aftermath*. Rowman & Littlefield, 2010.

Luft, Benjamin J., MD. *We're Not Leaving: 9/11 Responders Tell Their Stories of Courage, Sacrifice, and Renewal.* Cornell University Press, 2019.

Mattei, Suzanne. "Pollution and Deception at Ground Zero: How the Bush Administration's Reckless Disregard of 9/11 Toxic Hazards Poses Long-Term Threats for New York City and the Nation." Sierra Club, 2005. https://www.gothamgazette.com/rebuilding_nyc/sierraclub_report.pdf.

Mukherjee, Siddhartha. *The Emperor of All Maladies: A Biography of Cancer*. Scribner, 2010.

Murakami, Haruki. *Underground: The Tokyo Gas Attack and the Japanese Psyche.* Translated by Alfred Birnbaum and Philip Gabriel. Vintage International, 2001.

National Commission on Terrorist Attacks upon the United States. *The 9/11 Commission Report: Final Report of the National Commission on Terrorist Attacks upon the United States.* US Government Printing Office, 2004.

Nelson, Eliot. *The Beltway Bible: A Totally Serious A–Z Guide to Our No-Good, Corrupt, Incompetent, Terrible, Depressing, and Sometimes Hilarious Government*. Diversion Books, 2016.

Nordstrom, Lila. *Some Kids Left Behind: A Survivor's Fight for Health Care in the Wake of 9/11*. Apollo Publishers, 2021.

Pfeifer, Joseph. *Ordinary Heroes: A Memoir of 9/11*. Portfolio, 2023.

Smith, Chris, with Jon Stewart. *The Daily Show (The Book): An Oral History as Told by Jon Stewart, the Correspondents, Staff and Guests.* Grand Central Publishing, 2016.

Van Der Kolk, Bessel. *The Body Keeps the Score: Brain, Mind, and Body in the Healing of Trauma*. Penguin Books, 2015.

ACKNOWLEDGMENTS

First of all, to Ray Pfeifer, Luis Alvarez, and John McNamara. Cancer didn't define you, in life or in death. You made me a better man and a better leader. I'm jealous because you got to Valhalla before me, and you don't have to bury any more of your friends.

To my team leaders and team members, friends who became family, a diverse group of uniform and non-uniform responders and survivors, who walked side-by-side wherever they were needed, enduring my relentless ball busting and harsh nicknames, those who went with us and those who have gone before. I am humbled by your example and your work . . . see you in Valhalla.

To anyone who has suffered in the aftermath of 9/11 or from burn pit exposure. Your pain is why I do what I do.

Jon Stewart, not because you're famous or funny . . . Thank you for being my brother, for standing with us when you didn't have to (even though you're taller than me). Thank you for finding words for what was in our hearts and for making the whole world listen. *Don't ever make me miss you, because I love you dearly.*

Ben Chevat, who created FrankenFeal. Thank you… I think.

Michael Barasch, your resources, your loyalty, your commitment, and most of all your friendship have helped us move mountains.

Bridget Gormley, I met you under the worst circumstances, and I've seen you take life's rotten lemons and make limoncello. You are a gift to anyone who's lucky enough to cross your path.

Michael O'Connell, it feels good to finally be taller than someone. *Shumani tutanka*, you are my friend.

To the citizens who wrote in and called their representatives, the high school kids who reach out to me seeking advice on activism, this book is for you. You can do what we did and do it so much better. Trust me.

To the politicians who became my friends, I thank you for your friendship but not for doing your job.

To Charlie, you're not my fucking co-author, you're my fucking brother; Lucinda Halpern, our agent; BenBella Books, the publisher who gave this book a good home; Rick Chillot, our wise and fearless editor; and Charlie's mom, Christine Sullivan Daly, who was the only person, besides me and Charlie, allowed to see the rough draft. Christine worked for Speaker "Tip" O'Neill back in the day and was a resource for understanding how Congress works and how congressional aides deal with angry constituents. She contributed the old DC adage "assumption is the mother of fuckup," and Tip's classic line "all politics is local." Charlie's parents had a lot to do with the man and the writer he became. I never met Charlie's father. But his life's body of work would eclipse my twenty-five years. I have met Charlie's mother, and her strength and resolve make me look weak. This book was to cleanse me, and guide me home. I now think this book is to show how small I really am compared to others. Charlie's pen and the life he has shared with me prove my belief in our collaboration.

Thank you to our first readers for their attention and feedback: Dominique Müller, Dan Engel, Dan & Noelle O'Leary, Joshua Maloney, Aodhán Hurley, and Kevin Daly.

Charlie's research wouldn't have been possible without Dominique's love and support and help from Faye Murman-Dorsey, Ken Feinberg,

Dr. Wilkenfeld, the law offices of Barasch & McGarry, Amy Weinstein and the folks at the 9/11 Memorial and Museum, Sealy & Tim, Michael Daly, FDNY Ladder 7, Fergal Gallagher, and everyone who told Charlie their stories. My dear friends Chris Foerster, Marzena Feal, James Tonra, Charles Hume, Major Doctor David Hume (US Army), Coaches Bob Schuster and Richard Morrison, and to everyone who ever doubted. I hope I failed you.

Yaz, thank you for loving me, thank you for believing in me, thank you for accepting me and my flaws (trust me, there's many). Thank you for the permanent distraction (seven minutes—if you know you know). My heart knew you before my eyes met you. I hope we're together when this book comes out, or I'm gonna look stupid.

ABOUT THE AUTHORS

John Feal is a Long Islander who served in the 101st Airborne Division and worked as a demolition supervisor at Ground Zero until a disabling injury five days into the cleanup. He lobbied Congress to pass the James Zadroga 9/11 Health and Compensation Act of 2010, which he subsequently fought to defend and expand in 2015 and 2019 with the help of dozens of his fellow 9/11 responders, post-9/11 illness survivors, and comedian Jon Stewart. Through the FealGood Foundation, he continues to advocate for the health needs of first responders nationwide. A clip of his appearance on Fox News with Jon Stewart has gone viral.

Rudy Giuliani has blocked him on Twitter/X. John has spoken at the 9/11 Memorial Museum, Princeton University, and Quinnipiac University in Connecticut. *Vanity Fair* has covered his story along with NPR, *The Daily Beast*, *The Wall Street Journal,* all major news networks and many local affiliates nationwide, and two documentaries.

Charles Daly (co-author) is the co-author of *Make Peace or Die: A Life of Service, Leadership, and Nightmares*, which was featured on *Jocko Podcast*. He has worked as a collaborator on bestselling military memoirs. His work has appeared in *The Boston Globe*, *We Are the Mighty*, and Kōkatat. He lives in a cottage on the west coast of Ireland with his wife, a Swiss crime novelist, and their son and their black cat. He serves as a maritime first responder on his local Lifeboat.